THE JOHN ADAMS PAPERS

Selected, edited and interpreted
FRANK DONOVAN

Illustrated with photographs

JOHN ADAMS was a member of the first tinental Congresses and the drafting commit Declaration of Independence, a commiss France, a negotiator of the Treaty of Paris, Great Britain, George Washington's Vice and second President of the United States. the least known of the Founding Fathers. Overshadowed in history by Franklin, Washington, and Jefferson, he has remained a Puritanical enigma, almost ignored by historians. His relative anonymity is attributable in a large part to the passion of his descendants for privacy. It is a paradox of American letters that the papers of John Adams have been preserved better and read less than those of any of the other Founding Fathers because for a century they were totally inaccessible.

Frank Donovan, author of THE BENJAMIN FRANKLIN PAPERS, etc., has selected the most significant writings by or to John Adams that are available and has presented them in their historical context. This new volume in THE PAPERS OF THE FOUNDING FATHERS series serves to re-create the man who, in the words of the inscription on his epitaph written by his son John Quincy, "Pledged his life, fortune, and sacred honor to the independence of his country."

D1270160

FRANK DONOVAN

FRANK DONOVAN was born in New York City and went to work as a copy writer for an advertising agency at the age of sixteen. He later had his own advertising agency and became Business Manager of *The Magazine of Wall Street*. He joined Pathe News as a script writer and was made Vice-President in Charge of Production. Subsequently he formed his own company as an independent producer of films.

He is the author of a number of books on historical subjects, including *The Medal: The Story of the Medal of Honor, Mr. Lincoln's Proclamation,* and *The Papers of the Founding Fathers* series. He currently lives in Weston, Connecticut, where he is working on his next book and is chairman of the local Cub Scouts.

THE JOHN ADAMS PAPERS

By Frank Donovan

THE MEDAL
THE TALL FRIGATES
THE EARLY EAGLES
THE UNLUCKY HERO
THE AMERICANISM OF BARRY GOLDWATER
MR. MONROE'S MESSAGE
MR. LINCOLN'S PROCLAMATION
MR. MADISON'S CONSTITUTION

The Papers of the Founding Fathers

THE BENJAMIN FRANKLIN PAPERS
THE THOMAS JEFFERSON PAPERS
THE GEORGE WASHINGTON PAPERS
THE JOHN ADAMS PAPERS

Juveniles

THE IRONCLADS
THE BRAVE TRAITOR
THE CUTTER
THE MANY WORLDS OF BENJAMIN FRANKLIN
FAMOUS TWENTIETH CENTURY LEADERS
IRONCLADS OF THE CIVIL WAR
THE VIKINGS

From my Chamber in Worcester Septr 1st 1755

John Adams,

Phyladelphia June 1775

John Adams —

Philadelphia June 20. 1797

John Adams

Quincy April 15. 1815

John Adams.

J. Adams

Facsimiles of the signature of John Adams written
in 1755, 1775, 1797, 1815 and 1823.

THE PAPERS OF THE FOUNDING FATHERS

THE
JOHN ADAMS
PAPERS

Selected, edited, and interpreted by

FRANK DONOVAN

ILLUSTRATED

DODD, MEAD & COMPANY

NEW YORK

The extended quotations on pages 312 to 318 are from
Correspondence of John Adams and Thomas Jefferson by Paul
Wilstach, copyright 1925 by The Bobbs-Merrill Company, R. 1953
by Arthur Hellen, reprinted by permission of the publishers.

Library of Congress Catalog Card Number: 65-24686

Printed in the United States of America
by The Cornwall Press, Inc., Cornwall, N. Y.

IN EXPLANATION AND
ACKNOWLEDGMENT

Although, during his long lifetime, much of what John Adams wrote was misunderstood, most of his political theorizing was profoundly true. But nothing that he wrote was more truly prophetic than this statement from a letter to Benjamin Rush: "Mausoleums, Statues, Monuments will never be erected to me. I wish them not. Panegyrical Romances will never be written, nor flattering orations spoken to transmit me to posterity in brilliant colors."

John Adams is the Founding Father whom nobody knows. He has been, in a sense, "brushed off" by history. Enough has been written about Benjamin Franklin to fill a small library; in fact, the Franklin Collection at Yale University Library has a room to itself. George Washington has been idolized and debunked and examined in print from every angle. Thomas Jefferson has been a favorite subject of many pens. But Adams has remained a puritanical enigma, almost ignored by historians. There are some who explain this by saying that he was overshadowed by his great predecessor in the presidency, Washington, and by his brilliant successor, Jefferson. Others point out that he had no political party to keep his name alive after he presided over the demise of his own party, the Federalists. But the main reason for Adams' relative anonymity is that his descendants had a positive passion for privacy.

It is an interesting minor paradox of American letters that the papers of John Adams have been preserved better and read less than those of any of the other Founding Fathers, because, for a century, they were totally inaccessible.

v

In 1787 Adams wrote, from Holland, to his friend Cotton Tufts, back home in Massachusetts, saying:

THERE IS SO MUCH appearance of war, that I thought it a precaution of prudence to send my manuscript letter books, and collections of papers, relative to all my transactions in France and Holland, home by Mr. Jenks. They are contained in a large trunk, and are so numerous as to fill it, so that there is no room for anything else in it. I suppose the custom house officers will let it pass: but they may open it if they please. Yet I hope they will not disturb the order of the papers. These I suppose are neither prohibited goods, nor liable to duties. Let me pray you, sir, to send them to Braintree, to the care of Mr. Cranch till my return.

These foreign documents were added to a collection which he maintained throughout his life, including copies of everything that he wrote and everything that was written to him. In his last years he tried to put this material in some kind of order and carefully deeded "all my manuscript letter books, and account books, letters, journals, and manuscript papers" to his son, John Quincy Adams.

After his years in the White House, John Quincy started to organize further his father's papers and to write a biography. He seemed happy to drop this work at the end of the second chapter, when he went back into Congress. John Quincy's son, Charles Francis Adams, found such labor much more congenial. He completed the biography and published it as the first of ten volumes of *The Works of John Adams, Second President of the United States,* in 1856. The remaining nine volumes were very well edited by the standards of the mid-nineteenth century, but they are woefully incomplete. John Adams left an unfinished autobiography and a rather spotty diary. His grandson combined these, interlarding excerpts from the autobiography in the diary at their proper chronological points. This makes a rather confusing document. He then completed the work with most, but not all, of John Adams' published writings, his official papers, messages to Congress, etc., and a seemingly random "smattering" of letters.

From that time on the Adams papers, housed in the Stone Library in Quincy, Massachusetts, were virtually inaccessible. In 1905 they were deeded to the Adams Manuscript Trust, which was to run for fifty years under the supervision of male members of the family. The material was moved to the vaults of the Massachusetts Historical Society. Here Brooks Adams, last surviving son of the first Charles Francis, guarded his great-grandfather's writings with jealous zeal. After his death, Henry Adams, II, would sometimes honor a request from a scholar by typing a copy of a letter *to* John Adams, but no further publication of the works of the Founding Father was permitted.

This naturally made John Adams a difficult subject for twentieth-century biographers and historians. The only good biography written about him, until recently, has been the very readable *Honest John Adams* by Gilbert Chinard, published in 1933. An indication of the writer's problems in dealing with his subject is his statement: "Of the childhood of John Adams very little is known." When he wrote this, Chinard did not have access to the section of the autobiography in which Adams described his childhood because this had been omitted from the edition prepared by Charles Francis.

The veil of secrecy was at long last rent in 1952 when the Massachusetts Historical Society acquired the ownership of the Adams papers and reproduced them on 608 reels of microfilm. This includes the writings of the descendants of John Adams and their wives down to 1889. Copies of these microfilm reels are available in most good research libraries. Currently some of this material is being published in book form by the Belknap Press of Harvard University, edited by L. H. Butterfield. This has so far resulted in the publication of four volumes containing the complete autobiography and diary. Future plans call for the publication of autobiographical and diary material of John Quincy Adams and Charles Francis Adams; a separate series of volumes containing letters from all members of the family; and a third series of public and official papers of the three Adams statesmen.

When it is completed, which may not be during the current century, this work will still leave the picture of John Adams somewhat confused. The focal point of this vast compilation is the family, rather than the second President. Also, unlike the editions of Franklin, Jefferson, and Hamilton papers which are currently being done at Yale, Princeton, and Columbia Universities respectively, the letter-press edition of Adams papers will not be complete. It is described as a "comprehensive selection," presumably much more comprehensive than the edition by Charles Francis Adams, but still the microfilm reels will be the only complete reference source. Finally, the first serial rights to the Adams papers have been sold to *Life* magazine, which creates a copyright situation under which the reproduction of the material is still restricted.

In recent years a few books have thrown some new light on John Adams, although most were published before the microfilm was available. A half volume of excerpts from his writings was edited in 1946 by Adrienne Koch and William Peden and published under the title *The Selected Writings of John and John Quincy Adams. New Letters of Abigail Adams,* edited by Stewart Mitchell, was published in 1947. *John Adams and the Prophets of Progress,* by Zoltan Haraszti, 1952, is a collection of some lengthy marginal notes made by Adams on the books in his library. *The Adams Federalists,* by Manning J. Dauer, 1953, comments on events and some of John Adams' theories and ideas which affected the rise and fall of the Federalist party. *The Political Writings of John Adams,* edited by George A. Peek, Jr., in 1954, is a slim volume containing selections from Adams' most important writings on government. *The Adams-Jefferson Letters* were edited in two volumes by Lester J. Cappon in 1959, and *John Adams* is a biography by Page Smith published in two lengthy volumes in 1962.

In this volume the writer has been faced with the usual conflict between the purist and the popularizer as to changes in spelling, punctuation, and capitalization. Customs have changed in these areas since the eighteenth century. In a work which is purely for scholarly research it is important to preserve the idiosyncrasies of the original writer and carefullly reproduce his unique spelling and capitalization and his characteristic punctuation. In this volume, which is intended for the reader rather than the scholar (although one may be both) these details have been conformed to modern practice in the interest of readability. No changes in wording or grammatical construction have been made.

The writer wishes to express his debt to the Sterling Library at Yale University, the Yale Law Library, and Pequot Library in Southport, Connecticut, for their cooperation in the research on this volume.

CONTENTS

ℰ

ILLUSTRATIONS

ℰ

Extended quotations from John Adams and others appear in the larger of the two sizes of type used for the text.

CHAPTER I

THE LAWYER

༙

When he was writing his autobiography in the eighteenth century John Adams could not have known that in the nineteenth century a poet would immortalize his mother's great-great-grandparents; otherwise he might have mentioned his descent from John and Priscilla Alden rather than from a certain Henry Adams who secured a grant of land in Braintree, Massachusetts, in 1636. True, this Henry Adams may have been a brother of Thomas Adams whose name appeared on the original charter of the province and who later became Lord Mayor of London. There had been Adamses in Braintree for a century before John was born on October 19, 1735.

During that century the family had prospered mildly since the first Henry left an estate of £17.13.0, a house and barn, three beds, a cow, a heifer, some swine, some old books, and one silver spoon. John's great-grandfather's worldly wealth totaled £349.4.0, and he established a precedent by sending his oldest son to Harvard. The family social position was improved by the marriage of John's father—also John—to a Boylston, one of the most prominent families in the province. Of his male parent the younger John said that he had

. . . a good education, though not at college, and was a very capable and useful man. In his early life he was an officer of militia, afterward a deacon of the church and a selectman of the town; almost all of the business of the town being managed by him in that department for twenty years together; a man of strict piety, and great integrity; much esteemed and beloved wherever he was known, which was not far, his sphere of life being not very extensive.

In a biography of his father which John Quincy Adams started —and left for grandson Charles Francis Adams to finish—he described his forebears by writing:

IT IS IN the order of the dispensations of Providence to adapt the characters of men to the times in which they live. The grandfather of John Adams had given to the eldest of his twelve children a college education for his only inheritance. And a precious inheritance it was; it made him for nearly seventy years an instructor of religion and virtue. And such was the anticipation and the design of the father of John Adams, who, not without urgent advice and even solicitation, prevailed upon his son to prepare himself for college.

According to John, his parent's "solicitation" was occasioned by the son's juvenile interest in sailing boats, flying kites, driving hoops, playing with marbles, quoits, and particularly shooting, at which young Adams was expert. Unlike fellow Founding Fathers Franklin, Jefferson, and Madison, Adams showed no early fondness for books, a condition which he attributed to his first schoolmaster, a Mr. Joseph Clevery, who ran the public school in Braintree. John was convinced that he wanted to be a farmer like his dad, and late in life, told an anecdote of how he lost his first love:

WHEN I WAS A BOY, I had to study the Latin grammar; but it was dull and I hated it. My father was anxious to send me to

college, and therefore I studied the grammar till I could bear
with it no longer; and going to my father, I told him I did not
like study, and asked for some other employment. It was opposing his wishes, and he was quick in his answer. "Well,
John," said he, "if Latin grammar does not suit you, you may
try ditching, perhaps that will; my meadow yonder needs a
ditch, and you may put by Latin and try that."

This seemed a delightful change, and to the meadow I went
—but I soon found ditching harder than Latin, and the first
forenoon was the longest I ever experienced. That day I ate
the bread of labor, and glad was I when night came on. That
night I made comparison between Latin grammar and ditching, but said not a word about it. I dug the next forenoon, and
wanted to return to Latin at dinner, but it was humiliating,
and I could not do it. At night toil conquered pride, and I
told my father, one of the severest trials of my life, that, if he
chose, I would go back to Latin grammar. He was glad of it;
and if I have since gained any distinction it has been owing to
the two days' labor in that abominable ditch.

Under a more congenial tutor named Marsh, John was prepared
for Harvard and entered that institution in 1751, at the age of
fifteen, where his name appeared in fourteenth place on a list in
which precedence was determined by social position. Edward
Holyoke, Harvard's president, was considered by many as a rather
dangerous liberal, if not a radical. In one sermon he had said: "All
forms of government originate from the people. . . . As these
forms have originated from the people, doubtless they may be
changed whensoever the body of them choose to make such an
alteration." On another occasion he departed from the strict tenets
of Calvinism by preaching: "The minister or pastor should have
no hand in making any laws with regard to the spiritual affairs of
their people . . . [and] have no right to impose their interpreta-
tions of the laws of Christ upon their flocks. . . . Every man is to
judge for himself in these things." The molding mind of teen-age

John Adams was receptive to such ideas in both politics and theology.

His son wrote that John was "distinguished as a scholar, in a class which . . . contained as many men afterward eminent in the civil and ecclesiastical departments as any class that ever was graduated at that institution." John admitted his growing interest in study but expressed regret that his early fondness for mathematics and science in preference to the classics was not the best preparation for his later life, but he did put books before sports and girls. At this point in his somewhat spotty autobiography he digressed to praise his teen-age morality:

HERE IT may be proper to recollect something which makes an article of great importance in the life of every man. I was of an amorous disposition and very early, from ten or eleven years of age, was very fond of the society of females. I had my favorites among the young women and spent many of my evenings in their company, and this disposition, although controlled for seven years after my entrance into college, returned and engaged me too much till I was married. I shall draw no characters nor give any enumeration of my youthful flames. It would be considered as no compliment to the dead or the living: This I will say—they were all modest and virtuous girls and always maintained this character through life. No virgin or matron ever had cause to blush at the sight of me, or to regret her acquaintance with me. No father, brother, son, or friend ever had cause of grief or resentment for any intercourse between me and any daughter, sister, mother, or any other relation of the female sex. . . . These reflections, to me consolatory beyond all expression, I am able to make with truth and sincerity and I presume I am indebted for this blessing to my education.

The professions open to a Harvard graduate of 1755 were medicine, law, teaching, and the ministry, of which the last was by far the most highly regarded. John's parents had almost certainly assumed that he would be a clergyman, and the young man was probably of the same mind until the mild heresies at Harvard unsettled him. He attributed the beginning of his doubts of a clerical life to an incident while he was in college. The Braintree minister had been accused of misconduct, "partly on account of his principles, which were called Arminian, and partly on account of his conduct, which was too gay and light, if not immoral." A hearing was held in John's home where, wrote John:

I SAW such a spirit of dogmatism and bigotry in clergy and laity that, if I should be a priest, I must take my side and pronounce as positively as any of them or never get a parish, or getting it must soon leave it. Very strong doubts arose in my mind whether I was made for a pulpit in such times, and I began to think of other professions. I perceived very clearly, as I thought, that the study of theology and the pursuit of it as a profession would involve me in endless altercations, and make my life miserable, without any prospect of doing any good to my fellow men.

Choosing a profession presented a problem. He would not ask his father to support him while he studied law or medicine. So the nineteen-year-old Bachelor of Arts was happy to accept a position teaching Latin in a school at Worcester, from whence he wrote, in one of his earliest letters, an amusing description of life as a schoolmaster:

WHEN THE NIMBLE HOURS have tackled Apollo's coursers, and the gay deity mounts the eastern sky, the gloomy pedagogue arises, frowning and lowering like a black cloud begrimed with uncommon wrath, to blast a devoted land. When the destined time arrives, he enters upon action, and as a haughty monarch ascends his throne, the pedagogue mounts his awful *great chair,* and dispenses right and justice through his whole empire. His obsequious subjects execute the imperial mandates with cheerfulness, and think it their high happiness to be employed in the service of the emperor. Sometimes paper, sometimes his penknife, now birch, now arithmetic, now a ferule, then A B C, then scolding, then flattering, then thwacking, calls for the pedagogue's attention. At length, his spirits all exhausted, down comes pedagogue from his throne and walks out in awful solemnity through a cringing multitude. In the afternoon, he passes through the same dreadful scenes, smokes his pipe, and goes to bed. Exit muse.

John further described his pupils by writing:

IN THIS little state I can discover all the great geniuses, all the surprising actions and revolutions of the great world, in miniature. I have several renowned generals but three feet high, and several deep projecting politicians in petticoats. I have others catching and dissecting flies, accumulating remarkable pebbles, cockleshells, etc., with as ardent curiosity as any virtuoso in the Royal Society. . . . At one table sits Mr. Insipid, foppling and fluttering, spinning his whirligig, or playing with his fingers, as gaily and wittily as any Frenchified coxcomb brandishes his cane or rattles his snuffbox. . . . In short, my little school, like the great world, is made up of kings, politicians, divines, L.D.'s, fops, buffoons, fiddlers, sycophants, fools, coxcombs, chimney sweepers, and every other character drawn in history, or seen in the world.

Schoolmaster Adams first lived with a doctor in Worcester who had

. . . a pretty library. . . . I read a good deal in these books, and entertained many thoughts of becoming a physician and a surgeon. But the law attracted my attention more and more; and, attending the courts of justice, where I heard Worth-

ington, Hawley, Trowbridge, Putnam, and others, I felt myself irresistibly impelled to make some effort to accomplish
my wishes. I made a visit to Mr. Putnam and offered myself
to him. He received me with politeness and even kindness,
took a few days to consider of it, and then informed me that
Mrs. Putnam had consented that I should board in his house,
that I should pay no more than the town allowed for my
lodgings, and that I should pay him a hundred dollars when
I should find it convenient. I agreed to his proposals without
hesitation, and immediately took possession of his office.

Two years later, in 1758, John was admitted to the bar in Boston and returned to Braintree to hang out his shingle.

Although the youth had renounced the narrow theology of the
"frigid Calvin," he was very much the Puritan. A basic paradox
of John Adams' life is that he proclaimed the principles of free
thought but was guided by the dictates of Puritanism. In a wider
world than New England his Puritan promptings would cause him
many of the difficulties which he encountered in later life. With
Calvin, he was convinced that man is fundamentally sinful. In his
diary he wrote: "Vice and folly are so interwoven in all human
affairs that they could not possibly be wholly separated from them
without tearing and rending the whole system of human nature
and state; nothing would remain as it is." And before he was
twenty, he longed to purify his own character.

OH! that I could wear out of my mind every mean and base
affectation; conquer my natural pride and self-conceit; expect
no more deference from my fellows than I deserve; acquire
that meekness and humility which are the sure mark and characters of a great and generous soul; subdue every unworthy
passion, and treat all men as I wish to be treated by all. How
happy should I then be in the favor and good will of all
honest men and the sure prospect of a happy immortality!"

In this he never succeeded and throughout his writings are many castigations of his own departures from grace.

I HAVE NOT conversed enough with the world to behave rightly. I talk to Paine about Greek; that makes him laugh. I talk to Samuel Quincy about resolution, and being a great man, and study, and improving time, which makes him laugh. I talk to Ned about the folly of affecting to be a heretic, which makes him mad. I talk to Hannah and Esther about the folly of love . . . which makes them laugh. All this is affectation and ostentation. It is affectation of learning, and virtue, and wisdom, which I have not; and it is a weak fondness to show all that I have, and to be thought to have more than I have. Besides this, I have insensibly fallen into a habit of affecting wit and humor; of shrugging my shoulders and moving and distorting the muscles of my face; my motions are stiff and uneasy, ungraceful; and my attention is unsteady and irregular. These are reflections on myself that I make; they are faults, defects, fopperies, and follies, and disadvantages. Can I mend these faults and supply these defects?

The conflict in his religious and moral motivation is indicated by two passages written only four days apart in February 1756. In the first he asks: "Where do we find a precept in the Gospel, requiring ecclesiastical synods, convocations, councils, decrees, creeds, confessions, oaths, subscriptions, and whole cartloads of other trumpery, that we find religion encumbered with in these days?" And in the second:

SUPPOSE a nation in some distant region should take the Bible for their only law book, and every member should regulate his conduct by the precepts there exhibited. Every member would be obliged in conscience to temperance and frugality and industry, to justice and kindness and charity toward his fellow men, and to piety and love, and reverence toward almighty

God. In this Commonwealth, no man would impair his health
by gluttony, drunkenness, or lust—no man would sacrifice his
most precious time to cards, or any other trifling and mean
amusement—no man would steal or lie or any way defraud his
neighbor, but would live in peace and good will with all men
—no man would blaspheme his Maker or profane his worship,
but a rational and manly, a sincere and unaffected, piety and
devotion would reign in all hearts. What a Utopia, what a
Paradise would this region be.

Puritanism, or Bostonian provincialism, also lay at the root of
Adams' tendency to criticize adversely his peers, another habit
which remained throughout his life and contributed to contre-
temps, great or small, with most of the other Founding Fathers.
Indicative of this are certain early diary passages such as a portrait
of a female who "is awkward, shamefaced, bashful, yet would fain
seem sprightly, witty, etc. She is a squatty, masculine creature,
with a swarthy pale face, a great staring, rolling eye, a rare collection of disagreeable qualities." At about the same time he wrote of
a legal associate: "Bob Paine is conceited, and pretends to more
knowledge and genius than he has. . . . He is an impudent, illbred,
conceited fellow." Another was "like a little knurly, ill-natured
horse, that kicks at every horse of his own size and sheers off from
every one that is larger."

Few letters have survived from Adams' youth, and most of
these betoken the serious, purposeful student of law and politics.
At an age when Franklin bemoaned the "intrigues with low
women" in which his "hard-to-be-governed passions" had involved
him, when Washington was writing of "my former passion for your
Lowland Beauty," and when Jefferson was telling a friend that he
was "as merry as agreeable company and dancing with Belinda in
the Appollo could make me," Adams was concerned, at the age
of twenty, with far more weighty matters. In one of his earliest
letters he unknowingly prophesied the future of his country.

IF WE LOOK into history, we shall find some nations rising from contemptible beginnings, and spreading their influence till the whole globe is subjected to their sway. When they have reached the summit of grandeur, some minute and unsuspected cause commonly effects their ruin, and the empire of the world is transferred to some other place. . . . England . . . is now the greatest nation upon the globe. Soon after the Reformation, a few people came over into this new world for conscience's sake. Perhaps this apparently trivial incident may transfer the great seat of empire into America. It looks likely to me: for if we can remove the turbulent Gallicks [the French] our people, according to the exactest computations, will in another century become more numerous than England itself. Should this be the case . . . the united force of all Europe will not be able to subdue us. The only way to keep us from setting up for ourselves is to disunite us. *Divide et impera.* Keep us in distinct colonies and then, some great men in each colony desiring the monarchy of the whole, they will destroy each other's influence and keep the country *in equilibrio.*

Adams principal thoughts in his early twenties had to do with self-analysis, moral self-improvement, and how to acquire a niche in the hall of fame—or at least a profitable legal practice. He did not seek praise or flattery. He wrote:

GOOD TREATMENT makes me think I am admired, beloved, and my own vanity will be indulged in me; so I dismiss my guard, and grow weak, silly, vain, conceited, ostentatious. But a check, a frown, a sneer, a sarcasm, rouses my spirits, makes me more careful and considerate. It may, in short, be made a question whether good treatment or bad is the best for me; that is, whether smiles, kind words, respectful actions, do not betray me into weaknesses and littlenesses, that frowns, satirical speeches and contemptuous behavior make me avoid.

He told his diary:

REPUTATION ought to be the perpetual subject of my thoughts
and aim of my behavior. How shall I gain a reputation? How
shall I spread an opinion of myself as a lawyer of distinguished genius, learning, and virtue? Shall I make frequent
visits in the neighborhood, and converse familiarly with men,
women, and children, in their own style, on the common tittle-
tattle of the town and the ordinary concerns of a family, and
so take every fair opportunity of showing my knowledge in
the law? But this will require much thought and time. . . .
Shall I endeavor to renew my acquaintance with those young
gentlemen in Boston who were at college with me, and to extend my acquaintance among merchants, shopkeepers, trades-
men, etc., and mingle with the crowd upon Change, and
traipse the town-house floor with one and another, in order to
get a character in town? But this, too, will be a lingering
method and will require more art, and address, and patience,
too, than I am master of.

Shall I, by making remarks and proposing questions to the
lawyers at the bar, endeavor to get a great character for understanding and learning with them? But this is slow and tedious,
and will be ineffectual; for envy, jealousy, and self-interest
will not suffer them to give a young fellow a free, generous
character, especially me. Neither of these projects will bear
examination, will avail.

Shall I look out for a cause to speak to, and exert all the
soul and all the body I own, to cut a flash, strike amazement,
to catch the vulgar; in short, shall I walk a lingering, heavy
pace, or shall I take one bold determined leap into the midst
of fame, cash, and business? That is the question—a bold
push, a resolute attempt, a determined enterprise, or a slow,
silent, imperceptible creeping; shall I creep or fly? I feel vexed,
fretted, chafed; the thought of no business mortifies me, stings

me. But let me banish these fears; let me assume a fortitude, a greatness of mind.

One thing at which young Adams flew was the demon rum. Although not a temperance man himself, he saw in the taverns of Braintree a cause on which he could act. There were twelve ordinaries in the small town, far more than were necessary for the needs of a sober people. Adams campaigned against the public houses and drafted a speech which he may have made at a town meeting.

AT THE PRESENT DAY, such houses are become the eternal haunt of loose disorderly people of the . . . town, which renders them offensive and unfit for the entertainment of a traveler of the least delicacy. . . . Such multitudes have been lately licensed that none can afford to make provision for any but the tippling, nasty, vicious crew that most frequent them. The consequences of these abuses are obvious. Young people are tempted to waste their time and money and to acquire habits of intemperance and idleness that we often see reduce many to beggary and vice, and lead some of them at last to prison and the gallows. . . . But the worst effect of all . . . , these houses are become in many places the nurseries of our legislators. An artful man . . . may, by gaining a little sway among the rabble of the town, multiply taverns and dram shops . . . , and the multiplication of taverns will make many who may be induced by flip and rum to vote for any man whatever. . . . I think for these reasons it would be well worth the attention of our legislature to confine the number . . . of licensed houses; lest that impiety and profaneness; that abandoned intemperance and prodigality; that impudence and brawling temper which these abominable nurseries daily propagate, should arise at length to a degree of strength that even the legislature will not be able to control.

As a result of Adams' campaigning, the town passed an ordinance limiting the number of taverns to three. This was a short-lived reform, and Adams later admitted that rum-inspired discussions in country taverns were an important stimulus to the revolutionary movement.

One of Adams' grievances with the taverns was that they contributed to the delinquency of his farmhands, of one of whom he wrote: "A terrible, drunken, distracted week he has made of the last. A beast associating with the worst beasts in the neighborhood, running to all the shops and private houses, swilling brandy, wine, and cider in quantities enough to destroy him." This was important to Adams, the practical farmer who, at this point, was more dependent for support on his acres than on his legal briefs. When not riding the circuit or dreaming of advancement he recorded:

MY THOUGHTS are running continually from the orchard to the pasture and from thence to the swamp, and thence to the house and barn and land adjoining. Sometimes I am at the orchard ploughing up acre after acre, planting, pruning apple-trees, mending fences, carting dung; sometimes in the pasture, digging stones, clearing bushes, pruning trees. . . . Sometimes I am at the old swamp, burning bushes, digging stumps and roots, cutting ditches across the meadows . . . and am sometimes ploughing the upland with six yoke of oxen.

When his father died in 1761 John, already gaining recognition as Braintree's only lawyer, became a property owner—a freeholder—and a young man of some substance. He was appointed surveyor of roads, a thankless job without pay. However, he diligently went to "ploughing and ditching and blowing rocks upon Penn's hill, and building another bridge of stone." The bridge washed out the next spring, but the workmen were blamed, not Adams. He developed a new system of taxation for road maintenance and sold it to the town meeting. He wangled an appointment as deputy sheriff for his brother Boylston. The rather pushing young lawyer was becoming a man of some importance in Braintree, a condition which caused him to comment, "I am creating enemies in every quarter of the town . . . multiplying and propagating enemies fast. I shall have the ill will of the whole town."

One who did not hate the young lawyer was a certain Hannah Quincy, whom John visited frequently in 1761. He mentioned courting her, but it would seem that Hannah, who was frankly hungry for a husband, did most of the courting. John finally recorded:

ACCIDENTS, as we call them, govern a great part of the world, especially marriages. S—— and E—— broke in upon H—— and me, and interrupted a conversation that would have terminated in a courtship, which would have terminated in a marriage, which marriage might have depressed me to absolute poverty and obscurity, to the end of my life; but that accident separated us.

It was surely with no original intention of paying court to seventeen-year-old Abigail Smith that John frequented the home of Reverend William Smith, to whom he talked "about despising gay dress, grand buildings and estates, fame, etc., and being content with what will satisfy the real wants of nature." At first he compared Abigail and her sister adversely to Hannah, writing that the latter had a fondness and compassion that "Parson Smith's girls" lacked. But Abby, although sickly, had a pertness, a keen mind and a will to speak it that attracted John. Of the culmination of a three-year courtship he wrote in his autobiography:

I PASSED THE SUMMER of 1764 in attending court and pursuing my studies with some amusement on my little farm to which I was frequently making additions, until the fall, when on the 25th day of October, I was married to Miss Smith, a daughter of the Reverend Mr. William Smith a minister of Weymouth . . . a connection which has been the source of all my felicity, although a sense of duty which forced me away from her and my children for so many years has produced all the griefs of my heart and all that I esteem real afflictions in life.

Years later John Quincy Adams would write, in a biography of his father:

BY THIS MARRIAGE, Mr. Adams became allied with a numerous connection of families, among the most respectable for their weight and influence in the province, and it was immediately perceptible in the considerable increase of his professional practice.

Whether or not the marriage was responsible, at about this time John started to become more influential at the bar in Boston. He did not join the radical Caucus Club of which his older cousin Samuel Adams was the leader, and of which John wrote:

THERE they smoke tobacco till you cannot see from one end of the garret to the other. There they drink flip, I suppose, and there they choose a moderator, who puts questions to the vote regularly; and selectmen, assessors, collectors, wardens, firewards, and representatives are regularly chosen before they are chosen in the town.

But he was proud to be invited into the Sodalitas Club which had been organized by the legal lights of the town to meet once a week "in order to read in concert the Feudal Law and Tully's Orations." The *Dissertation on the Canon and Feudal Law* which Adams presented at this junta was his first piece of writing to attract attention in Boston and London.

The title of *Dissertation* and the fact that it was initially prepared for a learned legal club would indicate a scholarly, profound treatise. Actually, the document was more in the nature of a popu-

lar application of the history of law to current events. At the time
of its publication the excitement caused by the Stamp Act was at
its height, and Adams took advantage of this with an attention-
getting appeal to patriots.

Dissertation started by claiming that the two greatest systems of
tyranny over men's minds were the feudal laws and the canons of
the Roman Catholic church which, said Adams, "kept the people
in sordid ignorance and staring timidity . . . by infusing in them a
religious horror of letters and knowledge." Under these two tyran-
nies priests and lords

. . . have accordingly labored, in all ages, to wrest from the
populace, as they are contemptuously called, the knowledge of
their rights and wrongs, and the power to assert the former or
redress the latter, I say *Rights,* for such they have, undoubtedly, antecedent to all earthly government—*Rights,* that cannot be repealed or restrained by human laws—*Rights,* derived
from the great Legislator of the universe.

This continued until, said Adams:

GOD IN HIS BENIGN PROVIDENCE raised up the champions who
began and conducted the Reformation. . . . It was this great
struggle that peopled America. It was not religion alone, as is
commonly supposed; but it was a love of universal liberty, and
a hatred, a dread, a horror, of the infernal confederacy described, that projected, conducted, and accomplished the
settlement of America.

With little regard for the niceties of historical accuracy Adams
then lauded the Puritans as the leaders, if not the sole combatants,
in the fight against tyranny. The Puritans

AFTER THEIR ARRIVAL HERE . . . formed their plan, both of
ecclesiastical and civil government, in direct opposition to the

John Adams in 1783. Portrait by John S. Copley.

canon and the feudal systems. . . . Their greatest concern
seems to have been to establish a government . . . more agreeable to the dignity of human nature than any they had seen
in Europe, and to transmit such a government down to their
posterity, with the means of securing and preserving it forever.

According to Adams these enlightened people realized that

. . . liberty cannot be preserved without a general knowledge
among the people . . . as their great Creator, who does nothing in vain, has given them understandings, and a desire to
know . . . the preservation of the means of knowledge among
the lowest ranks is of more importance to the public than all
the property of all the rich men in the country.

Next to education the Puritans loved a free press: ". . . none of
the means of information are more sacred, or have been cherished with more tenderness and care by the settlers of America
than the press." The trouble was, said Adams, that Americans
were too timid to claim their rights.

BELIEVE ME, my countrymen, they have imbibed an opinion
on the other side the water that we are an ignorant, a timid
and a stupid people; nay, their tools on this side have often the
impudence to dispute your bravery. But I hope in God the
time is near at hand when they will be fully convinced of your
understanding, integrity, and courage.

The governor of Massachusetts must have found this amazing or
amusing, plagued as he was by the continuing and increasing complaints and demands of the patriots and the depredations of
Samuel Adams' Sons of Liberty.

John continued to catalogue the woes of the colonies:

HAVE WE NOT been treated . . . with abominable insolence?
. . . Have not some generals from England treated us like

servants, nay, more like slaves than like Britons? Have we not been under the most ignominious contribution, the most abject submission, the most supercilious insults, of some custom-house officers? Have we not been *trifled* with, brow-beaten, and trampled on, by former governors? . . .

We have been told that "the word *rights* is an offensive expression"; "that the king, his ministry, and parliament will not endure to hear Americans talk of their *rights*"; "that Britain is the mother and we the children, that a filial duty and submission is due from us to her," and that "we ought to doubt our own judgment, and presume that she is right," even when she seems to us to shake the foundations of government. . . .

Are we the children of Great Britain any more than the cities of London, Exeter, and Bath? Are we not brethren and fellow subjects with those in Britain, only under a somewhat different method of legislation, and a totally different method of taxation? But admitting we are children, have not children a right to complain when their parents are attempting to break their limbs, to administer poison, or to sell them to enemies for slaves? Let me entreat you to consider, will the mother be pleased when you represent her as deaf to the cries of her children? . . .

Enough of this, said Adams:

LET US DARE to read, think, speak, and write. Let every order and degree among the people rouse their attention and animate their resolution. . . . Let us read and recollect and impress upon our souls the views and ends of our own more immediate forefathers, in exchanging their native country for a dreary, inhospitable wilderness. Let us examine into the nature of that power, and the cruelty of that oppression, which drove them from their homes. . . . Let us recollect it was liberty, the hope of liberty for themselves and us and ours, which conquered all discouragements, dangers, and trails. . . .

Let the pulpit resound with the doctrines and sentiments of religious liberty. . . . Let the bar proclaim, "the laws, the rights, the generous plan of power" delivered down from remote antiquity. . . . Let it be known that British liberties are not the grants of princes or parliaments, but original rights, conditions of original contracts, coequal with prerogative, and coeval with government; that many of our rights are inherent and essentially agreed on as maxims, and established as preliminaries, even before a parliament existed. . . .

Let the colleges join their harmony in the same delightful concert. Let every declamation turn upon the beauty of liberty and virtue, and the deformity, turpitude, and malignity of slavery and vice. Let the public disputations become researches into the grounds and nature and ends of government, and the means of preserving the good and demolishing the evil. . . .

In a word, let every sluice of knowledge be opened and set a-flowing. . . . The prospect now before us in America ought in the same manner to engage the attention of every man of learning to matters of power and of right, that we may be neither led nor driven blindfolded to irretrievable destruction.

The ideas expressed in *Dissertation* were not new. They represented the prevailing opinions of most of the moderates in the group which the British would soon call rebels and the Americans patriots. They are important because they are Adams' first public espousal of the cause to which he would devote the next twenty years of his life. John had not yet joined the radical partisans led by his cousin Samuel and James Otis, who used the mob as well as the mind to counter British wrongs. While John was advocating learning, Samuel's Sons of Liberty were burning Governor Hutchinson's books. When James Warren pressed John Adams to join with him and John Hancock in haranguing town meetings, John replied, "That way madness lies."

Although Adams condemned the Stamp Act, imposed on the colonies in 1765, as a burden on "the poorer sort of people" to give his *Dissertation* more popular appeal, the greatest real sufferers under it were lawyers, businessmen, and printers. When the controversy closed the law courts, Adams cried in his diary:

I WAS but just getting into my gears, just getting under sail, and an embargo is laid upon the ship. Thirty years of my life are passed in preparation for business. I have had poverty to struggle with; envy and jealousy, and malice of enemies to encounter, no friends, or but few, to assist me; so that I have groped in dark obscurity, till of late, and had but just become known, and gained a small degree of reputation, when this execrable project was set on foot for my ruin, as well as that of America in general, and of Great Britain.

Adams was the prime mover in calling a town meeting in Braintree to instruct the town's representative to the General Court in opposing the Stamp Act, and wrote the instructions. He started by saying: "In all the calamities which have ever befallen this country, we have never felt so great a concern, or such alarming apprehensions, as on this occasion." Then, for the first time, he played his variation of the theme "no taxation without representation." He wrote:

WE FURTHER APPREHEND this tax to be unconstitutional. We have always understood it to be a grand and fundamental principle of the Constitution that no freeman should be subject to any tax to which he has not given his own consent, in person or by proxy. And the maxims of the law, as we have constantly received them, are to the same effect, that no freeman can be separated from his property but by his own act or fault. We take it clearly, therefore, to be inconsistent with the spirit of the common law, and of the essential fundamental principles of the British constitution, that we should be subject to any tax imposed by the British Parliament; because we are not represented in that assembly.

Adams' instructions were published in the Boston *Gazette* and were used as a model by not less than forty other towns. The resulting publicity swelled his law practice and kept him so busy that he eschewed politics for some time. In the spring of 1767 he moved his family, which now included two-year-old Abigail, called Nabby, to Boston. Here John Quincy Adams was born in July, to be followed later by Charles, Susanna, and Thomas. Susanna lived but a year.

With an eye to suborning Adams from the patriot camp, the governor offered him the post of advocate general of the Court of Admiralty. Although the post was a "sure introduction to the most profitable business of the Province," John turned it down because "The office would be incompatible with my settled convictions." Yet, though he was doing well, he questioned his purpose, his abilities and his goal. In 1768 he asked himself:

TO WHAT OBJECT are my views directed? What is the end and purpose of my studies, journeys, labors of all kinds, of body and mind, of tongue and pen? Am I grasping at money or scheming for power? Am I planning the illustration of my family or the welfare of my country? These are great questions. In truth, I am tossed about so much from post to pillar that I have not leisure and tranquillity enough to consider distinctly my own views, objects, and feelings. . . . I am certain . . . that the course I pursue will neither lead me to fame, fortune, nor to the service of my friends, clients, or country.

Perhaps the most controversial act of Adams' career was his legal defense of the British soldiers who were prosecuted for perpetrating the so-called Boston Massacre in 1770. This started when a mob attacked a British sentry. The guard, under a Captain Thomas Preston, responded to the sentry's cries for help and faced

the mob with loaded rifles. The mob taunted the eight lobster-
backs, pelted them with stones and snowballs, and knocked one
down with a stick. Suddenly a shot rang out, then a ragged volley
which killed three and wounded eight members of the mob. When
this happened Adams was visiting on the south side of Boston. At
the ringing of the alarm bell he ran into the street, assuming there
was a fire. Here, he reported:

WE WERE INFORMED that the British soldiers had fired on the
inhabitants, killed some and wounded others, near the town
house. A crowd of people was flowing down the street to the
scene of action. When we arrived, we saw nothing but some
fieldpieces placed before the south door of the town house,
and some engineers and grenadiers drawn up to protect them.
Mrs. Adams [who was pregnant] was then in circumstances to
make me apprehensive of the effect of the surprise upon her,
who was alone, excepting her maids and a boy, in the house.
Having therefore surveyed round the town house, and seeing
all quiet, I walked down Boylston Alley into Brattle Square,
where a company or two of regular soldiers were drawn up . . .
with their muskets all shouldered, and their bayonets all fixed.
I had no other way to proceed but along the whole front in a
very narrow space which they had left for foot passengers.
Pursuing my way, without taking the least notice of them, or
they of me, any more than if they had been marble statues, I
went directly home to Cole Lane.

My wife . . . had recovered from her first apprehensions,
and we had nothing but our reflections to interrupt our repose.
These reflections were to me disquieting enough. Endeavors
had been systematically pursued for many months, by certain
busy characters, to excite quarrels, re-encounters, and combats,
single or compound, in the night, between the inhabitants of
the lower class and the soldiers, and at all risks to enkindle an
immortal hatred between them. I suspected that this was the
explosion which had been intentionally wrought up by design-

ing men, who knew what they were aiming at better than the instruments employed. If these poor tools should be prosecuted for any of their illegal conduct, they must be punished. If the soldiers, in self-defense, should kill any of them, they must be tried, and, if truth was respected and the law prevailed, must be acquitted. To depend upon the perversion of law, and the corruption of partiality of juries, would insensibly disgrace the jurisprudence of the country and corrupt the morals of the people.

Adams was approached, the next day, by a friend of British Captain Preston who told him:

". . . he wishes for counsel, and can get none. I have waited on Mr. Quincy, who says he will engage, if you will give him your assistance; without it, he positively will not." . . . I had no hesitation in answering, that counsel ought to be the very last thing that an accused person should want in a free country; that the bar ought, in my opinion, to be independent and impartial, at all times and in every circumstance . . . and that every lawyer must hold himself responsible not only to his country, but to the highest and most infallible of all tribunals for the part he should act. . . . If he thinks he cannot have a fair trial of that issue without my assistance, without hesitation, he shall have it.

Upon this, Forrest offered me a single guinea as a retaining fee, and I readily accepted. From first to last I never said a word about fees, in any of those cases, and I should have said nothing about them here, if calumnies and insinuations had not been propagated that I was tempted by great fees and enormous sums of money. Before or after the trial, Preston sent me ten guineas, and at the trial of the soldiers afterward, eight guineas more, which were all the fees I ever received or were offered to me, and I should not have said anything on the subject to my clients if they had never offered me anything. This was all the pecuniary reward I ever had for fourteen or fifteen days labor in the most exhausting and fatiguing causes I ever tried, for hazarding a popularity very general and very hardly earned, and for incurring a clamor, popular suspicions and prejudices, which are not yet worn out, and never will be forgotten as long as the history of this period is read.

Knowing that the Boston mob was feared and detested outside the city, defense counsel used its challenges against Bostonians to load the jury with countrymen, and Adams drew a dramatic picture of the type of delinquents who had caused the incident by telling the jury:

WE HAVE BEEN ENTERTAINED with a great variety of names to avoid calling the persons who gathered at the custom house a mob. Some have called them shavers, some call them geniuses. The plain English is, gentlemen, a motley rabble of saucy boys, Negroes and mulattoes, Irish teagues and outlandish jack tars. And why should we scruple to call such a set of people a mob? I cannot conceive, unless the name is too respectable for them. The sun is not about to stand still or go out, nor the rivers to dry up, because there was a mob in Boston on the fifth of March that attacked a party of soldiers. Such things are not new in the world, nor in the British dominions, though they are, comparatively, rarities and novelties in this town.

The defense was based entirely on self-defense.

WHEN THE MULTITUDE was shouting and hazzaing, and threatening life, the bells ringing, the mob whistling, screaming and rending an Indian yell; the people from all quarters throwing every species of rubbish they could pick up in the street . . . Montgomery [one of the soldiers] in particular smote

with a club and knocked down, and as soon as he could rise
and take up his firelock, another club from afar struck his
breast or shoulder . . . what could he do? You expect he
should behave like a stoic philosopher, lost in apathy? Patient
as Epictetus while his master was breaking his legs with a
cudgel? It is impossible you should find him guilty of murder.
You must suppose him divested of all human passions, if you
don't think him at least provoked, thrown off his guard, and
into the *furor brevis,* by such treatment as this.

Adams summarized by declaiming:

THE LAW, in all vicissitudes of government, fluctuations of the
passions, or flights of enthusiasm, will preserve a steady unde-
viating course; it will not bend to the uncertain wishes, imaginations and wanton tempers of men. . . . It does not enjoin
that which pleases a weak, frail man, but without any regard
to persons, commands that which is good and punishes evil in
all, whether rich or poor, high or low—'tis deaf, inexorable,
inflexible. On the one hand it is inexorable to the cries and
lamentations of the prisoners; on the other it is deaf, deaf as
an adder, to the clamors of the populace.

Preston and most of the soldiers were acquitted. Two were convicted of manslaughter, pleaded benefit of clergy, were branded
on the thumbs and released with their sore hands in cold and inhospitable Boston. Actually, the soldiers would have been better
off if they had been sentenced to hang. The governor would have
surely pardoned them and sent them back to Merry England.

In recent years several dramatizations of the "defense of the
soldiers" have made much of the moral courage displayed by
Adams in taking the case—and have ignored the fact that he was,
at best, but associate counsel. He agreed to *assist* Quincy in the
defense. The idea of great sacrifice is based on Adams' words in
his diary at the time, in several later letters, and in his autobiogra-

phy where he mentioned "hazarding a popularity" and incurring suspicions and prejudices. Three years after the trials he commented on a commemorative celebration by writing:

I HAVE REASON to remember that fatal night. The part I took in defense of Captain Preston and the soldiers procured me anxiety and obloquy enough. It was, however, one of the most gallant, manly, and disinterested actions of my whole life, and one of the best pieces of service I ever rendered my country.

There is no evidence, other than his own statements, that Adams' action represented a sacrifice or endangered his reputation. Part of his motivation was undoubtedly his respect of justice and the law, but he was also conscious that outlying Massachusetts and the other colonies were strongly opposed to the Boston mob, and a triumph for the mob would be a setback for the moderate course he favored. Also his action was good for business. It was popular with the better class Bostonians from whom his local clients were drawn and in the towns on the circuit where much of his practice lay. That he was, to the responsible element, a hero rather than a martyr as a result of the trial was evidenced by his prompt election in Boston, by a large majority, to the General Court. He recorded in his diary:

I HAD NEVER been at a Boston town meeting, and was not at this until messengers were sent to me to inform me that I was chosen. I went down to Faneuil Hall and [with] a few words expressive of my sense of the difficulty and danger of the times, of the importance of the trust, and of my own insufficiency to fulfill the expectations of the people, I accepted the choice. Many congratulations were offered, which I received civilly, but they gave no joy to me. I considered the step as a devotion of my family to ruin, and myself to death, for I could scarce perceive a possibility that I should ever go through the

thorns and leap all the precipices before me and escape with
my life.

At this time I had more business at the bar than any man
in the province. My health was feeble. I was throwing away as
bright prospects as any man ever had before him, and I had
devoted myself to endless labor and anxiety, if not to infamy
and to death, and that for nothing except what indeed was
and ought to be all in all, a sense of duty. In the evening I
expressed to Mrs. Adams all my apprehensions. That excellent
lady, who has always encouraged me, burst into a flood of
tears, but said she was very sensible of all the danger to her
and to our children, as well as to me, but she thought I had
done as I ought; she was very willing to share in all that was
to come, and to place her trust in Providence.

Just why John expected to die as a result of his service on the
General Court is not clear, unless from overwork. This, as well as
his comments of the soldiers' trial, is indicative of his unconscious
longing for martyrdom, an attitude which he never lost. He was a
psychological hypochondriac who would create a cross to carry if
there was none ready-made.

The early 1770s represented the lull before the storm in colonial politics. John busied himself with his practice, his concern
for Abigail's always precarious health and his own, and his farm.
He moved back to Braintree for eighteen months and became a
commuter by making a daily one-hour ride to Boston. When
cousin Samuel pressed him to speak publicly for the cause he
pleaded

. . . the feeble state of my health [which] rendered me quite
willing to devote myself forever to private life; that, far from
taking any part in public, I was desirous to avoid even thinking upon public affairs, and that I was determined to pursue
that course, and therefore that I must beg to be excused.

But it did not take much to arouse his ire at England. When the Crown sought to punish the Rhode Island patriots for burning the revenue cutter *Gaspee* at Providence, Adams flared:

I FOUND the old warmth, heat, violence, acrimony, bitterness, sharpness of my temper and expression, was not departed. I said there was no more justice left in Britain than there was in hell; that I wished for war, and that the whole Bourbon family was upon the back of Great Britain; avowed a thorough disaffection to that country; wished that anything might happen to them, and, as the clergy prayed of our enemies in time of war, that they might be brought to reason or to ruin. I cannot but reflect upon myself with severity for these rash, inexperienced, boyish, raw, and awkward expressions. A man who has no better government of his tongue, no more command of his temper, is unfit for everything but children's play and the company of boys.

When Hutchinson was confirmed as governor of the colony and seemed to be seeking a reconciliation, John did not trust him and was convinced that he and cousin Samuel were the only active patriots left. He asked himself:

Is IT NOT A PITY that a brace of so obscure a breed should be the only ones to defend the household, when the generous mastiffs and best-blooded hounds are all hushed to silence by the bones and crumbs that are thrown to them, and even Cerberus himself is bought off with a sop?

The "brace of so obscure a breed" were John and Sam; the Cerberus who had failed them was James Otis, who had endorsed certain of Hutchinson's acts.

Adams' opinion of Hutchinson was confirmed when Benjamin Franklin sent from England a packet of letters which had fallen into his hands and which disclosed that Hutchinson, although

native-born, had little love for the colony. Franklin had sent the
letters to Thomas Cushing, saying that he had promised that they
would not be copied or published. Cushing showed them to a
group of patriots, including Adams, who agreed that in view of
"such injunctions to secrecy . . . it is difficult to make any public
use of them!" But they proved that he was right about the governor whom, he wrote, was a "cool-thinking deliberate villain,
malicious and vindictive, as well as ambitious and greedy . . .
Bone of our bone, born and educated among us!" Others, probably cousin Samuel, were not so scrupulous about following
Franklin's injunctions, and the letters found their way to the press,
which resulted in Franklin's expulsion from England.

By the spring of 1773 Adams was back in politics when his
friends induced him to run for the Assembly so that he would be
available for nomination to the Governor's Council. On election
eve he contemplated what the morrow might bring.

TOMORROW IS our general election. The plots, plans, schemes,
and machinations of this evening and night will be very numerous. . . . For myself, I own, I tremble at the thought of an
election.

If I should be called in the course of Providence to take a
part in public life, I shall act a fearless, intrepid, undaunted
part at all hazards, though it shall be my endeavor likewise
to act a prudent, cautious, and considerate part. But if I
should be excused by a nonelection . . . I shall enjoy a sweet
tranquillity in the pursuit of my private business, in the education of my children, and in a constant attention to the preservation of my health. This last is the most selfish and pleasant
system, the first the more generous, though arduous and disagreeable. But I was not sent into this world to spend my days
in sports, diversions, and pleasures; I was born for business,
for both activity and study.

When Adams was elected, his appointment to the Governor's

Council was vetoed by Hutchinson because of "the very conspicuous part that Mr. Adams had taken in opposition."

As 1773 came to a close there occurred the dramatic act which history knows as the Boston Tea Party. Tea had become a test case in the controversy as to whether Parliament had the right to tax the colonies. When a shipload of it arrived at Boston, Abigail Adams wrote to her friend Mercy Warren:

THE TEA, that baneful weed, is arrived. Great and, I hope, effectual opposition has been made to the landing of it. . . . The flame is kindled, and like lightning it catches from soul to soul. Great will be the devastation, if not timely quenched or allayed by some more lenient measures.

Next day handbills circulated through the city:

FRIENDS! BRETHREN! COUNTRYMEN! That worst of plagues, the detested TEA . . . is now arrived in this harbor. The hour of destruction, or manly opposition to the machinations of tyranny, stares you in the face. Every friend to his country, to himself and posterity, is now called upon to meet at Faneuil Hall at nine o'clock THIS DAY . . . to make a united and successful resistance to this last, worst, and most destructive measure of administration.

Several meetings accomplished nothing except to excite the patriots and strengthen Hutchinson's resolve that the tea ship would not be allowed to return its cargo to England. When he turned down a final request for clearance, Samuel Adams roared from the dais in Faneuil Hall: "This meeting can do nothing more to save the country." A group of Sons of Liberty, disguised as Mohawk Indians, raced to the waterfront and threw 342 cases of tea into the harbor.

Few of the colonial leaders outside of Massachusetts endorsed this act. George Washington wrote that although the cause of

Boston was the cause of America, he did not "approve their conduct in destroying the tea." Franklin called the Tea Party "an act
of violent injustice" and offered to pay for the tea from his
pocket—after the tax law was repealed. It is rather surprising that
John Adams, with his great respect for law and order, took a very
different attitude:

LAST NIGHT, three cargoes of Bohea tea were emptied into
the sea. . . . There is a dignity, a majesty, a sublimity, in this
last effort of the patriots, that I greatly admire. The people
should never rise without doing something to be remembered,
something notable and striking. This destruction of the tea is
so bold, so daring, so firm, intrepid and inflexible, and it
must have so important consequences, and so lasting, that I
cannot but consider it as an epocha in history. This, however,
is but an attack upon property. Another similar exertion of
popular power may produce the destruction of lives. Many
persons wish that as many dead carcasses were floating in the
harbor as there are chests of tea. . . .
The question is, whether the destruction of this tea was
necessary? I apprehend it was absolutely and indispensably
so. . . . To let it be landed would be giving up the principle
of taxation by parliamentary authority, against which the continent has struggled for ten years. It was losing all our labor
for ten years, and subjecting ourselves and our posterity forever to Egyptian task-masters; to burthens, indignities; to
ignominy, reproach and contempt; to desolation and oppression; to poverty and servitude. . . .

While he waited for news of what action England might take
Adams was pessimistic about the progress of the patriot cause.

NEWS WE HAVE NONE. Still! silent as midnight! The first vessels
may bring us tidings which will erect the crests of the Tories
again, and depress the spirits of the Whigs. For my own part,

I am of the same opinion that I have been for many years, that there is not spirit enough on either side to bring the question to a complete decision, and that we shall oscillate like a pendulum and fluctuate like the ocean for many years to come, and never obtain a complete redress of American grievances, nor submit to an absolute establishment of parliamentary authority, but be trimming between both, as we have been for ten years past, for more years to come than you and I shall live. Our children may see revolutions, and be concerned and active in effecting them, of which we can form no conception.

In May the news that the port of Boston was to be closed to commerce seemed to cheer him. He wrote to Abigail:

WE LIVE, my dear soul, in an age of trial. What will be the consequence, I know not. The town of Boston for aught I can see, must suffer martyrdom. It must expire. And our principal consolation is that it dies in a noble cause—the cause of truth, of virtue, of liberty, and of humanity—and that it will probably have a glorious resurrection to greater wealth, splendor, and power, than ever. . . . Don't imagine from all this that I am in the dumps. Far otherwise. I can truly say that I have felt more spirits and activity since the arrival of this news than I had done before for years. I look upon this as the last effort of Lord North's despair, and he will as surely be defeated in it as he was in the project of the tea.

The reaction of the colonists was prompt. On June 17 the General Court appointed the two Adamses, Thomas Cushing, and Robert Treat Paine to meet with representatives of the other colonies in Philadelphia on September 1. John was about to make his bow on the national stage, a prospect which filled his pessimistic mind with its usual forebodings.

THERE IS a new and a grand scene opened before me: a Congress. This will be an assembly of the wisest men upon the continent, who are Americans in principle, that is, against the taxation of Americans by authority of Parliament. I feel myself unequal to this business. A more extensive knowledge of the realm, the colonies, and of commerce, as well as of law and policy, is necessary than I am master of. What can be done? Will it be expedient to propose an annual congress of committees? to petition? Will it do to petition at all?—To the King? To the Lords? To the commons? What will such consultations avail? Deliberations alone will not do.

And to his friend James Warren he expressed fears for his personal safety.

THERE IS ONE ugly reflection. Brutus and Cassius were conquered and slain. Hampden died in the field, Sidney on the scaffold, Harrington in jail, etc. This is cold comfort. Politics are an ordeal path among red hot ploughshares. Who, then, would be a politician for the pleasure of running about barefoot among them? Yet somebody must. And I think those whose characters, circumstances, educations, etc., call them, ought to follow.

With the other Massachusetts delegates Adams set out on August 10, 1774, on his first long journey. It was a slow and social procession with dinners, discussions, and entertainment by patriots along the route. He approved of the Connecticut delegates whom he met: Silas Deane was "a gentleman of liberal education"; Roger Sherman "a solid sensible man." The city of New York impressed him: "The streets of this town are vastly more regular and elegant than those in Boston, and the houses are more grand, as well as neat. They are almost all painted, brick buildings and all." He did not fully approve of the colony's leaders; after all, "Mr. Duane is an Episcopalian; so are all the delegates from New York except

Mr. Livingston." He admitted that John Jay was reputed to be "a hard student and a good speaker" and Peter Livingston "a sensible man and a gentleman," but "Phil Livingston is a great rough, rapid mortal. There is no holding any conversation with him."

But on balance the Massachusetts Puritan did not think highly of the Yorkers.

WITH ALL THE OPULENCE and splendor of this city, there is very little good breeding to be found. We have been treated with an assiduous respect; but I have not seen one real gentleman, one well-bred man, since I came to town. At their entertainments there is no conversation that is agreeable; there is no modesty, no attention to one another. They talk very loud, very fast, and altogether. If they ask you a question, before you can utter three words of your answer, they will break out upon you again and talk away.

From Princeton in New Jersey, John addressed his first letter to Abigail. They had corresponded before—while they were courting and when John was riding circuit—but this was the formal beginning of the most memorable husband and wife written dialogue in American history. A letter from Abigail expressed fears for the future.

THE GREAT ANXIETY I feel for my country, for you, and for our family renders the day tedious and the night unpleasant. The rocks and quicksands appear upon every side. What course you can or will take is all wrapped in the bosom of futurity. Uncertainty and expectation leave the mind great scope. Did ever any kingdom or state regain its liberty, when once it was invaded, without bloodshed? I cannot think of it without horror.

John tried to reassure her:

LET ME ENTREAT YOU, my dear, to make yourself as easy and quiet as possible. Resignation to the will of Heaven is our only resource in such dangerous times. Prudence and caution should be our guides. I have the strongest hopes that we shall yet see a clearer sky and better times.

The rest of the letter was personal. He sent his "tender love to little Abby," and of young John Quincy said: "Tell him I am glad to hear he is so good a boy as to read to his mamma for her entertainment, and to keep himself out of the company of rude children." He enjoined Abby to be a diligent farm manager:

I HOPE our husbandry is prudently and industriously managed. Frugality must be our support. Our expenses in this journey will be very great. Our only [recompense will] be the consolatory reflection that we toil, spend our time, and [encounter] dangers for the public good—happy indeed if we do any good. The education of our children is never out of my mind. Train them to virtue. Habituate them to industry, activity, and spirit. Make them consider every vice as shameful and unmanly. Fire them with ambition to be useful. Make them disdain to be destitute of any useful or ornamental knowledge or accomplishment. Fix their ambition upon great and solid objects, and their contemp upon little, frivolous, and useless ones.

On September 2, 1774, occurred a meeting in a Philadelphia tavern which would have great meaning for the colonies. Adams merely mentioned it in his diary:

AFTER COFFEE, we went to the tavern, where we were introduced to Peyton Randolph . . . Speaker of Virginia, Colonel Harrison, Richard Henry Lee, . . . and Colonel Bland. Randolph is a large, well-looking man; Lee is a tall, spare man; Bland is a learned, bookish man. These gentlemen from Virginia appear to be the most spirited and consistent of any. Harrison said he would have come on foot rather than not come. Bland said he would have gone, upon this occasion, if it had been to Jericho.

Here were the two groups which, more than any others, would lead the colonies to independence: the somewhat stiff and staid merchants and lawyers of Massachusetts, and the easygoing, gracious aristocrats of Virginia. Opposites in every detail of appearance, manners, and customs they would, through years of travail, be foils for each other in freeing their country and establishing its new government.

The Congress in Philadelphia started with a squabble—which would not be finally settled for thirteen years—as to whether the colonies should have one vote each or be rated by population or wealth. The small colonies wanted the former, the large ones the latter, until Patrick Henry, from populous Virginia, delivered one of his famous orations in favor of the plan of the small colonies, which Adams tersely noted in his diary by writing:

MR. HENRY. Government is dissolved. Fleets and armies and the present state of things show that government is dissolved. Where are your landmarks, your boundaries of Colonies? We are in a state of nature, sir. I did propose that a scale should be laid down; that part of North America which was once Massachusetts Bay, and that part which was once Virginia, ought to be considered as having weight. Will not people complain? Ten thousand Virginians have not outweighed one thousand others. I will submit, however; I am determined to submit, if I am overruled. . . . The distinctions between Virginians, Pennsylvanians, New Yorkers, and New Englanders are no more. I am not a Virginian, but an American.

Many years later Adams thus described his first formal contribution to American independence as a member of a congressional committee to prepare a bill of rights:

IT WAS, indeed, very much against my judgment that the committee was so soon appointed, as I wished to hear all the great topics handled in Congress at large in the first place. They were very deliberately considered and debated in the committee, however.

The two points which were labored the most were:

WHETHER WE SHOULD recur to the law of nature, as well as to the British constitution, and our American charters and grants. . . . The other great question was, what authority we should concede to Parliament; whether we should deny the authority of Parliament in all cases; whether we should allow any authority to it in our internal affairs; or whether we should allow it to regulate the trade of the empire with or without any restrictions. . . . After several days deliberation, we agreed upon all the articles excepting one, and that was the authority of Parliament, which was indeed the essence of the whole controversy. . . . After a multitude of motions had been made, discussed, negatived, it seemed as if we should never agree upon anything. Mr. John Rutledge of South Carolina, one of the committee, addressing himself to me, was pleased to say, "Adams, we must agree upon something; you appear to be as familiar with the subject as any of us, and I like your expressions. . . . Come, take the pen and see if you can't produce something that will unite us." Some others of the committee seconding Mr. Rutledge, I took a sheet of paper and drew up an article. When it was read, I believe not one of the committee was fully satisfied with it; but they all soon acknowledged that there was no hope of hitting on anything in which we could all agree with more satisfaction. All therefore agreed to this, and upon this depended the union of the Colonies.

Adams' article stated that the colonial legislatures had jurisdiction in "all cases of taxation and internal polity," and added:

... from the necessity of the case, and a regard to the mutual interest of both countries, we cheerfully consent to the operation of such acts of the British Parliament as are *bona fide* restrained to the regulation of our external commerce . . . excluding every idea of taxation, internal or external, for raising a revenue on the subjects in America without their consent.

Early in September a false report reached Philadelphia that Boston had been bombarded, probably based on the peaceful seizure by the British of some gunpowder. John was concerned for his family but not entirely displeased at an act which might strengthen the support of the other colonies. He wrote Abigail:

WHEN OR WHERE this letter will find you I know not. In what scenes of distress and terror I cannot foresee. We have received a confused account from Boston of a dreadful catastrophe. The particulars we have not heard. We are waiting with the utmost anxiety and impatience for further intelligence. The effect of the news we have, both upon the Congress and the inhabitants of this city, was very great. Great indeed! Every gentleman seems to consider the bombardment of Boston as the bombardment of the capital of his own province. Our deliberations are grave and serious indeed.

He was further encouraged when he heard that Washington had said, "I will raise one thousand men, subsist them at my own expense, and march myself at their head for the relief of Boston."

While his optimism prevailed, Adams was, for him, rather gay. During the middle of the month he wrote, "This was one of the happiest days of my life. In Congress we had generous, noble sentiments, and manly eloquence. This day convinced me that

America will support Massachusetts or perish with her." He forgot his diet in a series of dinners which included: "Turtle, and every other thing, flummery, jellies, sweetmeats of twenty sorts, trifles, whipped sillabubs, floating islands, fools, etc., and then a dessert of fruits, raisins, almonds, pears, peaches. Wines most excellent and admirable." He wrote Abigail:

I SHALL BE KILLED with kindness in this place. We go to Congress at nine, and there we stay most earnestly engaged in debates upon the most abstruse mysteries of state until three in the afternoon; then we adjourn, and go to dine with some of the nobles of Pennsylvania at four o'clock, and feast upon ten thousand delicacies, and sit drinking madeira, claret, and Burgundy, till six or seven, and then go home fatigued to death with business, company, and care. Yet I hold out surprisingly.

Then, as days passed without any positive action by the delegates, the pendulum of Adams' mood swung in the opposite direction. He wrote his wife:

I AM WEARIED to death with the life I lead. The business of the Congress is tedious beyond expression. This assembly is like no other that ever existed. Every man in it is a great man, an orator, a critic, a statesman; and therefore every man upon every question must show his oratory, his criticism, and his political abilities. The consequence of this is that business is drawn and spun out to an immeasurable length. I believe if it was moved and seconded that we should come to a resolution that three and two make five, we should be entertained with logic and rhetoric, law, history, politics, and mathematics, and then—we should pass the resolution unanimously in the affirmative. The perpetual round of feasting, too, which we are obliged to submit to, makes the pilgrimage more tedious to me.

Perhaps John's return of pessimism was engendered by the Pennsylvania conservative Joseph Galloway, who proposed that the Colonies make peace with the mother country under a plan which provided for supervision of their external affairs by Parliament and the control of internal affairs by a general Assembly selected by the colonial legislatures under a president with veto power appointed by the Crown. James Duane seconded; Richard Henry Lee opposed; John Jay thought the plan reasonable; Patrick Henry condemned it; Edward Rutledge of South Carolina thought it "an almost perfect plan." A move to table Galloway's resolution was defeated by a clear majority, and it seemed that the work of the Congress might be nullified. That evening, in smoke-filled rooms, John and cousin Samuel gathered enough wavering delegates to defeat the plan by the narrow vote of six to five.

The next day, John came forward with his own motion, which began with the resolve that Massachusetts and the town of Boston "are now struggling in the common cause of American freedom, and, therefore, that it is the indispensable duty of all the colonies to support them by every necessary means, and to the last extremity." The motion further resolved that:

. . . in case hostilities should be further pursued against that Providence, and submission be attempted to be compelled by force of arms, as soon as intelligence of this shall be communicated to the several Colonies, they ought immediately to cease all exportations of goods, wares, and merchandise, to Great Britain, Ireland, and the West Indies.

Also it provided that:

. . . in case any person or persons should be arrested, in Massachusetts Bay or any other colony . . . in order to be sent to Great Britain to be there tried for any crime whatsoever, committed in America . . . this ought to be considered as a declaration of war and a commencement of hostilities against all the Colonies, and reprisals ought to be made in all the Colonies and held as hostages for the security of the person or persons so arrested.

Adams' motion was tabled without a vote; this was farther than the Congress was willing to go.

John envisioned a long, slow road to united action when he wrote Abigail:

PATIENCE, FORBEARANCE, LONG SUFFERING are the lessons taught here for our Province, and, at the same time, absolute and open resistance to the new government. I wish I could convince gentlemen of the danger or impracticability of this, as fully as I believe it myself. The art and address of ambassadors from a dozen belligerent powers of Europe, nay, of a conclave of cardinals at the election of a Pope, or of the princes in Germany at the choice of an Emperor, would not exceed the specimens we have seen; yet the Congress all profess the same political principles. They all profess to consider our province as suffering the common cause, and indeed they seem to feel for us, as if for themselves. We have had as great questions to discuss as ever engaged the attention of men, and an infinite multitude of them.

And in his diary he recorded his usual adverse opinion of all which did not stem from Puritan New England.

PHILADELPHIA, with all its trade and wealth and regularity, is not Boston. The morals of our people are much better, their manners are more polite and agreeable, they are purer English, our language is better, our persons are handsomer, our spirit is greater, our laws are wiser, our religion is superior, our education is better. We exceed them in everything but in a market, and in charitable, public foundations.

The Congress finally passed the Declaration of Rights and Grievances and appointed Adams to a committee to draw up a petition to present it to His Majesty. They also agreed that a policy of nonimportation from Britain should start in December, and if Parliament did not repeal the objectionable statutes, non-exportation should start the next December. On the face of it the results of the conclave were inconclusive, yet the consequences were of vital importance for Massachusetts. By tact and moderation Adams and his colleagues had secured the assurance of some support from other colonies of widely diverse interests. The most important aspect of the first Congress to John, for the future, was expressed in a letter to Abigail:

I HAD THE CHARACTERS and tempers, the principles and views, of fifty gentlemen, total strangers to me, to study; and the trade, policy, and whole interest of a dozen provinces to learn, when I came here. I have multitudes of pamphlets, news-papers, private letters to read. I have numberless plans of policy and many arguments to consider. I have many visits to make and receive, much ceremony to endure, which cannot be avoided, which you know I hate.

When the Congress adjourned on October 28, John apparently forgot that Philadelphians had poor taste and inferior manners, as he had recorded but two weeks before. Now he wrote:

TOOK OUR DEPARTURE, in a very great rain, from the happy, the peaceful, the elegant, the hospitable, and polite city of Philadelphia. It is not very likely that I shall ever see this part of the world again, but I shall ever retain a most grateful, pleasing sense of the many civilities I have received in it.

CHAPTER II

THE CONGRESSMAN

ᘉ

ABOUT THIS TIME . . . among an immense quantity of meaner productions, appeared a writer under the signature of Massachusettensis. . . . These papers were well written; abounded with wit, discovered good information, and were conducted with a subtlety of art and address wonderfully calculated to keep up the spirits of their party, to depress ours . . . and to make proselytes among those whose principles and judgment give way to their fears; and these compose at least one third of mankind. . . . No answer appeared, and indeed some who were capable were too busy, and others too timorous. I began at length to think seriously of the consequences, and began to write under the signature of Novanglus, and continued every week in the Boston *Gazette,* till the 19th of April, 1775.

Adams' *Novanglus* (New England) papers contained a rather pedantic compendium of the rights of the people of Massachusetts to self-government and a historical account of the abuses of the royal governors, and presented, as in a legal brief, a support of the patriot position. Although they display Adams' considerable erudition—with references to Aristotle, Plato, Livy, and Cicero among the ancients and the moderns Sidney, Harrington, and Locke—they are noteworthy as examples of his legal and historical knowledge rather than of his felicity with a pen. The design of the series is indicated by these brief quotations:

I . . . MAY, PERHAPS . . . show the wicked policy of the Tories; trace their plan from its first rude sketches to its present complete draught; show that it has been much longer in contemplation than is generally known—who were the first in it—their views, motives, and secret springs of action, and the means they have employed. . . . From such a research and detail of facts, it will clearly appear who were the aggressors and who have acted on the defensive from first to last; who are still struggling, at the expense of their ease, health, peace, wealth, and preferment, against the encroachments of the Tories on their country, and who are determined to continue struggling . . . in the last ditch.

I would ask by what law the Parliament has authority over America? By the law of God in the Old and New Testament it has none. By the law of nature and nations it has none. By the common law of England it has none; for the common law, and the authority of Parliament founded on it, never extended beyond the four seas. By statute law it has none, for no statute was made before the settlement of the Colonies for this purpose; and the declaratory act, made in 1766, was made without our consent, by a Parliament which had no authority beyond the four seas. What religious, moral, or political obligations then are we under to submit to Parliament as a supreme legislative? None at all. When it is said that, if we are not subject to the supreme authority of Parliament Great Britain will make us so, all other laws and obligations are given up and recourse is had . . . to the law of brickbats and cannon balls, which can be answered only by brickbats and balls.

Adams wrote nothing directly about the event which terminated the publication of *Novanglus* except this notation in his diary:

THE BATTLE OF LEXINGTON, on the 19th of April, changed the instruments of warfare from the pen to the sword. A few days after this event I rode to Cambridge, where I saw . . . the New England army. There was great confusion and much distress. Artillery, arms, clothing were wanting, and a sufficient supply of provisions not easily obtained. Neither the officers nor men, however, wanted spirits of resolution. I rode from thence to Lexington, and along the scene of action for many miles, and inquired of the inhabitants the circumstances. These were not calculated to diminish my ardor in the cause; they, on the contrary, convinced me that the die was cast, the Rubicon passed, and . . . if we did not defend ourselves, they would kill us.

By the tenth of May, 1775, Adams was back in Philadelphia for the second session of the Continental Congress, to which he promptly offered a plan of action which he recalled in his autobiography:

I THOUGHT the first step ought to be to recommend to the people of every state in the Union to seize on all the Crown officers and hold them with civility, humanity, and generosity, as hostages for the security of the people of Boston, and to be exchanged for them as soon as the British army would release them; that we ought to recommend to the people of all the States to institute governments for themselves, under their own authority, and that without loss of time; that we ought to declare the Colonies free, sovereign, and independent states, and then to inform Great Britain we were willing to enter into negotiations with them for the redress of all grievances, and a restoration of harmony between the two countries, upon permanent principles . . . ; that we ought immediately to adopt the army in Cambridge as a continental army, to appoint a general and all other officers, take upon ourselves the pay, subsistence, clothing, armor, and munitions of the troops. . . . From conversation with the members of Congress, I was then convinced, and have been ever since convinced, that it was the general sense at least of a considerable majority of that body.

Counter to Adams' opinion this proposal was far too extreme for Congress in the spring of 1775, a condition which he attributed to "The gentlemen in Pennsylvania, who had been attached to the proprietary interest, and owed their wealth and honors to it, and the great body of the Quakers." Adams had particular contempt for Pennsylvania's John Dickinson, who had won fame as a patriot with his "Farmer's Letters" the year before but who now countered Adams' proposal with the suggestion for another appeal to the King. Adams later said:

. . . the Quakers had intimidated Mr. Dickinson's mother and his wife, who were continually distressing him with their remonstrances. His mother said to him, "Johnny, you will be hanged; your estate will be forfeited and confiscated; you will leave your excellent wife a widow, and your charming children orphans, beggars, and infamous." From my soul I pitied Mr. Dickinson. . . . I was very happy that my mother and my wife and my brothers, my wife's father and mother . . . and all her near relations, as well as mine, had uniformly been of my mind, so that I always enjoyed perfect peace at home.

At the time Adams had less sympathy for Dickinson. He created trouble for himself and his cause by one of his typical ouspoken criticisms. In a letter to James Warren, which also contained strong statements on independence, he said of Dickinson: "A certain great fortune and piddling genius, whose fame has been trumpeted so loudly, has given a silly cast to our whole doings."

The letter was intercepted by the British and published in the press because, said Adams:

. . . they thought they should produce quarrels among the members of Congress and a division of the Colonies. Me they expected utterly to ruin, because, as they represented, I had explicitly avowed by designs of independence. I cared nothing for this. I had made no secret, in or out of Congress, of my opinion that independence was become indispensable, and I was perfectly sure that in a little time the whole continent would be of my mind. I rather rejoiced in this as a fortunate circumstance, that the idea was held up to the whole world, and that the people could not avoid contemplating it and reasoning about it. Accordingly, from this time at least, if not earlier, and not from the publication of *Common Sense,* did the people in all parts of the continent turn their attention to this subject.

When *Common Sense* was first published anonymously, some attributed it to Franklin or Adams. Adams liked the document well enough to send it to several friends, but when it started to become America's first best-seller Adams decided that he should tell his wife just what she should think about Thomas Paine's work. As a contemporary literary critic he did not share posterity's reverence for the document.

SENSIBLE MEN think there are some whims, some sophisms, some artful addresses to superstitious notions, some keen attempts upon the passions, in this pamphlet. But all agree there is a great deal of good sense delivered in clear, simple, concise, and nervous style. His sentiments of the abilities of America, and of the difficulty of a reconciliation with Great Britain, are generally approved. But his notions and plans of continental government are not much applauded. Indeed, this writer has a better hand in pulling down than in building. It has been very generally propagated through the continent that I wrote this pamphlet. But although I could not have written anything in so manly and striking a style, I flatter myself I should have made a more respectable figure as an architect, if I had undertaken such a work. This writer seems to have very inadequate ideas of what is proper and necessary to be done in order to form constitutions for single colonies, as well as a great model of union for the whole.

Adams' most important positive move, in the early days of the second Congress, was his proposal that the body take the army at Cambridge under its wing and appoint a commanding general. In view of the historical concept that Washington was really a unanimous choice, Adams' recollection of the matter is of interest. He later wrote:

. . . we were embarrassed with more than one difficulty, not only with the party in favor of the petition to the King, and the party who were jealous of independence, but a third party, which was a southern party against a northern, and a jealousy against a New England army under the command of a New England general. Whether this jealousy was sincere, or whether it was mere pride and a haughty ambition of furnishing a southern general to command the northern army [I cannot say?]; but the intention was very visible to me that Colonel Washington was their object, and so many of our staunchest men were in the plan that we could carry nothing without conceding to it. Another embarrassment, which was never publicly known, and which was carefully concealed by those who knew it, the Massachusetts and other New England delegates were divided. Mr. Hancock and Mr. Cushing hung back, Mr. Paine did not come forward, and even Mr. Samuel Adams was irresolute. Mr. Hancock himself had an ambition to be appointed commander-in-chief. Whether he thought an election a compliment due to him, and intended to have the honor of declining it, or whether he would have accepted, I know not. . . . In canvassing this subject out of doors I found too that even among the delegates of Virginia there were difficulties. . . . In several conversations, I found more than one very cool about the appointment of Washington. . . .

Full of anxieties concerning these confusions, and apprehending daily that we should hear very distressing news from Boston, I walked with Mr. Samuel Adams in the State House yard for a little exercise and fresh air before the hour of Congress, and there represented to him the various dangers that surrounded us. He agreed to them all, but said, "What shall we do?" I answered him that he knew I had taken great pains to get our colleagues to agree upon some plan that we might be unanimous; but he knew that they would pledge themselves to nothing; but I was determined to take a step which should compel them and all the other members of Congress to declare themselves for or against something. "I am determined this morning to make a direct motion that Congress should adopt the army before Boston, and appoint Colonel Washington commander of it." Mr. Adams seemed to think very seriously of it, but said nothing.

Accordingly, when Congress had assembled, I rose in my place, and in as short a speech as the subject would admit, represented the state of the Colonies. . . . I concluded with a motion, in form, that Congress would adopt the army at Cambridge and appoint a general. . . . I had no hesitation to declare that I had but one gentleman in my mind for that important command, and that was a gentleman from Virginia who was among us and very well known to all of us. . . . Mr. Washington, who happened to sit near the door, as soon as he heard me allude to him, from his usual modesty, darted into the library-room.

Mr. Hancock, who was our President, which gave me an opportunity to observe his countenance while I was speaking . . . heard me with visible pleasure; but when I came to describe Washington for the commander I never remarked a more sudden and striking change of countenance. Mortification and resentment were expressed as forcibly as his face could exhibit them. Mr. Samuel Adams seconded the motion, and that did not soften the President's physiognomy at all. The subject came under debate, and several gentlemen declared themselves against the appointment of Mr. Washington, not on account of any personal objection against him, but because the army were all from New England, had a general of their own, appeared to be satisfied with him, and had proved themselves able to imprison the British army in Boston, which was all they expected or desired at that time. The subject was postponed to a future day. In the meantime, pains were taken out of doors to obtain a unanimity, and the voices were generally so clearly in favor of Washington that the dissentient members were persuaded to withdraw their opposition, and Mr. Washington was nominated . . . and the army adopted.

At the time of Washington's selection, John wrote to his wife:

THIS APPOINTMENT will have a great effect in cementing and securing the union of these colonies. . . . I hope the people of our province will treat the General with all that confidence and affection, that politeness and respect, which is due to one of the most important characters in the world. The liberties of America depend upon him, in a great degree. . . .

I have found this Congress like the last. When we first came together, I found a strong jealousy of us from New England and the Massachusetts in particular; suspicions entertained of designs of independency; an American republic; Presbyterian principles, and twenty other things. Our sentiments were heard in Congress with great caution, and seemed to make but little impression; but the longer we sat, the more clearly they saw the necessity of pushing vigorous measures. . . . But America is a great, unwieldy body. Its progress must be slow. It is like a large fleet sailing under convoy. The fleetest sailors must wait for the dullest and slowest. Like a coach and six, the swiftest horses must be slackened, and the slowest quickened, that all may keep an even pace.

Late in June, John had news from Abigail of the Battle of Bunker Hill and the destruction of Charlestown by the British, so that, "Scarcely one stone remaineth upon another; but in the midst of sorrow we have abundant cause of thankfulness, that so few of our brethren are numbered with the slain, whilst our enemies were cut down like the grass before the scythe. . . ." The people of Boston, she wrote were treated as "the most abject slaves under the most cruel and despotic of tyrants." To which John replied:

YOUR DESCRIPTION of the distresses of the worthy inhabitants of Boston and the other seaport towns is enough to melt a heart of stone. Our consolation must be this, my dear, that cities may be rebuilt, and a people reduced to poverty may acquire fresh property. But a constitution of government, once changed from freedom, can never be restored. Liberty, once lost, is lost forever.

But all of the couple's thoughts were not of war. Signing herself "Portia," Abigail wrote:

I HAVE A REQUEST to make of you; something like the barrel of sand, I suppose you will think it, but really of much more importance to me. . . . It is that you . . . purchase me a bundle of pins and put them in your trunk for me. The cry for pins is so great that what I used to buy for seven shillings and sixpence are now twenty shillings, and not to be had for that. A bundle contains six thousand, for which I used to give a dollar; but if you can procure them for fifty shillings, or three pounds, pray let me have them.

There was much contention between factions in Congress, even among the Massachusetts delegates. In disgust John wrote his wife:

I WISH I had given you a complete history . . . of the behavior of my compatriots. No mortal tale can equal it. I will tell you in future, but you shall keep it secret. The fidgets, the whims, the caprice, the vanity, the superstition, the inability of some of us is enough to—"

But perhaps there was some excuse for the slow progress in Congress. In the same letter he said:

WHEN FIFTY OR SIXTY MEN have a Constitution to form for a great empire, at the same time that they have a country of fifteen hundred miles in extent to fortify, millions to arm and train, a naval power to begin, an extensive commerce to regulate, numerous tribes of Indians to negotiate with, a standing army of twenty-seven thousand men to raise, pay, victual, and officer, I really shall pity those fifty or sixty men.

One thorny problem for the Congress during the fall of 1775 was that of foreign trade and international relations. A resolution had been passed in the first Congress calling for nonimportation. Should this policy be continued effective or should the Colonies seek supplies abroad? Trading with nations other than Great Britain would, said the timid souls, be tantamount to a declaration of independence. Adams did not agree. He said so vehemently, in and out of Congress. His theme was "God helps those who help themselves": American vessels should risk the dangers of British seizure to carry commodities to other countries, and foreign nations should be invited to trade with America. For this American harbors must offer safe haven. Adams admitted that the States could not cope with Britain on the high seas; but they could build floating batteries and arm small boats for harbor defense.

Congress wrangled for over a month but the conservatives prevailed; the ports were kept closed. But Congress did appoint a committee, at Adams' suggestion, to establish an American navy, an act which may entitle Adams to the appellation "father of the United States navy." Approval was granted to purchase and equip two vessels "to be employed . . . for the protection of the United Colonies." Adams was on the naval committee to effectuate this and probably wrote the *Rules for the Regulation of the Navy of the United States of North America,* which the committee submitted to Congress.

John's correspondence with his wife provided his principal surcease from the cares of Congress. These letters mixed politics and personal affairs with future plans and gossip and, principally, expressed a longing to have her with him:

REALLY, it is very painful to be four hundred miles from one's family and friends, when we know they are in affliction. . . . Upon my word, I think, if ever I were to come here again, I must bring you with me. I could live here pleasantly, if I had you with me. Will you come and have the smallpox here?

The reference to smallpox was occasioned by Abigail's announcement that she was going to be vaccinated against the disease.

The publication of the intercepted letter to Warren caused Adams to be temporarily more circumspect on public matters in his correspondence, but he wrote at length about morality, social responsibilities, and the relation of these to the education of their children. On a single day in October he wrote his wife three letters on these themes. In the first he said:

MY OPINION of the duties of religion and morality comprehends a very extensive connection with society at large and the great interest of the public. Does not natural morality and . . . Christian benevolence make it our indispensable duty to

lay ourselves out to serve our fellow creatures to the utmost
of our power in promoting and supporting those great political systems and general regulations upon which the happiness
of multitudes depends? The benevolence, charity, capacity,
and industry which, exerted in private life, would make a
family, a parish, or a town happy, employed upon a larger
scale in support of the great principles of virtue and freedom
of political regulations, might secure whole nations and generations from misery, want, and contempt. Public virtues and
political qualities, therefore, should be incessantly cherished
in our children.

In the second, education was lauded.

EDUCATION MAKES a greater difference between man and man
than nature has made between man and brute. The virtues and
powers to which men may be trained, by early education and
constant discipline, are truly sublime and astonishing. . . . It
should be your care, therefore, and mine, to elevate the
minds of our children and exalt their courage; to accelerate
and animate their industry and activity; to excite in them an
habitual contempt of meanness, abhorrence of injustice and
inhumanity, and an ambition to excel in every capacity, fac-
ulty, and virtue. If we suffer their minds to grovel and creep
in infancy, they will grovel all their lives. But their bodies
must be hardened, as well as their souls exalted. Without
strength and activity and vigor of body, the brightest mental
excellences will be eclipsed and obscured.

In the third letter of the day he bemoaned his Yankee provincialism, and then proceeded to justify it.

THERE IS in the human breast a social affection which extends
to our whole species, faintly indeed, but in some degree. The
nation, kingdom, or community to which we belong is em-

braced by it more vigorously. . . . It is stronger and stronger as we descend to the county, town, parish, neighborhood, and family, which we call our own. And here we find it often so powerful as to become partial, to blind our eyes, to darken our understandings, and pervert our wills.

It is to this infirmity in my own heart that I must perhaps attribute that local attachment, that partial fondness, that overweening prejudice in favor of New England, which I feel very often, and which, I fear, sometimes leads me to expose myself to just ridicule.

New England has, in many respects, the advantage of every other colony in America, and indeed, of every other part of the world that I know anything of.

1. The people are purer English blood . . . than any other; and descended from Englishmen, too, who left Europe in purer times than the present, and less tainted with corruption than those they left behind them.

2. The institutions in New England for the support of religion, morals, and decency exceed any other. . . .

3. The public institutions in New England for the education of youth . . . are not equaled, and never were, in any part of the world.

Abigail was probably teasing her husband when she wrote:

IN THE NEW CODE OF LAWS which I suppose it will be necessary for you to make, I desire you would remember the ladies and be more generous and favorable to them than your ancestors. Do not put such unlimited power into the hands of the husbands. Remember, all men would be tyrants if they could. If particular care and attention is not paid to the ladies, we are determined to foment a rebellion, and will not hold ourselves bound by any laws in which we have no voice or representation.

To which John replied:

As to your extraordinary code of laws, I cannot but laugh. We have been told that our struggle has loosened the bonds of government everywhere; that children and apprentices were disobedient; that schools and colleges were grown turbulent; that Indians slighted their guardians, and Negroes grew insolent to their masters. But your letter was the first intimation that another tribe, more numerous and powerful than all the rest, were grown discontented. . . . Depend upon it, we know better than to repeal our masculine systems. . . . We have only the name of masters, and rather than give up this, which would completely subject us to the despotism of the petticoat, I hope General Washington and all our brave heroes would fight. . . . I begin to think the ministry as deep as they are wicked. After stirring up Tories, land-jobbers, trimmers, bigots, Canadians, Indians, Negroes, Hanoverians, Hessians, Russians, Irish Roman Catholics, Scotch renegadoes, at last they have stimulated the [women] to demand new privileges and threaten to rebel.

There was much talk in Congress of forms of government, and late in 1775 Virginia's George Wyeth asked Adams to set down his thoughts on this subject. He complied in a long letter which became a widely circulated pamphlet. It started:

We ought to consider what is the end of government before we determine which is the best form. Upon this point all speculative politicians will agree that the happiness of society is the end of government, as all divines and moral philosophers will agree that the happiness of the individual is the end of man.

Of course, to Puritan Adams, happiness had a somewhat different meaning than to most: "All sober inquirers after truth,

ancient and modern, pagan and Christian, have declared that the
happiness of man, as well as his dignity, consists in virtue."

After making the point that good government must be founded
on virtue, he continued:

THERE IS NO good government but what is republican . . .
because the very definition of a republic is "an empire of
laws, and not of men." . . . Of republics there is an inex-
haustible variety, because the possible combinations of the
powers of society are capable of innumerable variations.

As good government is an empire of laws, how shall your
laws be made? In a large society, inhabiting an extensive
country, it is impossible that the whole should assemble to
make laws. The first necessary step, then, is to depute power
from the many to a few of the most wise and good. . . . The
principal difficulty lies, and the greatest care should be employed, in constituting this representative assembly. It should
be in miniature an exact portrait of the people at large. It
should think, feel, reason, and act like them. . . . Great care
should be taken to effect this, and to prevent unfair, partial,
and corrupt elections. . . .

A representation of the people in one assembly being obtained, a question arises whether all the powers of government, legislative, executive, and judicial, shall be left in this
body? I think a people cannot be long free, nor very happy,
whose government is in one assembly.

Adams then gave six reasons for his opinion. "A single assembly
is liable to all the vices, follies, and frailties of an individual; subject to fits of humor, starts of passion, flights of enthusiasm, par-
tialities, or prejudice." It was apt to be avaricious. It was apt to
grow ambitious. It was "unfit to exercise the executive power, for
want of two essential properties, secrecy and dispatch." And it
was "still less qualified for the judicial power, because it is too
numerous, too slow, and too little skilled in the laws." Finally, "A

single assembly, possessed of all the powers of government, would make arbitrary laws for their own interest, execute all laws arbitrarily for their own interest, and adjudge all controversies in their own favor."

Adams then concluded that a single assembly would not be satisfactory even as the sole legislative body, because it would be too powerful and conflict with the executive until

. . . the contest shall end in war, and the whole power, legislative and executive, be usurped by the strongest. The judicial power, in such case, could not mediate, or hold the balance, between the two contending powers, because the legislative would undermine it. And this shows the necessity, too, of giving the executive power a negative upon the legislative, otherwise this will be continually encroaching upon that.

The solution, Adams believed, was:

LET THE representative assembly then elect by ballot, from among themselves or their constituents, or both, a distinct assembly which, for the sake of perspicuity, we will call a council. It may consist of any number you please, say twenty or thirty, and should have a free and independent exercise of its judgment, and consequently a negative voice in the legislature. These two bodies . . . integral parts of the legislature, let them unite, and by joint ballot choose a governor, who, after being stripped of most of those badges of domination called prerogatives, should have a free and independent exercise of his judgment. . . . As the governor is to be invested with the executive power, with consent of council, I think he ought to have a negative upon the legislative. . . . The dignity and stability of government in all its branches, the morals of the people, and every blessing of society depends so much upon an upright and skillful administration of justice that the judicial power ought to be distinct from both the legislative and executive, and independent upon both, that so it may be a check upon both, as both should be checks upon that.

In both the legislative and executive branches

. . . all . . . elections, especially of representatives and counselors, should be annual, there not being in the whole circle of the sciences a maxim more infallible than this, "where annual elections end, there slavery begins." [Judges, because] their minds should not be distracted with jarring interest, . . . should not be dependent upon any man, or body of men. To these ends, they should hold estates for life in their offices.

Adams' proposal contained the fundamentals of the charter of government which the Constitutional Convention produced eleven years later. At the time he wrote to Abigail that he had

. . . written about ten sheets of paper, with my own hand, about some trifling affairs. . . . What will come of this labor, time will discover. I shall get nothing by it, I believe, because I never get anything by anything that I do. I am sure the public or posterity ought to get something. I believe my children will think I might as well have thought and labored a little, night and day, for their benefit. But I will not bear the reproaches of my children. I will tell them that I studied and labored to procure a free constitution of government for them to solace themselves under, and if they do not prefer this to ample fortune, to ease and elegance, they are not my children, and I care not what becomes of them.

In his plan for government Adams made it clear there must be limitations on the voting privilege. He believed that women should be excluded from the franchise:

. . . because their delicacy renders them unfit for practice and experience in the great business of life, and the hardy enterprises of war, as well as the arduous cares of state. Besides, their attention is so much engaged with the necessary nurture of their children, that nature has made them fittest for domestic cares. . . . Men in general, in every society, who are wholly destitute of property, are also too little acquainted with public affairs to form a right judgment, and too dependent upon other men to have a will of their own. . . . If you give to every man who has no property a vote, will you not make a fine encouraging provision for corruption? . . .

Depend upon it, sir, it is dangerous to open so fruitful a source of controversy and altercation as would be opened by attempting to alter the qualifications of voters; there will be no end of it. New claims will arise; women will demand a vote . . . and every man who has not a farthing will demand an equal voice with any other in all acts of state. It tends to confound and destroy all distinctions and prostrate all ranks to one common level.

Through the spring of 1776 the business of Congress was impeded by the persistent rumors that British commissioners were coming to try to effect a reconciliation. To Abby, John wrote:

WE ARE WAITING, it is said, for commissioners; a Messiah that will never come. This story of commissioners is as arrant an illusion as ever was hatched in the brain of an enthusiast, a politician, or a maniac. I have laughed at it, scolded at it, grieved at it, and I don't know but I may, at an unguarded moment, have rip'd at it. But it is vain to reason against such delusions.

When the commissioners did not come Congress dispatched Silas Deane as an emissary to France, and Adams made notes in his diary which were his first expressions of his "no entangling alliances" foreign policy which would guide America for many years.

IS ANY ASSISTANCE attainable from France? What connection may we safely form with her? 1. No political connection. Submit to none of her authority; receive no governors or officers from her. 2. No military connection. Receive no troops from her. 3. Only a commercial connection; that is, make a treaty to receive her ships into our ports; let her engage to receive our ships into her ports; furnish us with arms, cannon, saltpeter, powder, duck, steel.

There were several recurrent themes in his letters to Abby. He found much to criticize, voiced many complaints. There were self-pity and self-analysis and frequent comments on the moral weaknesses of mankind over which he tried to triumph. After writing that his letters were an *omnium gatherum,* a "collection of all things," he continued:

AMIDST ALL THE RUBBISH that constitutes the heap, you will see a proportion of affection for my friends, my family, and country, that gives a complexion to the whole. I have a very tender, feeling heart. This country knows not, and never can know, the torments I have endured for its sake. . . .

I have seen in this world but a little of that pure flame of patriotism which certainly burns in some breasts. There is much of the ostentation and affectation of it. I have known a few who could not bear to entertain a selfish design, nor to be suspected by others of such a meanness; but these are not the most respected by the world. A man must be selfish, even to acquire great popularity. He must grasp for himself, under specious pretenses for the public good, and he must attach himself to his relations, connections, and friends, by becoming a champion for their interests, in order to form a phalanx about him for his own defense, to make them trumpeters of his praise, and sticklers for his fame, fortune, and honor. . . . Thus it always is and has been and will be. Nothing has ever given me more mortification than a suspicion that has been propagated of me, that I am actuated by private views and have been aiming at high places. . . . There are very few people in this world with whom I can bear to converse. I can treat all with decency and civility, and converse with them, when it is necessary, on points of business. But I am never happy in their company. This has made me a recluse and will one day make me a hermit.

In May 1776 a resolution that each colony should set up a new government was proposed by a committee consisting of Adams, Richard Henry Lee, and Edward Rutledge. The preamble read, "it is necessary that the exercise of every kind of authority under the said crown should be totally suppressed, and all the powers of government exerted, under the authority of the people of the colonies." Adams later said that this "was . . . considered by men of understanding as equivalent to a declaration of independence." At the time he expressed his pride in his accomplishment to Abigail by writing:

Is IT NOT a saying of Moses, "Who am I, that I should go in and out before this great people?" When I consider the great events which are passed, and those greater which are rapidly advancing, and that I may have been instrumental in touching some springs and turning some small wheels, which have had and will have such effects, I feel an awe upon my mind which is not easily described.

Then in June and July, came the big events, which Adams described in his autobiography by writing:

NOT LONG AFTER THIS, the three greatest measures of all were carried. Three committees were appointed, one for preparing a declaration of independence, another for reporting a plan of a treaty to be proposed to France, and a third to digest a system of articles of confederation to be proposed to the

States. I was appointed on the committee of independence and on that for preparing the form of a treaty with France. . . . The committee of independence were Thomas Jefferson, John Adams, Benjamin Franklin, Roger Sherman, and Robert R. Livingston. . . .

The committee had several meetings, in which were proposed the articles of which the declaration was to consist, and minutes made of them. The committee then appointed Mr. Jefferson and me to draw them up in form, and clothe them in a proper dress. The subcommittee met, and considered the minutes, making such observations on them as then occurred, when Mr. Jefferson desired me to take them to my lodgings, and make the draught. This I declined, and gave several reasons for declining. 1. That he was a Virginian and I a Massachusettensian. 2. That he was a southern man and I a northern one. 3. That I had been so obnoxious for my early and constant zeal in promoting the measure that any draught of mine would undergo a more severe scrutiny and criticism in Congress than one of his composition. 4. And lastly, and that would be reason enough if there were no other, I had a great opinion of the elegance of his pen, and none at all of my own. I therefore insisted that no hesitation should be made on his part. He accordingly took the minutes, and in a day or two produced to me his draught. Whether I made or suggested any correction, I remember not. The report was made to the committee of five, by them examined, but whether altered or corrected in anything, I cannot recollect. But, in substance at least, it was reported to Congress, where, after a severe criticism, and striking out several of the most oratorical paragraphs, it was adopted on the fourth of July, 1776, and published to the world.

When he was eighty-eight years old Adams wrote another letter on this subject to Timothy Pickering. Before commenting on the Declaration, he describes the situation in which he found himself in Congress and seeks to explain why it was Virginia, rather than his beloved Massachusetts, which proposed independence. He says that, en route to Philadelphia:

CUSHING, two Adamses and [Robert Treat] Paine, all destitute of fortune, four poor pilgrims, proceeded in one coach. . . . We were met at Frankfort by Dr. Rush, Mr. Miflin, Mr. Bayard, and several other of the most active Sons of Liberty in Philadelphia who . . . asked leave to give us some information and advice, which we thankfully granted. They represented to us that the friends of government in Boston and in the Eastern States, in their correspondence with their friends in Pennsylvania and all the Southern States, had represented us as four desperate adventurers. "Mr. Cushing was a harmless kind of man, but poor, and wholly dependent on his popularity with the lowest vulgar for his living. John Adams and Mr. Paine were two young lawyers of no great talents, reputation, or weight, who had no other means of raising themselves into consequence than by courting popularity." We were all suspected of having independence in view. "Now," said they, "you must not utter the word independence, nor give the least hint of insinuation of the idea, either in Congress or any private conversation; if you do, you are undone; for the idea of independence is as unpopular in Pennsylvania and in all the Middle and Southern States as the Stamp Act itself. No man dares to speak of it. . . . You must be . . . very cautious; you must not come forward with any bold measures, you must not pretend to take the lead. You know Virginia is the most populous State in the Union. They are very proud of their ancient dominion, as they call it; they think they have a right to take the lead, and the Southern States, and Middle States too, are too much disposed to yield it to them."

This was plain dealing, Mr. Pickering; and I must confess that there appeared so much wisdom and good sense in it that it made a deep impression on my mind, and it had an equal effect on all my colleagues. This conversation, and the principles, facts, and motives suggested in it, have given a color, complexion, and character to the whole policy of the United States from that day to this. Without, Mr. Washington would never have commanded our armies; nor Mr. Jefferson have been the author of the Declaration of Independence; nor Mr. Richard Henry Lee the mover of it; nor Mr. Chase the mover of foreign connections. . . .

You inquire why so young a man as Mr. Jefferson was placed at the head of the Committee for Preparing a Declaration of Independence? I answer: it was the Frankfort advice, to place Virginia at the head of everything.

In this same letter Adams evaluated Jefferson's Declaration of Independence in much the same manner as he had criticized Thomas Paine's *Common Sense;* it was all right to a point—but all that was good in it had originated in Massachusetts.

I WAS DELIGHTED with its high tone and the flights of oratory with which it abounded, especially that concerning Negro slavery, which, though I knew his southern brethren would never suffer to pass in Congress, I certainly never would oppose. There were other expressions which I would not have inserted, if I had drawn it up, particularly that which called the King tyrant. I thought this too personal; for I never believed George to be a tyrant in disposition and in nature; I always believed him to be deceived by his courtiers on both sides of the Atlantic and, in his official capacity only, cruel. I thought the expression too passionate and too much like scolding, for so grave and solemn a document. . . .

We reported it to the committee of five. It was read, and I do not remember that Franklin or Sherman criticized anything. We were all in haste. Congress was impatient, and the instrument was reported, as I believe, in Jefferson's handwriting, as he first drew it. Congress cut off about a quarter of it, as I expected they would; but they obliterated some of the best of it, and left all that was exceptionably, if anything in it was. . . .

As you justly observe, there is not an idea in it but what had been hackneyed in Congress for two years before. The substance of it is contained in the declaration of rights and the violation of those rights, in the Journals of Congress in 1774. Indeed, the essence of it is contained in a pamphlet voted and printed by the town of Boston, before the first Congress met, composed by James Otis, as I suppose, in one of his lucid intervals, and pruned and polished by Samuel Adams.

Adams' letter drew a comment from octogenarian Jefferson.

THESE DETAILS are quite incorrect. The committee of five met; no such thing as a subcommittee was proposed, but they unanimously pressed on myself alone to undertake the draft. I consented; I drew it; but before I reported it to the committee, I communicated it separately to Doctor Franklin and Mr. Adams, requesting their corrections because they were the two members of whose judgments and amendments I wished most to have the benefit before presenting it to the committee; and you have seen the original paper now in my hands, with the corrections of Doctor Franklin and Mr. Adams interlined in their own handwritings.

On Jefferson's draft of the Declaration there are two inconsequential changes in Adams' hand, five in Franklin's, and sixteen changes and three added paragraphs in Jefferson's hand, which may have been proposed by his colleagues. Of Adams' accusation of plagiarism, the Virginian wrote:

PICKERING'S OBSERVATIONS, and Mr. Adams in addition, "that it contained no new ideas, that it is a commonplace compilation, its sentiments hackneyed in Congress for two years before, and its essence contained in Otis' pamphlet," may all be true. Of that I am not to be the judge. . . . Otis' pamphlet I never saw, and whether I had gathered my ideas from reading or reflection I do not know. I know only that I turned to neither book nor pamphlet while writing it. I did not consider it as any part of my charge to invent new ideas altogether.

In the minds of the members of the second Congress the important act of early July 1776 was not the signing of the Declaration of Independence but the actual fact of independence brought about by the adoption on July 2 of Richard Henry Lee's motion "that these united colonies are, and of right ought to be free and independent states." Regardless of his relation to the declaration, there is no doubt that John Adams was the strong man on the floor of Congress who carried the fight for independence when the motion was debated on July 1. He later described the scene by writing:

I AM NOT ABLE to recollect whether it was on this or some preceding day that the greatest and most solemn debate was had on the question of independence: . . . Mr. Dickinson . . . was determined to bear his testimony against it. . . . He had prepared himself apparently with great labor and ardent zeal and in a speech of great length, and with all his eloquence he combined together all that had before been written in pamphlets and newspapers and all that had from time to time been said in Congress by himself and others. He conducted the debate not only with great ingenuity and eloquence, but with equal politeness and candor, and was answered in the same spirit. No member rose to answer him, and after waiting some time in hopes that someone less obnoxious than myself, who . . . was represented and believed to be the author of all the mischief, would move, I determined to speak.

It has been said, by some of our historians, that I began by an invocation to the god of eloquence. This is a misrepresentation. Nothing so puerile as this fell from me. I began by saying that this was the first time of my life that I had ever wished for the talents and eloquence of the ancient orators of Greece and Rome, for I was very sure that none of them ever had before him a question of more importance to his country and to the world. They would probably, upon less occasions than this, have begun by solemn invocations to their divinities for assistance; but the question before me appeared so simple that I had confidence enough in the plain understanding and common sense that had been given me to believe that I could answer, to the satisfaction of the House, all the arguments which had been produced. . . . I had made no preparation beforehand, and never committed any minutes . . . to writing. . . . I summed up the reasons, objections, and answers, in as concise a manner as I could, till at length the . . . gentlemen . . . were fully satisfied and ready for the question, which was then put and determined in the affirmative.

There is much confirmation of the role that Adams played as the principal spokesman for independence. Jefferson later wrote, in connection with the contemplated publication of a decorated copy of the Declaration:

No MAN better merited than Mr. John Adams to hold a most conspicuous place in the design. He was the pillar of its support on the floor of Congress, its ablest advocate and defender against the multifarious assaults it encountered; for many excellent persons opposed it on doubts, whether we were provided sufficiently with the means of supporting it [and] whether the minds of our constituents were yet prepared to receive it.

Although he was not there at the time, James Madison recorded:

. . . the reports from Mr. Adams' fellow laborers in the cause, from Virginia, filled every mouth in that state with the praises due to the comprehensiveness of his views, the force of his arguments, and the boldness of his patriotism.

Richard Stockton, delegate from New Jersey, told his son:

THE MAN TO WHOM the country is most indebted for the great measure of independence is Mr. John Adams of Boston. I call him the Atlas of American independence. He it was who sustained the debate, and by the force of his reasoning demonstrated not only the justice, but the expediency, of the measure.

To his wife Adams wrote, on July 3, an account of the event, and accurately predicted the manner in which the country would henceforth celebrate Independence Day—except that he envisioned a "grand and glorious second" rather than a grand and glorious fourth.

YESTERDAY the greatest question was decided which ever was debated in America, and a greater, perhaps, never was nor will be decided among men. The second day of July 1776 will be the most memorable epocha in the history of America. I am apt to believe that it will be celebrated by succeeding generations as the great anniversary festival. It ought to be commemorated as the day of deliverance by solemn acts of devotion to God Almighty. It ought to be solemnized with pomp and parade, with shows, games, sports, guns, bells, bonfires, and illuminations, from one end of this continent to the other from this time forward forevermore.

You will think me transported with enthusiasm, but I am not. I am well aware of the toil and blood and treasure that it will cost us to maintain this Declaration and support and defend these States. Yet, through all the gloom, I can see the rays of ravishing light and glory. I can see that the end is more than worth all the means. And that posterity will triumph in that day's transaction, even although we should rue it, which I trust in God we shall not.

On the committee to draft a proposed French treaty, Adams apparently dominated the proceedings. He drafted and forced through Congress a form of a treaty which offered France nothing but the right to trade with the Colonies, a concession which, thought Adams:

. . . would be ample compensation to France for acknowledging our independence and for furnishing us, for our money, or upon credit for a time, with such supplies of necessaries as we should want, even if this conduct should involve her in a war. . . . When it [the treaty draft] came before Congress . . . many motions were made to insert in it articles of entangling alliance, of exclusive privileges, and of warranties of possessions; and it was argued that the present plan reported by the committee held out no sufficient temptation to France, who would despise it and refuse to receive our ambassador. It was chiefly left to me to defend my report, though I had some able assistance, and we did defend it with so much success that the treaty passed without one particle of alliance, exclusive privilege, or warranty.

The treaty which Benjamin Franklin negotiated with France in 1777 bore little resemblance to Adams' draft.

One clause written by Adams which did stay in the final treaty —although in Franklin's far more diplomatic language—expressed the basis of the famous Doctrine which John Adams' son, as James Monroe's Secretary of State, would help to formulate forty-seven years later.

IN CASE OF ANY WAR between the most Christian King and the King of Great Britain, the most Christian King shall never invade, nor under any pretence attempt to possess himself of Labrador, New Britain, Nova Scotia, Accadia, Canada, Florida, nor any of the Countries, Cities, or Towns, on the Continent of North America. . . . it being the true intent and meaning of this treaty that the said United States shall have the sole, exclusive, undivided and perpetual possession of all the Countries, Cities, and Towns on the said Continent, and of all Islands near to it, which now are, or lately were under the Jurisdiction of or subject to the King or Crown of Great Britain."

One pleasant chore for Adams at this time was serving on a committee with Franklin and Jefferson to design a great seal for the United Colonies. To Abby he wrote:

DR. F. PROPOSES a device for a seal: Moses lifting up his wand and dividing the Red Sea, and Pharaoh in his chariot overwhelmed with the waters. This motto, "Rebellion to tyrants is obedience to God." Mr. Jefferson proposed the children of Israel in the wilderness, led by a cloud by day and a pillar of fire by night; and on the other side, Hengist and Horsa, the Saxon chiefs from whom we claim the honor of being descended, and whose political principles and form of government we have assumed. I proposed the choice of Hercules . . . resting on his club. Virtue pointing to her rugged mountain on one hand, and persuading him to ascend. Sloth, glancing at her flowery paths of pleasure, wantonly reclining on the ground, displaying the charms both of her eloquence and person, to seduce him into vice. But this is too complicated a group for a seal or medal, and it is not original.

Another important subject which occupied Congress during the summer of 1776 was the report of the Commitee on Articles of Confederation. Adams was not a member, but since the report was written by conservative Dickinson, he had much to say about it. The principal bone of contention was, he wrote Abby: "If a confederation should take place, one great question is, how we shall vote. Whether each colony shall count one; or whether each shall have a weight in proportion to its number, or wealth, or exports and imports, or a compound ratio of all."

Dickinson had proposed that "in determining questions each colony shall have one vote." Adams maintained that the delegates in Congress were representatives of the people, not of the states, and that voting therefore should be in proportion to population. The interests within Congress "should be the mathematical representatives of the interests without doors." The so-called individuality of the colonies was "mere sound." He would give an example: "A has £50, B £500, C £1,000 in partnership. Is it just they should equally dispose of the moneys of partnership?" The small state members argued that the colonies were as individuals making a bargain. But, asked Adams, what would happen "when our bargain shall be made?" He answered himself by saying, "The confederacy is to make us one individual only; it is to form us, like separate parcels of metal, into one common mass. We shall no longer retain our separate individuality, but become a single individual."

These debates touched on an essential difference in viewpoint in political philosophy which would continue throughout American history. Adams placed himself strongly in the camp which would later be known as nationalist and, still later, as Federalist. Here was the embryo of the two-party political system.

Much of Adams' time during the remainder of his stay in the Congress was devoted to his position as Chairman of the Board of War—in effect, the Secretary of Defense. He said, "The daily references to the Board of War rendered it necessary for me to spend almost my whole time in it; on mornings till Congress met, and on evenings till late at night." The dilatory Congress was delinquent in every aspect of providing for the army in the field, and there was not much that Adams could do about it. He thoroughly agreed with Washington's demand for long-term enlistments, but Congress would not—indeed, it had not the means to

—provide the bounties, better pay, and other inducements to achieve this end. There was much dissatisfaction among the officers about their pay, which Adams thought was already too high in relation to that of enlisted men; and the New England officers complained that they were being passed over for favored Southerners. This brought threats of resignation from Generals Sullivan and Lincoln; and Benedict Arnold's treachery can be traced to Congress' promoting southerners over his head.

In his capacity as Chairman of the War Board, Adams, with the help of Jefferson, undertook to revise the Articles of War. He wrote:

IT WAS A VERY DIFFICULT and unpopular subject, and I observed to Jefferson that whatever alteration we should report with the least energy in it, or the least tendency to a necessary discipline of the army, would be opposed with as much vehemence as if it were the most perfect. We might as well, therefore, report a complete system at once, and let it meet its fate. Something perhaps might be gained. There was extant one system of articles of war which had carried two empires to the head of mankind, the Roman and the British; for the British articles of war were only a literal translation of the Roman. . . . I was, therefore, for reporting the British articles of war *totidem verbis*. Jefferson, in those days, never failed to agree with me in everything of a political nature, and he very cordially concurred in this. The British articles of war were, accordingly, reported and defended in Congress by me assisted by some others, and finally carried. They laid the foundation of a discipline which, in time, brought our troops to a capacity of contending with British veterans and a rivalry with the best troops of France.

Early in September 1776 General Sullivan, who had been captured by the British at the Battle of Long Island, returned to

Philadelphia with a message from Admiral Lord Howe to the effect:

THAT HE, in conjunction with General Howe, had full powers to compromise the dispute between Great Britain and America, upon terms advantageous to both. . . . That in case Congress were disposed to treat, many things which they had not as yet asked might and ought to be granted them; and that if, upon the conference, they found any probable ground of accommodation, the authority of Congress must be afterward acknowledged, otherwise the compact would not be complete.

Congress replied that Howe would have to recognize the authority of Congress before they would deal with him officially, but that three members would meet with him in their capacities as private gentlemen. Adams wrote at length of this pointless meeting. In his autobiography he described the trip to meet the Admiral.

MR. FRANKLIN, Mr. Edward Rutledge, and Mr. John Adams proceeded on their journey to Lord Howe on Staten Island, the two former in chairs, and the latter on horseback. . . . The taverns were so full we could with difficulty obtain entertainment. At Brunswick but one bed could be procured for Dr. Franklin and me, in a chamber little larger than the bed, without a chimney, and with only one small window. The window was open, and I, who was an invalid and afraid of the air in the night, shut it close. "Oh!" says Franklin, "don't shut the window, we shall be suffocated." I answered, "I was afraid of the evening air." Dr. Franklin replied, "The air within this chamber will soon be, and indeed is now, worse than that without doors. Come, open the window and come to bed, and I will convince you. I believe you are not acquainted with my theory of colds." Opening the window and leaping into bed, I said I had read his letters to Dr. Cooper in which he had advanced that nobody ever got cold by going into a cold church or any other cold air, but the theory was so little consistent with my experience that I thought it a paradox. However, I had so much curiosity to hear his reasons that I would run the risk of a cold. The Doctor then began a harangue upon air and cold, and respiration and perspiration, with which I was so much amused that I soon fell asleep, and left him and his philosophy together, but I believe they were equally sound and insensible within a few minutes after me, for the last words I heard were pronounced as if he was more than half asleep. I remember little of the lecture, except that . . . by breathing over again the matter thrown off by the lungs and the skin we should imbibe the real cause of colds, not from abroad, but from within. I am not inclined to introduce here a dissertation on the subject. There is much truth, I believe, in some things he advanced, but they warrant not the assertion that a cold is never taken from cold air. . . . I have heard that in the opinion of his own able physician, Dr. Jones, he fell a sacrifice at last . . . to his own theory, having caught the violent cold which finally choked him by sitting for some hours at a window, with the cool air blowing upon him.

Lord Howe received his rebellious guests graciously and escorted them "between lines of guards of grenadiers looking fierce as ten Furies" to his headquarters on Staten Island which

. . . had been the habitation of military guards, and was as dirty as a stable; but his lordship had prepared a large handsome room by spreading a carpet of moss and green sprigs from bushes and shrubs in the neighborhood till he had made it not only wholesome, but romantically elegant; and he entertained us with good claret, good bread, cold ham, tongues, and mutton. . . .

His Lordship then entered into a discourse of considerable length, which contained no explicit proposition of peace, except one, namely: That the Colonies should return to their allegiance and obedience to the government of Great Britain. The rest consisted, principally, of assurances that there was an exceeding good disposition in the King and his ministers to make that government easy to us, with intimations that, in case of our submission, they would cause the offensive acts of Parliament to be revised and the instructions to governors to be reconsidered. . . .

We gave it as our opinion to his lordship that a return to the domination of Great Britain was not now to be expected. We mentioned the repeated humble petitions of the Colonies to the King and Parliament . . . the unexampled patience we had shown under their tyrannical government, and that it was not till the late act of Parliament, which denounced war against us and put us out of the King's protection, that we declared our independence; that this declaration had been called for by the people of the Colonies in general . . . so that it was not in the power of Congress to agree, for them, that they should return to their former dependent state. . . . His Lordship then, saying that he was sorry to find that no accommodation was like to take place, put an end to the conference.

Upon the whole, it did not appear to your committee that his lordship's commission contained any other authority than that . . . of granting pardons . . . and of declaring America . . . to be in the King's peace, upon submission.

With the failure of the conference the Howe brothers immediately landed troops in New York City and drove the Americans north. This, following the defeat on Long Island, loosed a flood of critical letters from Adams to officers in the army. The impropriety of the Chairman of the War Board writing such criticism to subordinates of the Commander-in-Chief did not then seem to occur to him. Of these letters he later wrote:

IF THESE PAPERS should hereafter be read by disinterested persons, they will perhaps think that I took too much upon

me, in assuming the office of preceptor to the army. To this
objection, I can only reply by asserting that it was high time
that the army had some instructor or other. It was a scene of
indiscipline, insubordination, and confusion. . . . I had formed
an opinion that courage and reading were all that were necessary to the formation of an officer. Of the courage of these
gentlemen, and the officers in general, I had no doubt; but I
was too well informed that most of the officers were deficient
in reading. . . . I will add without vanity, I had read as much
on the military art, and much more of the history of war, than
any American officer of that army, General Lee excepted. If
all these considerations are not a sufficient apology for my interference, I submit to censure. Certain it is, that these letters
. . . were not calculated to procure me popularity in the army.

The army lacked discipline, he wrote, and courage. The officers,
none of whom, he said, knew their business, were mostly to blame.
He told his wife:

WHEREVER THE MEN OF WAR have approached our militia
have most manfully turned their backs and run away, officers
and men, like sturdy fellows; and their panics have sometimes
seized the regular regiments. . . . You are told that a regiment
of Yorkers behaved ill, and it may be true; but I can tell you
that several regiments of Massachusetts men behaved ill too.
The spirit of venality you mention is the most dreadful and
alarming enemy America has to oppose. It is as rapacious
and insatiable as the grave. . . . This predominant avarice will
ruin America, if she is ever ruined. If God Almighty does not
interfere by His grace to control this universal idolatry to the
mammon of unrighteousness we shall be given up to the chas-
tisements of His judgments. I am ashamed of the age I live in.

And when Washington retreated across the Hudson, he expressed a temporary lack of faith in the great commander by writing:

O HEAVEN! grant us one great soul! One leading mind would extricate the best cause from that ruin which seems to await it for the want of it. We have as good a cause as ever was fought for; we have great resources; the people are well tempered; one active, masterly capacity would bring order out of this confusion, and save this country.

The generals of the army had another grave fault in Adams' opinion; atrocious literary style. He wrote Washington's aide, Colonel Tudor:

YOU MUST BE SENSIBLE that intelligence is of the last consequence to the Congress, to the Assemblies, and to the public at large. It ought, therefore, to be transmitted as quick and frequently, and with as much exactness and particularity, as possible. In time of war, the letters from generals and other officers of the army are usually the memorials and documents from whence annals are afterward compiled and histories composed. . . . Read the relation of the battle between Catiline and his adversaries, in Sallust. You see the combatants. You feel the ardor of the battle. You see the blood of the slain, and you hear the wounded sigh and groan. But if you read our American relations of battles and sieges, in our newspapers or in private letters, or indeed in public official letters, you see little of this accuracy. . . . A general officer should spare no pains to make himself master of the epistolary style, which is easy, natural, simple, and familiar, and of the historical style, too, which is equally simple, although a little more grave, solemn, and noble. Xenophon, Caesar, Wolfe, Lee, are all indebted for a very large share of their fame to their pens.

By the end of the summer of 1776 John Adams was most

unhappy in Philadelphia. "Oppressed with a load of business, without an amanuensis or any assistance, I was obliged to do everything myself . . . I had no secretary or servant whom I could trust to write, and everything must be copied by myself." He complained constantly of his poor health: "My face is grown pale, my eyes weak and inflamed again, my nerves tremulous, and my mind weak as water. Night sweats and feverous heats by day are returned upon me, which is an infallible symptom with me that it is time to throw off all care for a time, and take my rest." To Abby he wrote:

FROM FOUR O'CLOCK in the morning until ten at night, I have not a single moment which I can call my own. I will not say that I expect to run distracted, to grow melancholy, to drop in an apoplexy, or fall into a consumption; but I do say it is little less than a miracle that one or other of these misfortunes has not befallen me before now.

External evidence indicates that small, rotund John Adams had great stamina, despite his constant complaints of ill health; at least, he kept going far longer than many who considered themselves as rugged. But now he insisted on a rest and wrote the Secretary of the Massachusetts General Court:

NO GENTLEMAN CAN possibly attend to an incessant round of thinking, speaking, and writing upon the most intricate as well as important concerns of human society, from one end of the year to another, without injury to his mental and bodily health. . . . I must entreat the General Court to give me leave to resign and immediately to appoint some other gentleman in my room. The consideration of my own health and the circumstances of my family and private affairs would have little weight with me, if the sacrifice of these was necessary for the public; but it is not. Because those parts of the business of Congress for which, if for any, I have any qualifications, being now nearly completed, and the business that remains being chiefly military and commercial, of which I know very little, there are multitudes of gentlemen in the province much fitter for the public service here than I am.

When he received no prompt reply he wrote Warren:

GO HOME I will, if I leave the Massachusetts without a member here. You know my resolutions in these matters are as fixed as fate; or if you do not know it, I do.

When he returned to Congress after a three-month vacation John complained to Abigail of the grinding routine.

I HAVE GOT into the old routine of war office and Congress, which takes up my time in such a manner that I can scarce write a line. I have not time to think nor to speak. There is a United States lottery abroad. I believe you had better buy a ticket and make a present of it to our four sweet ones. Let us try their luck. I hope they will be more lucky than their papa has ever been, or ever will be. I am as well as can be expected. How it happens I don't know, nor how long it will last.

And, a few days later:

THIS CITY is a dull place in comparison of what it was. More than one half the inhabitants have removed into the country, as it was their wisdom to do. The remainder are chiefly Quakers, as dull as beetles. From these neither good is to be expected nor evil to be apprehended. They are a kind of neutral tribe, or the race of the insipids.

From the cares of war he took time to display his erudition to his wife in a brief essay on the genius of an ancient female.

I THINK I have sometimes observed to you in conversation that upon examining the biography of illustrious men you will generally find some female about them, in the relation of mother or wife or sister, to whose instigation a great part of their merit is to be ascribed. You will find a curious example of this in the case of Aspasia, the wife of Pericles. She was a woman of the greatest beauty and the first genius. She taught him, it is said, his refined maxims of policy, his lofty imperial eloquence, nay, even composed the speeches on which so great a share of his reputation was founded. The best men in Athens frequented her house and brought their wives to receive lessons from her of economy and right deportment. Socrates himself was her pupil in eloquence, and gives her the honor of that funeral oration which he delivers in the "Menexenus" of Plato. Aristophanes, indeed, abuses this famous lady, but Socrates does her honor. I wish some of our great men had such wives. By the account in your last letter, it seems the women in Boston begin to think themselves able to serve their country. What a pity it is that our generals in the northern districts had not Aspasias to their wives!

He was somewhat annoyed at the amount of time Congress devoted to selecting gifts for the ladies of the French court, although he allowed that some good might come of it. Congress was considering, he wrote Abby:

MR. RITTENHOUS'S PLANETARIUM, Mr. Arnold's collection of varieties . . . which I once saw at Norwalk in Connecticut, Narragansett pacing mares, mooses, wood-ducks, flying squirrels, red-winged blackbirds, cranberries, and rattlesnakes have all been thought of. Is not this a pretty employment for great statesmen as we think ourselves to be? Frivolous as it seems, it may be of some consequence. Little attentions have great influence. I think, however, we ought to consult the ladies upon this point. Pray what is your opinion?

The willingness of France to help the rebellious colonies to the point of risking war with England seemed to annoy Adams, who never trusted French motives. He wrote Warren:

I DO NOT love to be entangled in the quarrels of Europe. I do not wish to be under obligations to any of them, and I am very unwilling they should rob us of the glory of vindicating our own liberties. It is a cowardly spirit in our countrymen which makes them pant with so much longing expectation after a French war. I have very often been ashamed to hear so many Whigs groaning and sighing with despondency and whining out their fears that we must be subdued unless France should step in. Are we to be beholden to France for our liberties? France has done so much already that honor and dignity and reputation of Great Britain are concerned to resent it. . . . She has received our ambassadors, protected our merchant-men, privateers, men-of-war and prizes, admitted us freely to trade, lent us money, and supplied us with arms, ammunition, and warlike stores of every kind. This is notorious all over Europe. And she will do more, presently, if our dastardly despondency, in the midst of the finest prospects imaginable, does not discourage her. . . . I am more concerned about our revenue than the aid of France. Pray let the loan offices do their part that we may not be compelled to make paper money as plenty and of course as cheap as oak leaves. There is so much injustice in carrying on a war with a depreciating currency that we can hardly pray with confidence for success.

The year 1777 was, in the main, rather uneventful for Adams; or so his sparse correspondence and diary entries indicate. As the third anniversary of his service to the nation approached in July he wrote his wife:

OUR AFFAIRS are in a fine, prosperous train, and if they continue so I can leave this station with honor. Next month completes three years that I have been devoted to the service of liberty. A slavery it has been to me, whatever the world may think of it. To a man whose attachments to his family are as strong as mine, absence alone from such a wife and such children would be a great sacrifice. But in addition to this separation what have I not hazarded? What have I not done? What have I not suffered? These are questions that I may ask you, but I will ask such questions of none else. Let the cymbals of popularity tinkle still. Let the buterflies of fame glitter with their wings. I shall envy neither their music nor their colors. The loss of property affects me little. All other hard things I despise, but the loss of your company and that of my dear babes, for so long a time, I consider as a loss of so much solid happiness. The tender social feelings of my heart, which have distressed me beyond all utterance in my most busy, active scenes, as well as in the numerous hours of melancholy solitude, are known only to God and my own soul.

When Howe threatened Philadelphia John wrote:

THE MOMENTS are critical here. We know not but the next will bring us an account of a general engagement begun, and when once begun, we know not how it will end. . . . But if it should be the will of Heaven that our army should be defeated, our artillery lost, our best generals killed, and Philadelphia fall into Mr. Howe's hands, still America is not conquered. . . . It may, for what I know, be the design of Providence that this should be the case, because it would only lay the foundations of American independence deeper, and cement them stronger. It would cure Americans of their vicious and luxurious and effeminate appetites, passions, and habits; a more dangerous army to American liberty than Mr. Howe's.

As Burgoyne moved toward Saratoga, Adams rejoiced that "The New England troops and New York troops are every man of them at Peekskill and with Gates. The Massachusetts men are all with Gates. General Washington has none but southern troops with him." Then Howe defeated Washington, and Adams recorded:

IN THE MORNING of the 19th instant, the Congress were alarmed in their beds by a letter from Mr. [Alexander] Hamilton, one of General Washington's family, that the enemy was in possession of the ford over the Schuylkill and the boats, so that they had it in their power to be in Philadelphia before morning.

The Congress moved to York where Adams heard the good news of Saratoga and wrote his wife:

CONGRESS WILL APPOINT a thanksgiving; and one cause of it ought to be that the glory of turning the tide of arms is not immediately due to the Commander-in-Chief nor to southern troops. If it had been, idolatry and adulation would have been unbounded, so excessive as to endanger our liberties, for what I know. Now, we can allow a certain citizen [Washington] to be wise, virtuous, and good, without thinking him a deity or a savior.

Early in November John again left Congress, this time accompanied by cousin Samuel. He later wrote:

IT WAS MY INTENTION to decline the next election, and return to my practice at the bar. I had been four years in Congress, had left my accounts in a very loose condition, my debtors were failing, the paper money was depreciating; I was daily losing the fruits of seventeen years' industry; my family was living on my past acquisitions, which were very moderate . . . my children were growing up without my care in their education, and all my emoluments as a member of Congress, for four years, had not been sufficient to pay a laboring man upon my farm.

After his return to Braintree his legal practice started to thrive immediately, but his recess as an attorney was of short duration. He journey to Portsmouth to try a big case and reported:

WHILE I WAS SPEAKING in it, Mr. Langdon came in from Philadelphia, and leaning over the bar, whispered to me that Mr. Deane was recalled and I was appointed to go to France. As I could scarcely believe the news to be true, and suspected Langdon to be sporting with me, it did not disconcert me. . . . Upon my return to Braintree, I found to my infinite anxiety that Mr. Langdon's intelligence was too well founded. Large packets from Congress, containing a new commission to Franklin, [Arthur] Lee, and me as plenipotentiaries to the King of France, with our instructions and other papers, had been left at my house and waited my arrival. . . .

When the dispatches from Congress were read, the first question was whether I should accept the commission or return it to Congress. The dangers of the seas, and the sufferings of a winter passage, although I had no experience of either, had little weight with me. The British men-of-war were a more serious consideration. . . . The consequence of a capture would be a lodging in Newgate. . . . Their act of Parliament would authorize them to try me in England for treason, and proceed to execution too. . . . My family, consisting of a dearly beloved wife and four young children, excited sentiments of tenderness which a father and a lover only can conceive, and which no language can express; and my want of qualifications for the office was by no means forgotten.

On the other hand, my country was in deep distress and in great danger. . . . My wife, who had always encouraged and animated me in all antecedent dangers and perplexities, did not fail me on this occasion. . . . After much agitation of mind, and a thousand reveries unnecessary to be detailed, I resolved to devote my family and my life to the cause, accepted the appointment, and made preparation for the voyage.

While he was getting ready to sail on the frigate *Boston,* John had a visit from General Knox, who, he said, wanted

. . . to sound me in relation to General Washington. He asked me what my opinion of him was. I answered, with the utmost frankness, that I thought him a perfectly honest man, with an amiable and excellent heart, and the most important character at that time among us, for he was the center of our Union. He asked the question, he said, because, as I was going to Europe, it was of importance that the General's character should be supported in other countries. I replied that he might be perfectly at his ease on the subject, for he might depend upon it that, both from principle and affection, public and private, I should do my utmost to support his character, at all times and in all places. . . . I mention this incident because that insolent blasphemer of things sacred and transcendent libeler of all that is good, Tom Paine, has more than once asserted in print that I was one of a faction, in the fall of the 1777, against General Washington.

Paine was not alone in believing that Adams favored Gates over Washington during the famous "Conway Cabal." La Fayette recorded in his memoirs that among the *ennemis* of Washington *"on distingue les Lees, Virginiens, and les deux Adams."* At least two of Adams' letters indicate that he was less than enthusiastic about the great Virginian at that time, but he could have had no active part in the agitation to replace the Commander-in-Chief with General Gates because it did not take place until after Adams had left Congress.

Adams' autobiography for 1777 ends with the terse comment: "I was almost out of patience waiting for the frigate till the thirteenth day of February, 1778."

CHAPTER III

THE DIPLOMAT

During the first few days of the long and dangerous voyage of the frigate *Boston* Adams felt that he might have occasion to jettison the dispatches which he had packaged, "with weight proper for sinking them on any immediate prospect of their otherwise falling into the enemies' hands." The *Boston* was chased by three British ships, escaped in the night, and then ran into a violent storm. "The smoke and smell of sea-coal, the smell of stagnant, putrid water, the smell of the ship where the sailors lie," brought on a session of *mal de mer*. When he recovered Adams noted in his diary:

IT WOULD BE FRUITLESS to attempt a description of what I saw, heard, and felt during these three days and nights. To describe the ocean, the waves, the winds; the ship, her motions, rollings, grindings, and agonies; the sailors, their countenances, language, and behavior, is impossible. No man could keep upon his legs, and nothing could be kept in its place; a universal wreck of everything in all parts of the ship, chests, casks, bottles, etc. No place was dry. . . . every thing and place was so wet, every table and chair was so wrecked, that it was impossible to touch pen or paper. It is a great satisfaction to me, however, to recollect that I was myself perfectly calm during the whole.

As soon as he was able to write John noted the deficiencies of the vessel, its crew, and its administration: "Our captain is an able seaman, and a brave, active, vigilant officer, but I believe he has no great erudition." As to the frigate, there was not enough space between decks; the ship was

. . . over-metalled; her number of guns, and the weight of their metal, is too great for her tonnage. . . . The ship is furnished with no pistols, which she ought to be. . . . This ship is not furnished with good glasses. . . . There is the same general inattention, I find, to economy in the navy that there is in the army. . . . There is the same general relaxation of order and discipline. . . . There is the same inattention to the cleanliness of the ship, and the persons and health of the sailors, as there is at land to the cleanliness of the camp and the health and cleanliness of the soldiers. . . . The practice of profane cursing and swearing, so silly as well as detestable, prevails in a most abominable degree.

Adams sought to remedy some of these faults by

. . . constantly giving hints to the captain concerning order, economy, and regularity, and he seems to be sensible of the necessity of them, and exerts himself to introduce them. . . . This ship would have bred the plague or the jail fever if there had not been great exertions since the storm to wash, sweep, air, and purify clothes, cots, cabins, hammocks, and all other things, places, and persons. The captain yesterday went down into the cockpit and ordered up everybody from that sink of devastation and putrefaction. . . . This was in pursuance of the advice I gave him in the morning: "If you intend to have

any reputation for economy, discipline, or anything that is
good, look to your cockpit!"

Ten-year-old John Quincy accompanied his father, and two
other boys of about the same age were aboard in Adams' care, the
sons of Silas Deane and William Vernon of the Navy Board. The
statesman found some consolation in the "guardianship of two
promising young gentlemen, besides my own son. This benevolent
office is peculiarly agreeable to my temper." Two French officers
started the boys on French lessons, but Adams *père* could not
accomplish much in this direction and concluded, "I believe very
little of anything was ever learned on a passage. There must be
more health and better accommodations." He watched the sailors
frolic when "the captain ordered a dance upon the main deck, and
all hands, Negroes, boys, and men, were obliged to dance." Some
of the men were "tolerably expert," but Adams concluded that
"there is not in them the least ray of elegance, very little wit, and
a humor of the coarsest kind. It is not superior to Negro and
Indian dances."

After six weeks at sea Adams was happy to land at Bordeaux
to be feted by the local officials in a garden that "was beautifully
illuminated with an inscription, 'God save the Congress, Liberty
and Adams.' " He recorded that, at dinner, "The language was
altogether incomprehensible. . . . I had much rather have remained in silent observation and reflection. . . . About 10 o'clock
we commenced our journey to Paris." If he was frustrated by the
news that Franklin had concluded an alliance with the Court of
Versailles before his arrival, he made no record of his feelings.

Four days after his arrival in Paris, John wrote his first impres-
sions to Abigail:

THE RECEPTION I have met in this kingdom has been as
friendly, as polite, and as respectful, as was possible. . . . The
delights of France are innumerable. The politeness, the elegance, the softness, the delicacy, are extreme. In short, stern

and haughty republican as I am, I cannot help loving these people for their earnest desire and assiduity to please.

It would be futile to attempt descriptions of this country, especially of Paris and Versailles. The public buildings and gardens, the paintings, sculpture, architecture, music, etc., of these cities have already filled many volumes. The richness, the magnificence and splendor are beyond all description. This magnificence is not confined to public buildings, such as churches, hospitals, schools, etc., but extends to private houses, to furniture, equipage, dress, and especially to entertainments. But what is all this to me? I receive but little pleasure in beholding all these things, because I cannot but consider them as bagatelles, introduced by time and luxury in exchange for the great qualities and hardy, manly virtues of the human heart. I cannot help suspecting that the more elegance, the less virtue, in all times and countries. Yet I fear that even my own dear country wants the power and opportunity more than the inclination to be elegant, soft, and luxurious.

A year later, in his diary, Adams recorded a somewhat different impression of his reception by the French:

WHEN I ARRIVED IN FRANCE, the French nation had a great many questions to settle. The first was, whether I was the famous Adams? *le fameux Adams? Ah, le fameux Adams* . . . The pamphlet entitled *Common Sense* had been printed in the *Affaires de l'Angleterre et de l'Amérique,* and expressly ascribed to Mr. Adams, the celebrated member of Congress—*le célèbre membre du Congrès.* . . . When I arrived at Bordeaux, all that I could say or do would not convince anybody but that I was the *fameux* Adams. . . .

But when I arrived at Paris I found a very different style. I found great pains taken, much more than the question was worth, to settle the point that I was not the famous Adams.

. . . All parties, both in France and England . . . differing in many other things, agreed in this, that I was not the famous Adams. . . . I behaved with as much prudence and civility and industry as I could; but still it was a settled point at Paris and in the English newspapers that I was not the famous Adams; and therefore the consequence was settled, absolutely and unalterably, that I was a man of whom nobody had ever heard before—a perfect cipher; a man who did not understand a word of French; awkward in his figure, awkward in his dress; no abilities; a perfect bigot and fanatic.

Adams found discord and animosity among the Americans who had preceded him to Paris. Before there was any formal agreement with France, Silas Deane, the first to arrive, had been successful in getting arms and ammunition from French arsenals through a dummy commercial company while the French government conveniently looked the other way. Obviously there were no damning records kept of this cloak and dagger operation. When Franklin and Arthur Lee arrived, the latter accused Deane of feathering his own nest. Deane was recalled by Congress and replaced by Adams. Lee also charged that Franklin would not tell him what was going on. This was to some extent true, but it was done at the request of the French foreign minister, the Comte de Vergennes, who was convinced that Lee was a British spy. Two days after his arrival Adams recorded Franklin's description of the situation in his diary:

THE FIRST MOMENT Dr. Franklin and I happened to be alone he began to complain to me of the coolness, as he very coolly called it, between the American ministers. He said there had been disputes between Mr. Deane and Mr. Lee; that Mr. Lee was a man of an anxious, uneasy temper, which made it disagreeable to do business with him; that he seemed to be one of those men, of whom he had known many in his day, who went on through life quarreling with one person or another till they commonly ended with the loss of their reason. He said, Mr. Izard was there too, and joined in close friendship with Mr. Lee; that Mr. Izard was a man of violent and ungoverned passions; that each of these had a number of Americans about him, who were always exciting disputes and propagating stories that made the service very disagreeable; that Mr. Izard, who, as I knew, had been appointed a minister to the Grand Duke of Tuscany, instead of going to Italy, remained with his lady and children at Paris; and instead of minding his own business, and having nothing else to do, he spent his time in consultations with Mr. Lee and in interfering with the business of the commission to this court; that they had made strong objections to the treaty, and opposed several articles of it; that neither Mr. Lee nor Mr. Izard was liked by the French. . . .

I heard all this with inward grief and external patience and composure. I only answered . . . that it would not become me to take any part in them; that I ought to think of nothing in such a case but truth and justice, and the means of harmonizing and composing all parties.

Although Adams expressed his impartiality in the disputes between the other commissioners, he was soon joined with Lee in opposing Franklin. Except for their mutual desire for independence and a republican form of government for the Colonies, the puritanical Adams and the sybaritic Franklin were in opposition on most things. There was a thirty-year difference in their ages, and the young man deplored what he considered the old man's loose conduct—such things as allowing the charming Madame Brillon to sit on his lap and playing chess with her while she bathed. Adams was undoubtedly jealous of the adoration of the French for Franklin and of the old man's great skill at personal diplomacy, an area in which Adams had little ability. To Franklin, the end result was all important. Adams, with his dedication to virtue as a principle, seemed to feel that the means were more important than the end. He even condemned Franklin's "policy never to say yes or no decidedly but when he cannot avoid it," not realizing that such a policy was the essence of diplomacy. Even in petty things Adams could not resist finding fault with the older man. He was trying, without marked success, to learn French and commented:

DR. FRANKLIN is reported to speak French very well, but I find, upon attending to him, that he does not speak it grammatically. . . . His pronunciation, too, upon which the French gentlemen and ladies compliment him, and which he seems to think is pretty well, I am sure is very far from being exact.

Adams poured his opinion of the great philosopher into his diary in recording a conversation with Marbois. They were discussing religion and the Frenchman said:

"ALL RELIGIONS are tolerated in America and the ambassadors have in all courts a right to a chapel in their own way; but Mr. Franklin never had any." "No," said I, laughing, "because Mr. Franklin had no——" I was going to say what I did not say, and will not say here. I stopped short, and laughed. "No," said M. Marbois, "Mr. Franklin adores only great Nature, which has interested a great many people of both sexes in his favor." "Yes," said I, laughing, "all the atheists, deists, and libertines, as well as the philosophers and ladies, are in his train." . . . "Yes," said M. Marbois, "he is celebrated as the great philosopher and the great legislator of America." "He is," said I, "a great philosopher, but as a legislator of America he has done very little. It is universally believed in France, England, and all Europe that his electric wand has accomplished all this revolution. But nothing is more groundless. He has done very little. It is believed that he made all the American constitutions and their confederation; but he made neither. He did not even make the constitution of Pennsylvania, bad as it is.

Adams ended this conversation with a nasty allusion to the illegitimacy of Franklin's son William and grandson Temple.

MR. MARBOIS ASKED, are natural children admitted in America to all privileges like children born in wedlock. . . . I said, they were not excluded from commissions in the army, navy, or state, but they were always attended with a mark of disgrace. M. Marbois said this, no doubt, in allusion to Mr. F.'s natural son, and natural son of a natural son. I let myself thus freely into this conversation . . . because I am sure it cannot be my duty, nor the interest of my country, that I should conceal any of my sentiments of this man, at the same time that I do justice to his merits. It would be worse than folly to conceal my opinion of his great faults.

He wrote another comment on Franklin to Abigail's friend Mercy Warren, although this is perhaps an amusing anecdote rather than a symptom of jealousy. He had frequently commented, with disapproval, on the freedom with which the ladies of France showed their affection for the old Doctor. To Mercy he wrote:

WHAT SHALL I SAY, Madam, to your question whether I am as much in the good graces of the ladies as my venerable colleague? Ah, no! Alas, alas, no! The ladies of this country, Madam, have an unaccountable passion for old age, whereas our countrywomen, you know, Madam, have rather a complaisance for youth, if I remember right. This is rather unlucky for me, because here I have nothing to do but wish that I was seventy years old, and when I get back to America, I shall be obliged to wish myself back again to five-and-twenty.

I will take the liberty to mention an anecdote or two,

Madam, among a multitude, to show you how unfortunate I am in being so young. A gentleman introduced me, the other day, to a lady. *"Voila, Madame,"* said he, *"Monsieur Adams, notre ami, le collegue de Monsieur Franklin." "Je suis enchante de voir Monsieur Adams,"* answered the lady. *"Embrassez le donc,"* replied the gentleman. *"Ah, non, Monsieur,"* said the lady, *"il est trop jeune."* So that you see I must wait patiently full thirty years longer before I can be so great a favorite.

Arthur Lee's accusations against Silas Deane caused an embarrassing situation for Congress. The former's brother, Richard Henry, was an important leader of the Virginia faction and called for action against Deane, action which would be an implied criticism of Deane's supporter, Franklin. This would offend not only Pennsylvania but the great Doctor's fellow philosophers and the mass of people who revered Poor Richard in America and Bonhomme Richard in France. Congress tried to sweep the whole thing under the rug until Deane published an appeal to the American people in which he disclosed the discord in France and made counter accusations against Lee. Incidently, nothing has ever turned up to indicate dishonesty on the part of any of the commissioners.

When Adams heard of Silas Deane's appeal to the people he flew off the handle.

IN CONVERSATION with Dr. Franklin, in the morning, I gave him my opinion of Mr. Deane's address to the people of America with great freedom and perhaps with too much warmth. I told him that it was one of the most wicked and abominable productions that ever sprang from a human heart; that there was no safety in integrity against such a man; that I should wait upon the Count de Vergennes and the other ministers and see in what light they considered this conduct of Mr. Deane; that if they and their representatives in America were determined to countenance and support by their influence such men and measures in America, it was no matter how soon the alliance was broke; that no evil could be greater, nor any government worse, than the toleration of such conduct.

Since Vergennes approved of Deane it is obvious that Adams' attitude would not win friends and influence ministers at the Court of Versailles. Adams continued to tell his diary:

. . . such a contempt of Congress, committed in the city where they sit . . . appeared to me evidence of such a complication of vile passions, of vanity, arrogance, and presumption, of malice, envy, and revenge, and at the same time of such wickedness, indiscretion, and folly, as ought to unite every honest and wise man against him; that there appeared to me no alternative left but the ruin of Mr. Deane or the ruin of his country; that he appeared to me in the light of a wild boar, that ought to be hunted down for the benefit of mankind.

So much for Adams' impartiality. He concluded:

THERE IS NO MAN HERE that I dare trust at present. They are all too much heated with passions and prejudices and party disputes. Some are too violent, others too jealous, others too cool and too reserved at all times, and at the same time, every day, betraying symptoms of a rancor quite as deep. The wisdom of Solomon, the meekness of Moses, and the patience of Job, all united in one character, would not be sufficient to qualify a man to act in the situation in which I am at present; and I have scarcely a spice of either of these virtues. On Dr. Franklin the eyes of all Europe are fixed as the most important character in American affairs in Europe; neither Lee nor myself are looked upon [as of] much consequence.

A prime cause of Adams' failure as a diplomat in France was that, fundamentally, he did not approve of much that was inherent in the nature of the French; and he openly distrusted their ministers. He feared that the French alliance might be a case of "out of the frying pan into the fire" with France dominating the Colonies. When a Marshal Maillebois was lauded as a great general and Vergennes idly commented, "Ah, I wish he had the command with you," Adams saw in this:

. . . a confirmation strong of the design at court of getting the whole command of America into their own hands. . . . My feelings, on this occasion, were kept to myself, but my reflection was I will be buried in the ocean, or in any other manner sacrificed, before I will voluntarily put on the chains of France when I am struggling to throw off those of Great Britain.

He saw much merit in the connection with France and felt that it

. . . ought to be cultivated with perfect faith and much tenderness. . . . But [he added in a letter to Roger Sherman] still it is a delicate and dangerous connection. There is danger to the simplicity of our manners and to the principles of our constitution, and there may be danger that too much will be demanded of us. There is danger that the people and their representatives may have too much timidity in their conduct toward this power, and that your ministers here may have too much diffidence of themselves and too much complaisance for the court. There is danger that French councils and emissaries and correspondents may have too much influence in our deliberations.

Adams' basic feeling toward the French is indicated by a long diary entry which had nothing to do with diplomatic relations. He inquired about the beautiful palace of Bellevue which, he was told, had been built by Louis XV for his mistress, Madame de Pompadour. The monarch, Adams recorded, "visited here for twenty years, leaving a worthy woman, his virtuous queen, alone at Versailles." He then reported the iniquitous machinations that took place behind the noble façade of Madame Pompadour's domain:

HERE WERE MADE judges and counselors, magistrates of all sorts, nobles and knights of every order, generals and admirals, ambassadors and other foreign ministers, bishops, archbishops, cardinals, and popes. Hither were directed all eyes that wished and sought for employment, promotion, and every species of court favor. . . . Here *lettres de cachet,* the highest trust and most dangerous instrument of arbitrary power in France, were publicly sold to any persons who would pay for them, for any, the vilest purposes of private malice, envy, jealousy, revenge, or cruelty. . . . Here still lived the daughters of the last king, and the aunts of the present. Instead of wondering that the licentiousness of women was so common and so public in France, I was astonished that there should be any modesty or purity remaining in the kingdom. . . . Could there be any morality left among such a people, where such examples were set up to the view of the whole nation?

In his autobiography Adams used the feminine influence at Bellevue as the basis for a short essay on female virtue and, inferentially, the lack thereof in France.

FROM ALL THAT I HAD READ of history and government, of human life and manners, I had drawn this conclusion: that the manners of women were the most infallible barometer to ascertain the degree of morality and virtue in a nation. . . . The manners of women are the surest criterion by which to determine whether a republican government is practicable in a nation or not. The Jews, the Greeks, the Romans, the Dutch, all lost their public spirit, their republican principles and habits, and their republican forms of government, when they lost the modesty and domestic virtues of their women.

What havoc, said I to myself, would these manners make in America! Our governors, our judges, our senators or representatives, and even our ministers, would be appointed by harlots, for money; and their judgments, decrees, and decisions be sold to repay themselves or, perhaps, to procure the smiles of profligate females.

The foundations of national morality must be laid in private families. In vain are schools, academies, and universities, instituted if loose principles and licentious habits are impressed upon children in their earliest years. The mothers are the earliest and most important instructors of youth. The vices and examples of the parents cannot be concealed from the children. How is it possible that children can have any just sense of the sacred obligations of morality or religion if, from their earliest infancy, they learn that their mothers live in habitual infidelity to their fathers, and their fathers in as constant infidelity to their mothers? Besides the Catholic doctrine is that the contract of marriage is not only a civil and moral engagement, but a sacrament; one of the most solemn vows and oaths of religious devotion. Can they then believe religion, and morality too, anything more than a veil, a cloak, a hypocritical pretext, for political purposes of decency and conveniency?

When he arrived in Paris, Adams found Franklin comfortably ensconced in a house which had been graciously loaned to him in Passy, a suburb of Paris—although Adams did not know it was a loan. He righteously deplored the extravagance of his colleagues:

MY EXPENSES were very trifling. I had no house rent to pay

separate from Dr. Franklin. I kept no carriage, and used none but that of Dr. Franklin, and that only when he had no use for it. I had very little company more than Dr. Franklin would have had if I had not been there. But, before my arrival, Mr. Deane had his house and furniture and establishment of servants, as well as his carriage, in Paris, and another establishment for his apartments in the country at Passy, and another carriage and set of horses and servants. Mr. Lee had a house, furniture, carriage, and organization of servants at Chaillot. Dr. Franklin had his in the Basse-cour de Monsieur Le Ray de Chaumont [the house in Passy], at what rent I never could discover; but, from the magnificence of the place, it was universally suspected to be enormously high.

During his first stay in France, which lasted some fourteen months, Adams made a solid contribution toward straightening out the tangled bookkeeping and economic affairs and systems of the American commission. He was appalled at the casual way in which commercial affairs were handled by Deane and Franklin. They had appointed various commercial agents, some without the approval of Congress, and at least one of these, wrote Adams:

. . . expected us to advance him money to pay for his purchases, and yet did not think himself responsible to us, or obliged to send us his accounts, vouchers, or even his powers or orders. Whatever Mr. Deane or Dr. Franklin had done before my arrival, I thought this procedure . . . irregular [and] inconsistent with the arrangement of Congress. . . . Mr. Arthur Lee's opinion and mine were perfectly in unison upon this point.

Lee and Adams threw themselves into a feverish session of bookkeeping and letter writing. Adams recorded:

. . . public business had never been methodically conducted.

There never was, before I came, a minute-book, a letter-book, or an account-book; or, if there had been, Mr. Deane and Dr. Franklin had concealed them from Mr. Lee, and they were now nowhere to be found. . . . I was now determined to procure some blank books and to apply myself with diligence to business, in which Mr. Lee cordially joined me.

Most of his outgoing letters were of this tenor: "Sir, We are sorry to inform you that the state of our funds admits of no further expenditure. . . . It is, therefore, our desire, that you abstain from any further purchases." Or: "Sir, We have done by our friends at Amsterdam, who have followed our orders, everything that we thought incumbent on us to do, relative to your affairs, and we do not incline to have any further concern with them." Or, again: "Sir, Your bill upon our banker was not paid because it was drawn without our leave . . . and he could not regularly pay a bill on our account which he had not our orders to pay."

Most of these letters bore the signatures of all three commissioners; Lee and Adams drafted them and waited, sometimes for days, until they could get Franklin to spare a few moments from his socializing to sign them. In justice to the old Doctor it must be mentioned that, while his associates were keeping track of the bills, he was applying his skillful personal diplomacy at the French court to raise the money to pay them.

One of Adams' less fortunate letters demanding order, system, and economy was addressed to the naval hero John Paul Jones. When Jones brought in prizes from a successful cruise he wanted to advance part of the prize money to his crew for necessary clothing and presented a draft against the commission to a French banker, which caused Adams to write:

YOUR BILL OF EXCHANGE in favor of M. Bersolle, for twenty-four thousand livres, which you inform us you mean to distribute among the brave officers and men to whom you owe your late success, has been presented to us by M. Chaumont. We are sorry to inform you that we have been under the disagreeable necessity of refusing payment. . . . We have no authority to make presents of the public money to officers or men, however gallant or deserving.

The naval captain had explained that his men needed clothes, and Adams told him:

UPON A REPRESENTATION from you of the quantity of slops necessary for them, we should order Mr. Schweighauser to furnish your ship with them; not more, however, than one suit of clothes for each man . . . charging each man upon the ship's books with what he shall receive, that it may be deducted out of his pay.

It is not surprising that Jones considered Adams "that wicked and conceited upstart" and referred to him contemptuously as "Mr. Roundface."

In mid-1778 there was a persistent rumor in Paris that Great Britain was willing to recognize the independence of the United States on condition that the new country would renounce her alliance with France and, hopefully, join her former mother in war against her erstwhile sister.

Despite his suspicions of the motives of the French, Adams recognized the military and financial importance of the French connection; and, regardless of this, a treaty had been made in good faith, and the virtuous Puritan could not condone even thinking about violating it. To Henry Laurens, president of Congress, among others, he wrote:

THE KING OF GREAT BRITAIN and his council have determined to send instructions to their commissioners in America to offer us independency, provided we will make peace with them separate from France. This appears to me to be the last effort to seduce, deceive, and divide. They know that every man of honor in America must receive this proposition with indignation. But they think they can get the men of no honor to join them by such a proposal, and they think the men of honor are not a majority. What has America done to give occasion to the King and council to think so unworthily of her!

The proposition is, in other words, this: "America, you have fought me until I despair of beating you; you made an alliance with the first power of Europe, which is a great honor to your country and a great stability to your cause, so great that it has excited my highest resentment and has determined me to go to war with France. Do you break your faith with that power and forfeit her confidence, as well as that of all the rest of mankind forever, and join me to beat her, or stand by neuter and see me do it, and for all this I will acknowledge your independency because I think in that case you cannot maintain it, but will be easy prey to me afterward, who am determined to break my faith with you as I wish you to do yours with France." My dear countrymen, I hope you will not be allured upon the rocks by the siren song of peace.

Soon after his arrival in Paris Adams decided that it was ridiculous to keep three commissioners of equal rank in France, even if they could get along with each other. Franklin had reached this conclusion some time before and had written several letters on it. Now John wrote to cousin Samuel:

OUR AFFAIRS in this kingdom I find in a state of confusion and darkness that surprises me. . . . The truth is, in my humble opinion, our system is wrong in many particulars: In having three commissioners at this court: one in the character of envoy is enough. . . . My idea is this: Separate the offices of public ministers from those of commercial agents;

recall, or send to some other court, all the public ministers
but one at this court. . . . The inconveniences arising from
the multiplicity of ministers and the complication of business
are infinite.

Although Adams would have liked this job, he admitted that
Franklin was the more logical man for it. In his diary he queried:

WHAT WOULD BE THE CONSEQUENCE if my plan should be
adopted? Dr. Franklin's reputation was so high in America,
in the court and nation of France, and all over Europe, that
he would undoubtedly, as he ought, be left alone at the Court
of Versailles. . . . I thought . . . that there was no alternative
for me but to return to America; and I very deliberately determined that I had rather run the gauntlet again through all
the British men-of-war in the Bay of Biscay, the British
Channel, and the Gulf Stream, with all their storms and
calms, than remain where I was, under a system and circumstances so ruinous to the American cause.

When Congress took his advice and confirmed Franklin as sole
minister he complained to Abigail that they were ignoring him.

A NEW COMMISSION has arrived by which the Dr. is sole
minister. Mr. Lee continues commissioner for Spain, but I
am reduced to the condition of a private citizen. The Congress have not taken the least notice of me. On the 11th of
September they resolved to have one minister only in France.
On the 14th they chose the Dr. In October they made out his
commission, the *Alliance* sailed on the 14th January, and in
all that interval they never so much as bid me come home,
bid me stay, or told me I had done well or done ill. . . . The
Congress, I presume, expect that I should come home, and I
shall come accordingly. As they have no business for me in
Europe, I must contrive to get some for myself at home.

Prepare yourself for removing to Boston, into the old house, for there you shall go, and there I will draw writs and deeds, and harangue juries, and be happy.

While he waited for passage home Adams tutored John Quincy in Latin. "Yesterday and today in the forenoon, assisted my son in translating Cicero's First Philippic against Cataline." He wrote Abby:

MY LITTLE SON gives me great pleasure both by his assiduity to his books and his discreet behavior. The lessons of his mamma are a constant lesson to him, and the reflection that they are so to his sister and brothers is a never failing consolation to me at times when I feel more tenderness for them than words can express, or than I should choose to express if I had power.

He also spent time at what was always one of his favorite occupations, self-condemnation. To his diary he confided:

THERE IS A FEEBLENESS and a languor in my nature. My mind and body both partake of this weakness. By my physical constitution I am but an ordinary man. The times alone have destined me to fame; and even these have not been able to give me much. When I look in the glass, my eye, my forehead, my brow, my cheeks, my lips, all betray this relaxation. Yet some great events, some cutting expressions, some mean hypocrisies, have, at times, thrown this assemblage of sloth, sleep, and littleness into rage a little like a lion. Yet it is not like the lion; there is extravagance and distraction in it that still betray the same weakness.

Upon his return to Braintree in the summer of 1779 Adams' first concern was to send a long report to Congress on conditions in Europe, a sort of political Baedecker. This was the type of paper he did superbly well—when no personalities were involved. He reminded the legislature:

As THE TIME APPROACHES when our relations with the most considerable states in Europe will multiply and assume a greater stability they deserve the attention of Americans in general, but especially of those composing their supreme council.

France deserves the first place among those powers with which our connections will be the most intimate, and it is with pleasure I am able to assure Congress that from the observations I have made during my residence in that kingdom I have the strongest reasons to believe that their august ally, his ministers and nation, are possessed of the fullest persuasion of the justice of our cause, of the great importance of our independence to their interests, and the firmest resolution to preserve the faith of treaties inviolate, and to cultivate our friendship with sincerity and zeal. . . .

In the opinion of some the power with which we shall one day have a relation the most immediate, next to that of France, is Great Britain. But it ought to be considered that this power loses every day her consideration and runs toward her ruin. Her riches, in which her power consisted, she has lost with us and never can regain. . . . She resembles the melancholy spectacle of a great wide-spreading tree that has been girdled at the root. Her endeavors to regain these advantages will continually keep alive in her breast the most malevolent passions toward us. Her envy, her jealousy and resentment, will never leave us while we are what we must unavoidably be: her rivals in the fisheries, in various other branches of commerce, and even in naval power.

There followed vignettes of the political and commercial situations of other countries in relation to the rebellious colonies:

THE ACTIVE COMMERCE OF SPAIN is very inconsiderable; of her passive commerce we shall not fail to have a part. The vicinity of this power, her forces, her resources, ought to make us attentive to her conduct; but if we may judge of the future by the past I should hope we had nothing to fear from it. . . . Her conduct toward us at this time will perhaps appear equivocal and indecisive; her determinations appear to be solely the fruit of the negotiations of the court of Versailles. . . .

As Portugal has not known how to deliver herself entirely from the influence of England we shall have little to hope from her; on the other hand, such is her internal weakness that we have absolutely nothing to fear. . . .

It would be useless to consider that infinite number of little sovereignties into which Germany is divided and develop all their political interests. . . . The state of Germany with which we may have commerce of an honorable kind is the house of Austria, one of the most powerful in Europe. . . . This court would seize with eagerness the advantages that are presented to her by the independence of America, but an interest more powerful restrains her; and . . . there is reason to believe she will be one of the last powers to acknowledge our independence. . . .

The jealousy between the Emperor and the King of Prussia, and that between the houses of Bourbon and Austria, are a natural tie between France and Prussia . . . so Prussia will be one of the first to acknowledge our independence. . . . The rest of Germany, excepting Hamburg and Bremen, have no means of opening a direct commerce with us. . . .

Poland, depopulated by the war and a vicious government, reduced by a shameful treaty to two-thirds of her ancient dominion, destitute of industry and manufactures even of the first necessity, has no occasion for the productions of America. . . .

Russia, Sweden, and Denmark . . . have been thought by some to be interested in our return to the domination of Great Britain . . . yet the motive of humbling the pride of the English, who have endeavored to exercise their domination even over the northern seas and to render the Danish and Swedish flag dependent upon theirs, has prevailed over all others, and they are considered in Europe as having given their testimony against the English in this war.

Italy, a country which declines every day from its ancient prosperity, offers few objects for our speculations. . . .

Venice, heretofore so powerful, is reduced to a very inconsiderable commerce, and is in an entire state of decay.

Switzerland is another lender of money, but neither her position nor her commerce can occasion any near relation with us. . . .

The court of Rome, attached to ancient customs, would be one of the last to acknowledge our independence if we were to solicit for it, but Congress will probably never send a minister to his Holiness, who can do them no service, upon condition of receiving a Catholic legate or nuncio in return or in other words an ecclesiastical tyrant, which it is to be hoped the United States will be too wise ever to admit into their territories.

The most important potential alliance, after that with France, would be

. . . that which will probably be formed between the Hollanders and us. The similitude of manners, of religion, and in some respects of constitution; the analogy between the means by which the two republics arrived at independency; but above all the attractions of commercial interest will infallibly draw them together.

He then shrewdly pointed out:

FROM THE ESSAYS and inquiries of your commissioners at Paris it appears that some money may be borrowed there . . . and possibly Congress may think it expedient to send a minister there. If they should, it will be proper . . . to give him full powers and clear instructions concerning the borrowing of money; and the man himself, above all, should have a consummate prudence and a caution and discretion that will be proof against every trial.

Reading between the lines it seems more than probable that Adams had himself in mind as the man of "consummate prudence" who should be sent to Holland.

While awaiting a national assignment Adams was appointed to the convention to draft a constitution for Massachusetts, and to the committee of three which was to draw the preliminary draft. Actually, Adams personally wrote the constitution draft, which was adopted with but minor changes. Fundamentally, the charter of government was little different from those which several other colonies had already adopted; but it did have some peculiarly Adams' features. In the bill of rights, which was common to most constitutions, Adams wrote, "All men are born equally free and independent." The committee changed this to the conventional "born free and equal," an ambiguous phrase which annoyed lawyer Adams, since all men were decidedly not born equal in their inherent talents or their possessions.

In view of mid-twentieth century judicial decisions concerning prayers in schools, the third clause of Adams' bill of rights is interesting:

GOOD MORALS BEING NECESSARY to the preservation of civil society, and the knowledge and belief of the being of GOD, His providential government of the world, and of a future state of rewards and punishment, being the only true foundation of morality, the legislature hath, therefore, a right, and ought to provide, at the expense of the subjects if necessary, a suitable support for the public worship of GOD, and of the teachers of religion and morals; and to enjoin upon all the subjects an attendance upon their instructions at stated times and seasons, provided there be any such teacher on whose ministry they can conscientiously and conveniently attend.

The wording of this was changed by the convention without altering the meaning.

The fifth chapter of the Massachusetts constitution was unique in that it provided for the care of Adams' *alma mater:*

WHEREAS our wise and pious ancestors, so early as the year one thousand six hundred and thirty-six, laid the foundation of Harvard College, in which university many persons of great eminence have by the blessing of God been initiated in those arts and sciences which qualified them for public employments, both in church and state. And whereas the encouragement of arts and sciences, and all good literature, tends to the honor of God, the advantage of the Christian religion, and the great benefit of this and the other United States of America, it is declared that the PRESIDENT and FELLOWS OF HARVARD COLLEGE . . . shall have, hold, use, exercise, and enjoy, all the powers, authorities, rights, liberties, privileges, immunities, and franchises, which they now have, or are entitled to have, hold, use, exercise, and enjoy.

The article further stipulated that "gifts, grants, devises of houses, lands, tenements, goods, chattels, legacies, and conveyances, heretofore made . . . to Harvard College . . . are hereby forever confirmed unto the President and Fellows of Harvard College, and to their successors."

Under the title "The Encouragement of Literature, Etc." this section continued:

WISDOM AND KNOWLEDGE, as well as virtue, diffused generally among the body of the people, being necessary for the preservation of their rights and liberties, and as these depend on spreading the opportunities and advantages of education in the various parts of the country, and among the different orders of the people, it shall be the duty of legislators and magistrates, in all future periods of this commonwealth, to cherish the interests of literature and the sciences, and . . . to countenance and inculcate the principles of humanity and general benevolence, public and private charity, industry and frugality, honesty and punctuality . . . sincerity, good humor, and all social affections and generous sentiments among the people."

The latter part of the above, particularly the provision that the government should inculcate principles of "general benevolence" and "good humor" among the people, surely indicates that his stay in France had some influence on Adams.

The preamble to the constitution proclaimed:

THE END OF THE INSTITUTION, maintenance, and administration of government is to secure the existence of the body politic; to protect it, and to furnish the individuals who compose it with the power of enjoying, in safety and tranquillity, their natural rights and the blessings of life; and whenever these great objects are not obtained, the people have a right to alter the government, and to take measures necessary for their safety, happiness, and prosperity.

The government to do this was to consist of a two-house legislature, an executive, and an independent judiciary. The upper house, the senate, would represent men of substance, and membership was limited to those who had "a freehold estate . . . of at least three hundred pounds." The more representative lower house had a property qualification of one hundred pounds, and all money bills originated here. Both were elected annually, as was the governor, who must be a Christian with an estate of at least one thousand pounds and who had an absolute veto over the acts of the legislature. The judiciary served for life or during "good behavior." It has often been pointed out that the constitution which Adams drafted for Massachusetts was a prototype of the United States Constitution, framed seven years later. This is true; but the same can be said for several of the other state constitutions, particularly those of New York and Virginia.

Adams had scarcely finished his constitution writing when he heard that Congress was planning a new diplomatic assignment for him. Early in 1779 the French minister at Philadelphia, Conrad Gérard, had officially acquainted Congress with "the desire of His Most Christian Majesty that the United States would speedily put themselves in a condition to take that part in the negotiation for peace apparently about to take place which their dignity and interest required . . . by giving their plenipotentiary the most ample instructions and full powers." Congress decided to appoint a special minister, other than Franklin, for this purpose. The Virginians nominated Arthur Lee. The middle states blocked this by voting en masse for John Jay of New York. New England wanted John Adams. The vote deadlocked six states for Adams, five for Jay. To break this the Jay supporters proposed that Congress first elect a minister plenipotentiary to Spain. When Jay won this the way was clear to elect Adams to the peace commissionership, a procedure which prompted James Lovell to write to him, "What damned dirty work is this of politics."

Gérard wrote to Vergennes that the appointment of Adams was made on "the presumption that he would be agreeable" to the French foreign minister. This assumption was not valid. While Vergennes did not have the same active antipathy toward Adams that he had toward Lee, he neither liked nor fully trusted him. Despite Adams' protestations to the contrary, Vergennes thought that he favored a separate peace with England, which was untrue. Also there were temperamental differences. Vergennes was an expert, old-line, European diplomat—suave and gracious, deep and wily. He considered it bad policy to let his right hand know what his left was doing. Adams was stiff, somewhat awkward, and lacking in charm. If he considered an objective right by his strict Puritan standards, his method of diplomacy was to put his head down and bull his way toward that objective, but only by virtuous means, of course.

Adams had no inkling of Vergennes' attitude when, after arriving in Paris, he happily reported their first interview to Congress.

I NEVER HEARD the French ministry so frank, so explicit, so decided as [he] was in the course of this conversation in his declarations to pursue the war with vigor and to afford effectual aid to the United States. . . . I asked permission of the Count de Vergennes to write to him on the subject of my mission, which he cheerfully and politely agreed to.

Adams' letter to the French minister inquired

. . . whether, in the present state of things, it is prudent in me to acquaint the British ministry that I am arrived here, and that I shall be ready to treat whenever the belligerent powers shall be inclined to treat. . . . Or whether to remain on the reserve, as I have hitherto done since my arrival in Europe.

Adams' suspicions were not aroused by Vergennes' advice that he keep the purposes of his mission secret, "and to take every precaution that the British ministry may not have a premature knowledge of them." He perforce agreed and assured the foreign minister that "Our alliance with France is an honor and a security which have ever been near to my heart," and that if there were any British overtures for a separate peace he would "endeavor to hear them with decency and respect; but it would require much philosophy to hear wth patience such absurd and extravagant propositions as are published in pamphlets and newspapers and made in Parliament." To this Vergennes replied by expressing the "confidence we place on your principles and what security we feel beforehand as to the conduct you will hold in case the court of London should propose to you overtures of conciliation." The American accepted the Frenchman's polite assurances at face value, with no suspicion that they were merely a façade behind which Vergennes was working to frustrate his mission and secure the revocation of his commission.

While he waited for months Adams wrote, as always and on many subjects, to his beloved Abby. These letters were addressed to "My Dear Portia," although his usual salutation to his wife was the characteristically reserved "My Dearest Friend." To his friend Portia he wrote:

SINCE MY ARRIVAL THIS TIME, I have driven about Paris more than I did before. The rural scenes around this town are charming. The public walks, gardens, etc., are extremely beautiful. . . . I wish I had time to describe these objects to you . . . but my head is too full of schemes, and my heart of anxiety. . . . To observe these objects with taste, and describe them so as to be understood, would require more time and thought than I can possibly spare.

It is not indeed the fine arts which our country requires; the useful, the mechanic arts are those which we have occasion for in a young country as yet simple and not far advanced in luxury, although perhaps much too far for her age and character. I could fill volumes with descriptions of temples and palaces, paintings, sculptures, tapestry, porcelain, etc., etc., etc., if I could have time; but I could not do this without neglecting my duty. The science of government it is my duty to study, more than all other sciences; the arts of legislation and administration and negotiation ought to take place of, indeed to exclude, in a manner, all other arts. I must study politics and war, that my sons may have liberty to study mathematics and philosophy. My sons ought to study mathe-

matics and philosophy, geography, natural history and naval
architecture, navigation, commerce, and agriculture, in order
to give their children a right to study painting, poetry, music,
architecture, statuary, tapestry, and porcelain.

With time heavy on his hands Adams undertook to assume with
his pen some of the duties which, in his opinion, Franklin was
neglecting. He would give information to Congress. When he
heard a rumor that Britain had hired a Russian fleet and army to
serve in America he wrote to his French friend M. Genêt for
further information. Genêt showed his request to Vergennes, who
denied the danger from the Russians and asked Genêt to inform
Adams "that on every occasion he will be very happy to have you
address yourself directly to him, and that you will always find him
eager to satisfy your inquiries."

Adams also undertook to advise Vergennes on the conduct of
the war. He said that he was

. . . clearly of the opinion . . . that the English, both in North
America and in the West India Islands, have been for these
two years past absolutely in the power of their enemies, and
they are so now, and will continue to be so in such a degree
that nothing will be wanting but attention to their situation
and a judicious application of the forces of the allies to accomplish the entire reduction of their power in America.

For this "judicious application," "a French fleet should con-
constantly remain on that coast," and Adams therefore begged
leave

. . . to submit it to your excellency's consideration whether
there is any possible way that a marine force can be employed
against the English so much to the advantage of France and
the disadvantage of England as in this way, and whether upon
the principles of French interest and policy alone, even with-

out taking into consideration that of the United States, a fleet ought not to be constantly kept in North America.

He even told the French minister where the French vessels should be stationed:

TWO SHIPS OF THE LINE, with three frigates, stationed at Boston, with orders to cruise occasionally for the protection of French and American trade and the annoyance of the enemy; the same number at Rhode Island with the same orders; the same number at Delaware River with similar orders; and a like number in Chesapeake Bay with like orders. . . . Eight ships of the line and twelve frigates, I have a moral certainty, would in one year reduce the power of the English in North America to absolute annihilation without striking a blow on land.

There was, he pointed out, "a portion of the people in America who wish to return to the domination of Great Britain, many of whom are sensible and artful men." This faction would gain strength if France "considered her own interest alone in the conduct of the war." If France brought her fleet home for the winter, "I scruple not to give it as my opinion that it will disunite, weaken, and distress us more than we should have been disunited, weakened, or distressed if the alliance had never been made." He closed by reminding Vergennes of the importance to France of America's good will. "The United States of America are a great and powerful people, whatever European statesmen may think of them. . . . Breaking off such a nation as this from the English so suddenly and uniting it so closely with France is one of the most extraordinary events that ever happened among mankind."

Vergennes' reply was politely haughty.

THE CHEVALIER DE TERNAY and the Count de Rochambeau are sent with the express design which is the subject of your letter. They will concert their operations with Congress and with General Washington . . . they will employ the ships and troops under their command according to the plan that shall be settled between them and the American generals. You will perceive, sir, by this detail that the King is far from abandoning the cause of America, and that His Majesty, without having been solicited by Congress, has taken effectual measures to support the cause of America.

Adams next got into an unpleasant dispute with Vergennes about the decision of Congress to depreciate American loan certificates at the rate of forty to one. He advised the French minister of this, saying, "Although some Europeans may have considerable sums in loan-office certificates, yet I have reason to believe that the whole will be found much less than is imagined. They have realized their property generally as they went along." Vergennes viewed this action of Congress as a cheap trick to reduce debts of two hundred million dollars to five million dollars. He coldly replied, "I will not presume, sir, to criticize upon this operation, because I have no right to examine or comment upon the internal arrangements which Congress may consider as just and profitable."

This brought from Adams a curious five-thousand-word dissertation on international finance, concluding that private French creditors did not deserve much sympathy because all merchants were profiteers, which he proved by quoting the prices which Abigail was paying for French goods in Boston. He would not accept Vergennes' intimation that Congress had broken faith. He wrote:

NO MAN IS MORE READY than I am to acknowledge the obligations we are under to France; but the flourishing state of her marine and commerce, and the decisive influence of her councils and negotiations in Europe, which all the world will allow to be owing in a great measure to the separation of America from her [France's] inveterate enemy and to her new connections with the United States, show that the obligations are mutual.

Vergennes icily responded: "Details into which you have thought proper to enter have not changed my sentiments; but I think that all further discussion between us on this subject will be needless."

To Franklin the French minister wrote that Adams' dissertation "contains only abstract reasonings, hypotheses, and calculations which have no real foundation, or which at least do not apply to the subjects of the King and, in fine, principles than which nothing can be less analogous to the alliance subsisting between His Majesty and the United States."

Vergennes was becoming impatient with Adams' meddling in things which did not concern him, but he was too experienced a diplomat to permit his actions to be controlled by irritation. The real basis for his campaign to get rid of the man from Massachusetts is contained in the clause in Adams' letter to the effect that, between the United States and France, "obligations are mutual." John considered the Franco-American relationship as an alliance between equal partners in which France participated for her own self-interest. This was basically true, but it was not politic to say so at a time when France was doing all the giving. Vergennes considered France the senior partner by whose experience the new nation should be guided. Franklin did not openly challenge this. He made flattering protestations of gratitude for France's aid every time he asked for more money. Adams considered Franklin's attitude subservient, and in his mind, America should be subservient to no nation. Franklin requested, Adams demanded, and Vergennes much preferred to do business with the former.

The matter came to a head when Adams, in mid-July, reminded Vergennes that he had been waiting since February and said that the time had arrived for a "frank and decent communication of my full powers." This, he believed, would force England to come "to an explanation of their real intentions con-

cerning America; for there, sir, lies the obstacle to peace." Vergennes wrote a lengthy rebuttal of all Adams' arguments and
concluded:

I CONTINUE to be of opinion that the time to communicate
your plenipotentiary power to Lord Germain is not yet come.
. . . I pray you, and in the name of the King request you, to
communicate your letter and my answer to the United States,
and to suspend, until you shall receive orders from them, all
measures with regard to the English ministry.

Adams reluctantly agreed, but he could not leave well enough
alone. He harked back to a previous letter in which the French
minister had written "that the King, without being solicited by
the Congress, had taken measures the most efficacious to sustain
the American cause." Not so, said Adams. The idea of sending a
French fleet had been advanced by the American commissioners
who originated "the true plan, which is finally to humble the
English and give the combined powers the advantage."

To Vergennes this was the last straw. He considered it his
duty to inform Adams that "Mr. Franklin being the sole person
who has letters of credence to the King from the United States,
it is with him only that I ought and can treat of matters which
concern them, and particularly of that which is the subject of
your observation." Furthermore, he added curtly, "the King did
not stand in need of your solicitations to induce him to interest
himself in the affairs of the United States." He then sent all the
correspondence to Franklin with the request that he transmit it
to Congress so "that they may know the line of conduct which
Mr. Adams pursues with regard to us, and that they may judge
whether he is endowed, as Congress no doubt desires, with that
conciliating spirit which is necessary for the important and delicate business with which he is intrusted." This is as near as
Vergennes could come, without endangering diplomatic relations,
to demanding Adams' recall.

Franklin wrote to Congress:

MR. ADAMS HAS GIVEN OFFENSE to the court here by some
sentiments and expressions contained in several of his letters
written to the Count de Vergennes. I mention this with re-
luctance, though perhaps it would have been my duty to
acquaint you with such a circumstance, even were it not
required of me by the minister himself. . . . Mr. Adams did
not show me his letters before he sent them. . . .

It is true that Mr. Adams' proper business is elsewhere; but
the time not being come for that business, and having nothing
else here wherewith to employ himself, he seems to have endeavored supplying what he may suppose my negotiations
defective in. He thinks, as he tells me himself, that America
has been too free in expressions of gratitude to France, for
that she is more obliged to us than we to her, and that we
should show spirit in our applications. I apprehend that he
mistakes his ground, and that this court is to be treated with
decency and delicacy. The King, a young and virtuous prince,
has, I am persuaded, a pleasure in reflecting on the generous
benevolence of the action in assisting an oppressed people,
and proposes it as a part of the glory of his reign. I think it
right to increase this pleasure by our thankful acknowledg-
ments. . . . Mr. Adams, on the other hand, who at the same
time means our welfare and interest as much as I or any man
can do, seems to think a little apparent stoutness and a greater
air of independence and boldness in our demands will procure
us more ample assistance. . . . M. Vergennes, who appears
much offended, told me yesterday that he would enter into no
further discussions with Mr. Adams, nor answer any more of
his letters.

Elsewhere, Franklin summarized his opinion of Adams in a
thumbnail sketch by saying, "Mr. Adams is always an honest
man, and often a wise one, but he is sometimes completely out
of his senses." When he was in his late seventies Adams repeated this in the opening of a long article in the Boston *Patriot*

and then rehashed his entire controversy with Vergennes and the part which he alleged Franklin had played in it. He still thought that he had been entirely right and Franklin entirely wrong and sought to prove it in a ten-thousand-word legal-like brief. At this time Franklin, who had been dead for over twenty years, was a national hero. Adams quoted Jefferson's statement that Franklin was "an honor to human nature," and added, "and so indeed, he was. Had he been an ordinary man, I should never have taken the trouble to expose the turpitude of his intrigues, or to vindicate my reputation against his vilifications and calumnies." After castigating the dead philosopher for most of his article, he thought of all the favorable things which he could, in good conscience, say about him and concluded with:

FRANKLIN HAD A GREAT GENIUS, original, sagacious, and inventive, capable of discoveries in science no less than of improvements in the fine arts and the mechanic arts. He had a vast imagination, equal to the comprehension of the greatest objects, and capable of a steady and cool comprehension of them. He had wit at will. He had humor that, when he pleased, was delicate and delightful. He had a satire that was good-natured or caustic, Horace or Juvenal, Swift or Rabelais, at his pleasure. He had talents for irony, allegory, and fable, that he could adapt with great skill to the promotion of moral and political truth. He was master of that infantive simplicity which the French call Naïveté, which never fails to charm, in Phaedrus and La Fontaine, from the cradle to the grave. Had he been blessed with the same advantages of scholastic education in his early youth . . . as Sir Isaac Newton, he might have emulated the first philosopher. . . . He has added much to the mass of natural knowledge, and contributed largely to the progress of the human mind . . . in some parts of his life [he] has written pamphlets and essays upon public topics with great ingenuity and success; but after my acquaintance with him, which commenced in Congress in 1775, his excellence as a legislator, a politician, or a negotiator most certainly never appeared. No sentiment more weak and superficial was ever avowed by the most absurd philosopher than some of his. . . .

He was a man with whom I always wished to live in friendship . . . until I had unequivocal proofs of his hatred, for no other reason under the sun but because I gave my judgment in opposition to his in many points which materially affected the interests of our country, and in many more which essentially concerned our happiness, safety, and well-being. I could not and would not sacrifice the clearest dictates of my understanding and the purest principles of morals and policy in compliance to Dr. Franklin.

Since he was *persona non grata* in Paris, John went to Amsterdam, without authority or credentials from Congress. He thought that the time might be ripe for a treaty with the Dutch which would lessen America's dependence on France. He knew that Henry Laurens had been accredited to Holland, but did not know that he had been captured at sea and was languishing in the Tower of London. He was, at first, enthusiastic about the prospects in Holland and wrote the Congress:

SOME PRUDENT PERSON, authorized by Congress, is earnestly desired here. . . . There is not in Europe a better station to collect intelligence from France, Spain, England, Germany, and all the northern parts, nor a better situation from whence to circulate intelligence through all parts of Europe that this . . . and I have since my arrival here been more convinced than ever that Congress might open a considerable loan here. . . . We are still in daily hope and expectation that Mr. Laurens will arrive; but should he decline to come, or in case any accident has befallen him, I most earnestly recommend to Congress the appointment of some other gentleman, with a proper commission, with full powers, and especially to borrow money.

There was more than a hint in this that Adams would be a very suitable "other gentleman."

He was, for a time, highly pleased with the situation in Holland. He wrote Franklin:

I WAS NEVER MORE AMUSED with political speculations than since my arrival in this country. Every one has his prophecy, and every prophecy is a paradox. One says America will give France the go-by. Another, that France and Spain will abandon America. A third, that Spain will forsake France and America. A fourth, that America has the interest of all Europe against her. A fifth, that she will become the greatest manufacturing country, and thus ruin Europe. A sixth, that she will become a great military and naval power, and will be very ambitious, and so terrible to Europe. In short, it seems as if they had studied for every impossibility, and agreed to foretell it as a probable future event.

And to Abigail he wrote:

THE COUNTRY where I am is the greatest curiosity in the world. This nation is not known anywhere, not even by its neighbors. The Dutch language is spoken by none but themselves. Therefore they converse with nobody, and nobody converses with them. The English are a great nation, and they despise the Dutch because they are smaller. The French are a greater nation still, and therefore they despise the Dutch because they are still smaller in comparison to them. But I doubt much whether there is any nation of Europe more estimable than the Dutch in proportion. Their industry and economy ought to be examples to the world. They have less ambition, I mean that of conquest and military glory, than their neighbors, but I don't perceive that they have more avarice. And they carry learning and arts, I think, to greater extent. The collections of curiosities, public and private, are innumerable.

The initial honeymoon with the Dutch was brief. Adams did not at first understand the complex internal political situation in Holland, with a strong pro-English faction that was then exerting much influence. Private bankers were friendly, but without credentials Adams could not pry money from their vaults. He was soon writing Congress: "I was told very candidly that I might possibly be much mistaken in my information; that possibly I might think that money was more plentier here than it is; that America had more friends than she has." When Congress sent him formal authority to negotiate a loan he pointed out the obstacles to immediate success and penned a brief dissertation on languages.

THIS BUSINESS must be conducted with so much secrecy and caution and I meet so many difficulties for want of the language . . . I never saw the national benefit of a polished language generally read and spoken in so strong a light as since I have been here. . . .

I hope that Congress will profit by their example by doing what they have lost so much reputation and advantage by neglecting; I mean by doing everything in their power to make the language they speak respectable throughout the world. Separated as we are from the British dominion, we have not made war against the English language any more than against the old English character. An academy instituted by the authority of Congress for correcting, improving, and fixing the English language would strike all the world with admiration and Great Britain with envy.

In September 1780 Adams received the coveted commission as minister plenipotentiary to Holland and was encouraged by news from Franklin that the French King would personally guarantee the security of a Dutch loan and pay the interest. His optimism was short-lived, for the publication of dispatches captured with Laurens mentioning a proposed Dutch alliance threw the Hollanders into a panic. He wrote Congress:

I SEE EVERY DAY more and more of the inveterate prejudices of this nation in favor of the English and against the French . . . more and more of the irresolution, uncertainty, and confusion of the nation. How the whole will conclude I know not. One thing, however, is certain, that Congress can depend upon no money from hence.

His opinion of the Dutch had changed. He wrote Congress:

THIS COUNTRY is indeed in a melancholy situation, sunk in ease, devoted to the pursuits of gain, overshadowed on all sides by more powerful neighbors, unanimated by love of military glory or any aspiring spirit.

To a friendly Dutch banker he wrote:

I BELIEVE WITH YOU that the credit of America was never lower in the Low Countries than at this hour. . . . Everyone dreads the resentment of the English party, and no one dares to stand forth in opposition to it. So be it. Let them go on lending their money and hiring their ships to England to enable her to murder people of whom neither the lender nor the borrower is worthy. Time will show them how much wisdom there is in their unfeeling sacrifice of every sentiment and every principle upon the altar of Mammon. The less America has to do with such people the better it will be for her.

To Abigail, from the depths of his despair:

I BEG you would not flatter yourself with hopes of peace. There will be no such thing for several years. Don't distress yourself either about any malicious attempts to injure me in the estimation of my countrymen. Let them take their course and go the length of their tether. They will never hurt your husband, whose character is fortified with a shield of innocence and honor ten thousand fold stronger than brass or iron.

He said that he would never put his boys—both John Quincy and Charles were with him—in a Dutch public school.

THE MASTERS are mean-spirited wretches, pinching, kicking, and boxing the children upon every turn. There is besides a general littleness arising from the incessant contemplation of stivers and duits which pervades the whole people. Frugality and industry are virtues everywhere, but avarice and stinginess are not frugality.

When, in December 1780, the British ministry, with its usual contempt for a weak state, ordered "that general reprisals be granted against the ships, goods, and subjects of the States-General of the United Provinces," Adams took new heart; but the timid Dutch government still refused to deal with him. To Franklin he wrote his contempt for all of Europe:

GOD FORGIVE THEM, and enable America to forget their ungenerosity. . . . By heaven, I would make a bargain with all Europe if it lay with me. Let all Europe stand still, neither lend men nor money nor ships to England nor America, and let them fight it out alone. I would give my share of millions for such a bargain. America is treated unfairly and ungenerously by Europe. But thus it is; mankind will be servile to tyrannical masters and basely devoted to vile idols.

The Dutch Grand Pensionary, the States-General, and the Prince of Orange each refused to accept Adams' credentials and passed them back and forth like the hot potato that they were;

recognition of America meant open war with Britain. The forthright Adams then did something that made the European diplomats gasp—he had his credentials printed in Dutch, French, and English and distributed them to the people.

Meanwhile, Catherine the Great of Russia had proposed a congress in Vienna to work out a general peace among all the belligerents. Vergennes asked Adams to come to Paris that they "might have some consultations at leisure . . . that we might understand each other's views." Adams recorded that Vergennes' secretary told him:

> . . . it was necessary to consider certain points and make certain preparatory arrangements; to know whether we were British subjects, or in what light we were to be considered. . . . I said I was not a British subject; that I had renounced that character many years ago forever, and that I should rather be a fugitive in China or Malabar than ever reassume that character.

The Russians proposed that a year's truce be declared in America while the belligerents negotiated. This Adams rejected out of hand unless all British forces were withdrawn from America. He took offense at a Russian reference to negotiations between Great Britain and her "American colonies." Great Britain had no American colonies on the North American mainland except Canada. The United States was "a free, sovereign, and independent state, of right and in fact," which "can never consent that their independence shall be discussed or called in question by any sovereign or sovereigns, however respectable; nor can their interests be made a question in any congress in which their character is not acknowledged and their minister admitted."

Catherine of Russia was quite willing to throw the American States back to Britain as a sop for European peace. Adams' brusque rejection of the Russian plan may have helped to prevent its further development. Before returning to Amsterdam he made

the polished French diplomat shudder by one of his little homilies.
He wrote:

THE DIGNITY OF NORTH AMERICA does not consist in diplomatic ceremonials or any of the subtleties of etiquette; it consists solely in reason, justice, truth, the rights of mankind and
the interests of the nations of Europe. . . . I shall, therefore,
never make unnecessary difficulties on the score of etiquette.

Back home, the new French minister, the Chevalier de la
Luzerne, had succeeded beyond Vergennes' expectations in sabo-
taging Adams with Congress. He suavely pointed out that an
agent of Congress might do much damage "by aiming at impossible things, forming exorbitant demands . . . or perhaps by
misconstruing his instructions," and that Congress should therefore direct Adams "to take no step without the approbation of
His Majesty," and tell him "to receive his instructions from the
Count de Vergennes." The supine Congress resolved to instruct
Adams "ultimately to govern yourself by their advice and opinion, endeavoring in your whole conduct to make them sensible
how much we rely upon His Majesty's influence for the effectual support in everything that may be necessary for the present security of future prosperity of the United States of America."
In short, Vergennes was to be America's diplomatic representative
in dealing with the rest of Europe.

Congress' next move, again with French guidance, was to appoint a five-man peace commission representing all sections of the
country: Adams from Massachusetts, John Jay from New York,
Franklin from Pennsylvania, Jefferson from Virginia, and Henry
Laurens from the deep south. The American commissioners, said
Congress, were "to make the most candid and confidential communications upon all subjects to the ministers of our generous ally,
the King of France; to undertake nothing in the negotiations for
peace or truce without their knowledge and concurrence; and
ultimately to govern yourselves by their advice and opinion."

Back in Amsterdam, Adams' reaction to this news was surprisingly mild. "Congress has done very well," he wrote, "to join others in the commission for peace who have some faculties for it. My talent, if I have one, is for making war." In general he was again despondent and was

. . . apprehensive that this commission will lie a long time neglected and as useless as the former one. I am myself seriously of opinion that the English will not treat with the United States for many years. . . . My commission for borrowing money has hitherto been equally useless. . . .

Whether under all these circumstances Congress will think proper to continue me in Europe, whether it will be in their power to furnish me with the means of subsistence . . . I know not. . . . But . . . the state of my health . . . makes it very uncertain whether I shall be able to remain here. In short, my prospects both for the public and for myself are so dull, and the life I am likely to lead in Europe is likely to be so gloomy and melancholy and of so little use to the public, that I cannot but wish it may suit with the views of Congress to recall me.

This was the darkness before dawn. Word of Cornwallis' capitulation in October 1781 acted on the Dutch as the Battle of Saratoga had on the French. Adams' credentials were received by the States-General; he was feted by the diplomatic corps; graciously received by the Prince of Orange. The treaty of commerce which he drafted was approved, and he crowned his success by obtaining a Dutch loan of a million and a half guilders. At long last he could triumphantly write:

THE STANDARD OF THE UNITED STATES waves and flies at The Hague in triumph over . . . British pride. When I go to heaven, I shall look down over the battlements with pleasure upon the Stripes and Stars wantoning in the wind at the Hague.

CHAPTER IV

THE PEACEMAKER

Adams proudly displayed his newfound French in his diary by recording that he was off to Paris *"avec le rameau d'olive dans la bouche, dans le coeur, à la main."* Despite his recent pessimism for the prospect of peace, he had grasped the olive branch which he carried in his mouth, heart, and hand when he heard from John Jay in Madrid on October 6, 1782, that "Mr. Oswald received yesterday a commission to treat of a peace with the commissioners of the United States of America."

The background of the beginning of the peace negotiations highlights the contrast between Franklin's diplomacy and that of Adams. There had been a change in the British ministry which brought Lord Shelburne to the fore. This minister was friendly toward America and Franklin put forth the first feeler, a letter carried by a mutual friend whom he met at tea in Madame Brillon's salon, wherein he commented on "The returning good disposition of your country in favor of America," which he hoped would "tend to produce a general peace, which I am sure that your lordship, with all good men, desires." The letter closed by thanking Shelburne, in the name of Franklin's neighbor, Madame Helvètius, for some gooseberry bushes he had sent her. Such a procedure would not have occurred to Adams, who would never have been in Madame Brillon's salon to meet Shelburne's friend, nor would he have involved gooseberry bushes in a diplomatic communication.

Shelburne responded by sending a Mr. Oswald to see Franklin saying, "He is a pacifical man and conversant in those negotiations which are most interesting to mankind. This has made me prefer him . . . to any person of higher rank." Franklin was then the only American peace commissioner in Paris. Jefferson had stayed in America, Jay was in Spain, Adams and Laurens in Holland; the latter on parole and therefore not qualified to serve. Franklin introduced Oswald to Vergennes and then proceeded to negotiate with him privately, contrary to his instructions from Congress. The old Doctor was always most polite to the French, but in matters of importance he was by no means under their thumbs.

Franklin gave Oswald four points on which America would insist in any peace treaty—recognition of independence; settlement of boundaries; a confinement of the boundaries of Canada; and freedom of fishing on the banks of Newfoundland, for "fish as well as whales." He also proposed that it might be advisable for the British to indemnify Americans whose property had been destroyed; acknowledge their error in distressing the Americans; offer free trading privileges with Great Britain for American ships; and give up "every part of Canada." This was the situation when Jay arrived from Spain.

Meanwhile, Adams had spent some busy weeks in Holland spending the money he had borrowed. He wrote Jay that, before he could leave:

I MUST ALSO SIGN another thousand of obligations at least, that the loan may not stand still. All this shall be dispatched with all the diligence in my power, but it will necessarily take up some time, and my health is so far from being robust that it will be impossible for me to ride with as much rapidity as I could formerly. . . . If anything in the meantime should be in agitation concerning peace in which there should be any difference of opinion between you and your colleague, you have a right to insist upon informing me by express, or waiting till I come.

Adams felt that he could rely on Jay, a fellow lawyer who was rabidly anti-French, to cope with Franklin. He thought of himself as treading a middle ground and confided to his diary:

BETWEEN TWO as subtle spirits as any in this world, the one malicious, the other, I think, honest, I shall have a delicate, a nice, a critical part to act. Franklin's cunning will be to divide us; to this end he will provoke, he will insinuate, he will intrigue, he will maneuver. My curiosity will at least be employed in observing his invention and his artifice. Jay declares roundly that he will never set his hand to a bad peace.

For some reason which he did not explain Adams seemed deliberately to dawdle on his trip from Amsterdam to Paris. He toured Utrecht, Breda, and Antwerp, admiring works of art and visiting churches which, he noted, were clean, "no dust on any of my fingers." He socialized in Brussels and went sight-seeing in Cambrai and Chantilly. When he arrived in Paris he took a bath.

WENT INTO THE BATH upon the Seine not far from the Pont Royal, opposite the Tuileries. You are shown into a little room which has a large window looking over the river into the Tuileries. There is a table, a glass, and two chairs, and you are furnished with hot linen, towels, etc. There is a bell which you ring when you want anything.

He also made himself otherwise presentable before calling on his colleagues, and shrewdly predicted the future influence of French fashions in America.

THE FIRST THING TO BE DONE in Paris is always to send for a tailor, peruke-maker, and shoemaker, for this nation has established such a domination over the fashion that neither clothes, wigs, nor shoes made in any other place will do in Paris. This is one of the ways in which France taxes all Europe, and will tax America. It is a great branch of the policy of the court to preserve and increase this national influence over the *mode,* because it occasions an immense commerce between France and all the other parts of Europe. Paris furnishes the materials and the manner, both to men and women, everywhere else.

When he met Jay, Adams recorded that the New York lawyer had "refused to treat with Oswald, until he had a commission to treat with the commissioners of the United States of America; Franklin was afraid to insist upon it; was afraid we should be obliged to treat without; differed with Jay; refused to sign a letter, etc." Contrary to Jay's original advice, Oswald had not been authorized to deal with the commissioners of the United States but those of "said colonies and plantations." To Franklin this was of no moment, so long as the first article of the treaty recognized that these colonies and plantations were now the independent United States. Lawyer Jay insisted that Britain must first recognize the United States and *then* make a treaty. While Oswald made a round trip to London to have this inconsequential change made the British decisively defeated the Spaniards at Gibraltar and, in consequence, were in a somewhat less conciliatory mood.

Until he arrived in Paris, Adams had not seen the instructions from Congress that the American commissioners were "ultimately to govern yourselves by the advice and opinion of the French ministry." He promptly wrote to Robert Livingston, whom Congress had placed in charge of foreign affairs:

I NEVER SUPPOSED this to be the intention of Congress; if I had, I never would have accepted the commission, and if I now thought it their intention I could not continue in it. I cannot think it possible to be the design of Congress. If it is, I hereby resign my place in the commission and request that another person may be immediately appointed in my stead.

Adams further pointed out a problem that was to plague American diplomats abroad, who were bound by arbitrary orders, for years to come: distance and slow communications. He wrote Livingston:

THERE IS NO MAN more impressed with the obligation of obedience to instructions; but in ordinary cases the principal is so near the deputy as to be able to attend to the whole progress of the business and to be informed of every new fact and every sudden thought. Ambassadors in Europe can send expresses to their courts and give and receive intelligence in a few days with the utmost certainty. In such cases there is no room for mistake, misunderstanding, or surprise, but in our case it is very different. We are at an immense distance. Dispatches are liable to foul play and vessels are subject to accidents. New scenes open, the time presses, various nations are in suspense, and necessity forces us to act.

What can we do? . . . I see no way of doing my duty to Congress but to interpret the instruction, as we do all general precepts and maxims, by such restrictions and limitations as reason, necessity, and the nature of things demand.

Adams neglected to call on Vergennes upon his arrival in Paris. He had been in the French capital for two weeks when, he wrote:

ON SATURDAY LAST, the Marquis de la Fayette called upon me and told me he had been to Versailles, and that the Count de Vergennes had said to him that he had been informed by the returns of the police that I was in Paris, but not officially, and he should take it well if I would come and see him. I went

out to dine with Dr. Franklin the same day, who had just returned from delivering his memorial and repeated to me the
same message. I said to both I would go the next morning."

As to the general situation, Adams wrote a parable in his diary:

THE PRESENT CONDUCT of England and America resembles
that of the eagle and cat. An eagle scaling over a farmer's yard
espied a creature that he thought a hare; he pounced upon him
and took him up in the air. The cat seized him by the neck
with her teeth, and round the body with her fore and hind
claws. The eagle finding himself scratched and pressed, bids
the cat let go and fall down. No, says the cat, I won't let go
and fall; you shall stoop and set me down.

He expressed his opinion of general conditions by writing:

FOR MY OWN PART, I thought America had been long enough
involved in the wars of Europe. She had been a football between contending nations from the beginning, and it was easy
to foresee that France and England both would endeavor to
involve us in their future wars. I thought it our interest and
duty to avoid as much as possible, and to be completely independent, and have nothing to do, but in commerce, with either
of them. That my thoughts had been from the beginning
constantly employed to arrange all our European connections
to this end, and that they would continue to be so employed,
and I thought it so important to us that if my poor labors, my
little estate, or (smiling) sizy blood could effect it, it should be
done. But I had many fears.

The two main points of discussion in the daily bargaining sessions during November 1782 were England's claim for compensation to the American Tories for confiscated property and Adams'
claim for a more liberal clause on the fisheries—a matter of interest

only to New England. On the first issue Adams recorded at length an impassioned speech that he made to Oswald:

"How," SAID I, "will an independent man in one of our assemblies consider this?" We will take a man who is no partisan of England or France, one who wishes to do justice to both and to all nations, but is the partisan only of his own. . . . I don't know what you may have heard in England of Mr. S. Adams; you may have been taught to believe, for what I know, that he eats little children; but I assure he is a man of humanity and candor, as well as integrity. . . . I will make him my orator.

What will he say when the question of amnesty and compensation to the Tories comes before the Senate of Massachusetts, and when he is informed that England makes a point of it, and that France favors her? He will say, here are two old sagacious courts, both endeavoring to sow the seeds of discord among us, each endeavoring to keep us in hot water, to keep up continual broils between an English party and a French party in hopes of obliging the independent and patriotic party to lean to its side. England wishes them here and compensated, not merely to get rid of them and to save themselves the money but to plant among us instruments of their own, to make divisions among us, and between us and France, to be continually crying down the religion, the government, the manners of France, and crying up the language, the fashions, the blood, etc., of England.

England also means, by insisting on our compensating these worst of enemies, to obtain from us a tacit acknowledgment of the right of the war, an implicit acknowledgment that the Tories have been justifiable, or at least excusable, and that we only, by a fortunate coincidence of events, have carried a wicked rebellion into a complete revolution.

At the very time when Britain professes to desire peace, reconciliation, perpetual oblivion of all past unkindnesses, can she wish to send in among us a number of persons whose very countenances will bring fresh to our remembrance the whole history of the rise and progress of the war, and of all its atrocities? . . . What can be the design of France, on the other hand, by espousing the cause of these men? Indeed, her motives may be guessed at. She may wish to keep up in our minds a terror of England, and a fresh remembrance of all we have suffered; or she may wish to prevent our ministers in Europe from agreeing with the British ministers until she shall say that she and Spain are satisfied in all points.

Associated with the Tory question was the British demand that Congress guarantee the payment to British merchants of debts contracted by Americans before the Revolution. Adams claimed, "The question of paying debts, and that of compensating Tories, were two. . . . I proposed . . . that Congress should recommend it to the states to open their courts of justice for the recovery of all just debts." This reference to the courts of the states was the stumbling block in any agreement on Tory compensation and debts. The United States was united in name only. Congress could make a treaty for the whole country, but had no means of compelling the country's constituent parts to honor it.

Elsewhere in his diary Adams makes brief mention that, during breakfast with him and Jay, "Dr. Franklin read a letter, which he had prepared, to Mr. Oswald, upon the subject of the Tories, which we had agreed with him that he should read as containing his private sentiments." Actually, it was this letter that led to the settlement of the Tory question. In it Franklin said that, if there were going to be demands for reparations, America might demand payment for all the goods that Gage had seized in Boston and Howe in Philadelphia; for all tobacco, rice, indigo, and slaves taken by Arnold and Cornwallis in the South; for all the merchant ships and cargoes captured by the British navy and all the villages and farms burned or destroyed during the war.

The negotiators promptly reached a compromise which read:

WHEREAS it is *just* that private contracts made between individuals of the two countries before the war should be faithfully executed, and as the confiscation of the said lands may have a latitude not justifiable by the law of nations, it is agreed that British creditors shall, notwithstanding, meet with no lawful impediment to recovering all the full value, or sterling amount, of such *bona fide* debts as were contracted before the year 1775. And also, that Congress will recommend to the said states so to correct, if necessary, their said acts respecting the confiscation of lands in America belonging to real British subjects.

This bound Congress to nothing except to recommend a course of action to the states, but it did save British face.

During the negotiations Adams socialized more than was usual for him by accepting dinner invitations from many prominent Frenchmen. On such occasions, he gloatingly noted in his diary:

THE COMPLIMENT OF *"Monsieur, vois êtes le Washington de la négociations"* was repeated to me by more than one person. I answered, *"Monsieur, vous me faites le plus grand honneur, at le compliment le plus sublime possible." "Eh, Monsieur, en vérité, vous l'avez bien mérité."* A few of these compliments would kill Franklin, if they should come to his ears.

The last point to be settled was the fisheries. England was willing to grant the right for American fishing on the banks, but Adams demanded the further permission to dry fish on the coast of Nova Scotia, claiming that the former privilege was worthless without the latter. He was adamant on this and said that, unless it was granted, "he would never put his hand to any treaty." An example of the niggling that went on during the negotiations is given in Adams' diary. The British wanted to change the "right" of fishing to the "liberty" of fishing, on the grounds that the word "right" was an obnoxious expression. Adams recorded:

UPON THIS I rose up and said: "Gentlemen, is there or can there be a clearer right? . . . When God Almighty made the banks of Newfoundland, at three hundred leagues distance from the people of America and at six hundred leagues distance from those of France and England, did he not give as good a right to the former as to the latter? If Heaven in the creation gave a right it is ours at least as much as yours. If occupation, use, and possession give a right, we have it as clearly as you. If war, and blood, and treasure give a right, ours is as good as yours. We have been constantly fighting in Canada, Cape Breton, and Nova Scotia for the defense of this fishery, and have expended beyond all proportion more than you. If, then, the right cannot be denied, why should it not be acknowledged, and put out of dispute? Why should we leave room for illiterate fishermen to wrangle and chicane?

The final clause read:

. . . the people of the said United States shall continue to enjoy unmolested the right to take fish of every kind on the Grand Bank and on all the other banks of Newfoundland . . . and . . . shall have liberty to cure and dry their fish on the shores of Cape Sables and of any of the unsettled bays, harbors, or creeks of Nova Scotia.

This clause relating to drying fish was the only gain over the four essential points for peace which Franklin had originally submitted, the only tangible result of haggling from late August until the end of November. Franklin's four additional desirable points were never discussed. It is possible (very unlikely, perhaps, but still possible) that, had Jay and Adams supported Franklin instead of using their majority to thwart him, and had they moved fast and avoided lawyer-like hair-splitting on words, Canada would have become part of the United States.

In his diary on November 30 Adams rather grudgingly admitted that Franklin at least had not been a hinderance in their negotiations.

SATURDAY. St. Andrew's Day. We met first at Mr. Jay's, then at Mr. Oswald's; examinined and compared the treaties. . . . Then the treaties were signed, sealed, and delivered, and we all went out to Passy to dine with Dr. Franklin. Thus far has proceeded this great affair.

The unveiling of the plot has been to me the most affecting and astonishing part of the whole piece. As soon as I arrived in Paris I waited on Mr. Jay, and learned from him the rise and progress of the negotiations. Nothing that has happened since the beginning of the controversy in 1761 has ever struck me more forcibly, or affected me more intimately, than that entire coincidence of principles and opinions between him and me. In about three days I went out to Passy and spent the evening with Dr. Franklin, and entered largely into conversation with him upon the course and present state of our foreign affairs. I told him, without reserve, my opinion of the policy of this court, and of the principles, wisdom, and firmness with which Mr. Jay had conducted the negotiation in . . . my absence, and that I was determined to support Mr. Jay to the utmost of my power in the pursuit of the same system. The Doctor heard me patiently, but said nothing.

The first conference we had afterward, with Mr. Oswald, in considering one point and another, Dr. Franklin turned to Mr. Jay and said, "I am of your opinion, and will go on with these gentlemen in the business without consulting this court" [i.e., the French]. He has, accordingly, met us in most of our conferences, and has gone on with us in entire harmony and unanimity throughout, and has been able and useful, both by his sagacity and his reputation, in the whole negotiation.

The treaty that was signed was a provisional one which would become effective when treaties were signed by Great Britain and

France and Spain. But, counter to Congress' instructions, it had
been signed without consulting France. When Franklin sent Vergennes the treaty, the latter privately admitted to a colleague that
it was a good one: "You will notice that the English buy the peace
more than they make it. Their concessions, in fact, as much as to
the boundaries as to the fisheries and the loyalists, exceed all that
I should have thought possible." But he was not happy about the
way in which it had been handled and wrote Luzerne, French
minister to America:

I THINK IT PROPER that the most influential members of Congress should be informed of the very irregular conduct of their
commissioners in regard to us. You may speak of it not in the
tone of complaint. I accuse no person; I blame no one, not
even Dr. Franklin. He has yielded too easily to the bias of
his colleagues, who do not pretend to recognize the rules of
courtesy in regard to us.

Adams sent a copy of the treaty to Livingston and added: "As
the objects for which I ever consented to leave my family and
country are thus far accomplished, I now beg leave to resign all
my employments in Europe." It was left to Franklin to placate
Vergennes. The French minister rebuked the old philosopher by
writing:

I AM AT A LOSS, sir, to explain your conduct and that of your
colleagues on this occasion. You have concluded your preliminary articles without any communication between us, although the instructions from Congress prescribe that nothing
shall be done without the participation of the King. You are
about to hold out a certain hope of peace to America without
even informing yourself on the state of the negotiation on our
part. You are wise and discreet, sir; you perfectly understand
what is due to propriety; you have all your life performed your
duties. I pray you to consider how you propose to fulfill those
which are due to the King?

Franklin apologized for

. . . neglecting a point of *bienséance*. But as this was not from want of respect to the King, whom we all love and honor, we hope it will be excused, and that the great work which has hitherto been so happily conducted, is so nearly brought to perfection, and is so glorious to his reign, will not be ruined by a single indiscretion of ours.

He added, "The English, I just now learn, flatter themselves they have already divided us. I hope this little misunderstanding will therefore be kept a secret, and that they will find themselves totally mistaken." He then asked for another loan of twenty million livres. Vergennes gave him six million.

Livingston wrote the American commissioners that the treaty had been submitted to Congress and, "The articles have met with their warmest approbation, and have been generally seen by the people in the most favorable point of view." He added:

BUT, GENTLEMEN, though the issue of your treaty has been successful . . . I feel no little pain at the distrust manifested in the management of it, particularly in signing the treaty without communicating it to the court of Versailles till after the signature. . . . It gives me pain that the character for candor and fidelity to its engagements which should always characterize a great people should have been impeached thereby. The concealment was, in my opinion, absolutely unnecessary.

He concluded by sanctimoniously advising them, "Honesty is the best policy," which applied "with as much force to states as to individuals." Adams expressed his opinion of such criticisms from back home by confiding to his diary:

I AM WEARY, disgusted, affronted, and disappointed. This state of mind I must alter, and work while the day lasts. I have

been injured, and my country has joined in the injury; it has
basely prostituted its own honor by sacrificing mine. But the
sacrifice of me was not so servile and intolerable as putting
us all under guardianship. Congress surrendered their own
sovereignty into the hands of a French minister. Blush! blush!
ye guilty records! blush and perish! It is glory to have broken
such infamous orders. Infamous, I say, for so they will be to
all posterity. How can such a stain be washed out? Can we
cast a veil over and forget it?

On the part which he had played in Europe to date, he commented:

I HOPE it will be permitted to me, or to some other who can
do it better, some ten or fifteen years hence, to collect together
in one view my little negotiations in Europe. Fifty years hence
it may be published, perhaps twenty. I will venture to say however feebly I have acted my part, or whatever mistakes I
may have committed, yet the situations I have been in, between angry nations and more angry factions, have been some
of the most singular and interesting that ever happened to
any man. The fury of enemies, as well as of elements, the
subtlety and arrogance of allies, and, what has been worse
than all, the jealousy, envy, and little pranks of friends and
co-patriots, would form one of the most instructive lessons in
morals and politics that ever was committed to paper.

And to Abigail he wrote:

THE PEACE, which sets the rest of the world at ease, increases,
I think, my perplexities and anxiety. I have written to Congress a resignation, but I foresee there will not be a speedy
decison upon it, and I shall be left in a state of suspense that
will be intolerable. Foreseeing this, I am determined not to
wait for an acceptance of my resignation, but to come home

without it provided it does not arrive in a reasonable time. Don't think, therefore, of coming to Europe! If you do, we shall cross each other, and I shall arrive in America about the time that you may arrive in Europe. I shall certainly return home in the spring. With or without leave, resignation accepted or not, home I will come, so you have nothing to do but wait to receive your old friend.

But John did not come home. Six months after the provisional treaty was signed he was still writing Abigail:

I CAN NOW have no hopes of seeing you before late in the fall. . . . The affairs of the world have little complaisance for my happiness or yours, but it is not worth our while to be impatient, because it will do us no good. I am astonished, however, that we have nothing from Congress nor from you. If you and your daughter were with me, I could keep up my spirits; but idly and insipidly as I pass my time, I am weary, worn, and disgusted to death. I had rather chop wood, dig ditches, and make fence upon my poor little farm. Alas, poor farm and poorer family, what have you lost, that your country might be free, and that others might catch fish and hunt deer and beaver at their ease. . . .

But all this should not hinder me from going over the same scenes again upon the same occasion, scenes which I would not encounter for all the wealth, pomp, and powers of the world. Boys! if you ever say one word or utter one complaint, I will disinherit you. Work, you rogues, and be free. You will never have so hard work to do as papa has had. Daughter! get you an honest man for a husband and keep him honest. No matter whether he is rich, provided he be independent. Regard the honor and the moral character of the man, more than all other circumstances. Think of no other greatness but that of the soul, no other richness but those of the heart. An honest, sensible, humane man, above all the littlenesses of

vanity and extravagances of imagination, laboring to do good
rather than be rich, to be useful rather than make a show, living in a moderate simplicity clearly within his means, and free
from debts or obligations, is really the most respectable man in
society, makes himself and all about him the most happy.

While he waited, John had little to do and seemed to brood over
his treatment by Vergennes. He told his diary:

AN ATTACK HAD BEEN MADE on me by the Count de Vergennes, and Congress had been induced to disgrace me; that
I would not bear this disgrace, if I could help it; that I would
wear no livery with a spot upon it; the stain should be taken
out, or I would not wear the coat.

He finally decided that England should be warned against this
arch villain and advised about all French machinations.

I TOLD MR. HARTLEY [the British minister to France] the story
of my negotiation with the Comte de Vergennes, about communicating my mission to Lord George Germain, three years
ago, and the subsequent intrigues and disputes, etc. It is necessary to let the English ministers know where their danger lies,
and the arts used to damp the ardor of returning friendship.

He made similar disclosures to Oswald and unburdened himself at length to a third Englishman, Benjamin Vaughan.

I TOLD HIM I had some facts to communicate to him in confidence . . . that these facts were . . . so connected with public
affairs, with the interests of the House of Bourbon, and with
the essential interests of Great Britain and America, and the
true system of policy which the two last ought in future to
pursue toward each other, that it was my indispensable duty
to communicate them to some English gentleman, who might

put their government upon their guard. The two facts I should now mention were two instances of the policy of the Count de Vergennes to defeat the good intentions of Congress toward Great Britain. I then showed him my two original commissions, one, as minister plenipotentiary for making peace; the other, as minister plenipotentiary to make a treaty of commerce. . . .

Mr. Vaughan said he was astonished at my secrecy . . . in never communicating this before; that they never had any idea of this in London. I told him the Count de Vergennes had required me, in the name of the King, not to communicate it. . . . "You see here," said I, "Mr. Vaughan, a proof of a great confidence in me; and what was the cause of it? No other than this: my sentiments were known in Congress to be unalterable for independence . . . but it was known also to be a fixed principle with me to hurt Great Britain no farther than should be necessary to secure our independence . . . and other rights.

The Count de Vergennes knew my character . . . he knew me to be a man who would not yield to some of the designs he had in view; he accordingly sets his confidential friend, M. Marbois, to negotiating very artfully with Congress. They could not get me removed or recalled, and the next scheme was to get the power of the commission for peace into the hands of Dr. Franklin; to this end, the choice was made to fall upon him and four other gentlemen who could not attend. They have been, however, mistaken, and no wrestler was ever so completely thrown upon his back as the Count de Vergennes." Mr. Vaughan said this was very important information, and entirely new . . . that he would write it to the Earl of Shelburne, and his Lordship would make great use of it, without naming me.

This gratuitous information from Adams was conveyed to London at a time when America's ally, France, was negotiating a

peace with their joint enemy, England. It was on this occasion that
Franklin wrote to Livingston that Adams was "sometimes and in
some things absolutely out of his senses." He further told the
American Secretary of State:

HE MAKES NO SECRET of his having these opinions, expresses
them publicly, sometimes in presence of the English ministers,
and speaks of hundreds of instances which he could produce
in proof of them. None, however, have yet appeared to me.

I write this to put you on your guard (believing it my duty,
though I know that I hazard by it a mortal enmity), and to
caution you respecting the insinuations of this gentleman
against this court, and the instances he supposes of their ill
will to us, which I take to be as imaginary, as I know his fan-
cies to be, that Count de Vergennes and myself are continually plotting against him, and employing the newswriters of
Europe to depreciate his character, etc. But, as Shakespeare
says, "Trifles light as air."

While he waited Adams also made some scientific speculations
in his diary. This was Franklin's or Jefferson's province and a
somewhat unusual area of thought for Adams, yet some of his
thoughts were shrewd. He wondered:

WHAT IS IT IN THE AIR which burns? When we blow a spark
with the bellows, it spreads. We force a current of air to the
fire, by this machine, and in this air are inflammable articles.
Can it be in the same manner that life is continued by the
breath? Are there any particles conveyed into the blood of
animals through the lungs which increase the heat of it? . . .
The external air drawn into the lungs in breathing through
the mouth or nostrils, either leaves some particles behind in
the lungs or in the blood, or carries some particles off with it;
it may do both; that is, carry in some particles that are salu-
brious, and carry out others which are noxious. The air once

breathed is certainly altered; it is unfit to be breathed again
. . . which shows the necessity of keeping the windows open,
and of frequently airing your dining rooms, keeping rooms,
and bedchambers. I suspect that the health of mankind is
much injured by their inattention to this subject.

On another day he wrote:

THE LOADSTONE is in possession of the most remarkable, wonderful, and mysterious property in nature. This substance is
in the secret of the whole globe. It must have a sympathy with
the whole globe. It is governed by a law, and influenced by
some active principle, that pervades and operates from pole
to pole, and does not lose its virtue. . . . Has it been tried,
whether the magnet loses any of its force in vacuo—in a bottle
charged with electrical fire, etc.? This metal called iron may
one day reveal the secrets of nature. The primary springs of
nature may be too subtle for all our senses and faculties. I
should think, however, that no subject deserved more the
attention of philosophers, or was more proper for experiment.

He confided to his diary some observations on geography based
on the inaccurate maps of the day and made a speculation for the
future which was only slightly in error.

THE SEPARATION OF AMERICA from Asia is between the six-
tieth and seventieth degree of north latitude, precisely at the
Arctic polar circle. It is called in the French maps, *Détroit du
Nord*—the northern Strait, or Strait of the North; it is near
the *Archipel du Nord,* or Northern Archipelago. The point of
land in Asia is under the dominion of Russia, and is called
Russian Tartary. The Strait forms the communication between the Eastern and the Frozen Oceans,—the *Mer Orien-
tale* and the *Mer Glaciale.* There are a number of islands in
the Archipelago, and one in the Strait itself, called on the map

Alaska Island. There is a sea and a promontory called Kamschatka, situated on the Eastern Ocean, within ten or twelve
degrees of the Strait. The three Tartarys—Independent Tartary, Chinese Tartary, and Russian Tartary—form a vast
country, extending from Persia, Hindostan, and China, to the
point of Asia at the Straits of the North, which divide Asia
from America.

What should hinder the Empress of Russia from establishing a trading city on the sea of Kamschatka, and opening a
commerce with Pekin, Nankin, and Conton—the cities of
China? It is so near the islands of Japan, the Philippines, the
Moluccas, that a great scene may one day be opened here.

Russia established its trading post not on the sea of Kamschatka
but on the "island" of Alaska.

Adams also wrote letters during this period—many letters to
several members of Congress giving his opinion on many subjects.
One dealt with union and pointed out the faults of the Confederation that would finally lead to the United States Constitution.

IF THE UNION OF THE STATES is not preserved, and even their
unity in many great points, instead of being the happiest people under the sun, I do not know but we may be the most
miserable. . . . If there is not an authority sufficiently decisive
to draw together the minds, affection, and forces of the states
in their common . . . concerns, it appears to me we shall be
the sport of transatlantic politicians of all denominations, who
hate liberty in every shape, and every man who loved it, and
every country that enjoys it. If there is no common authority,
nor any common sense to secure a revenue for the discharge
of our engagements abroad for money, what is to become of
our honor, our justice, our faith, our universal, moral, political, and commercial character? If there is no common power
to fulfill engagements with our citizens, to pay our soldiers
and other creditors, can we have any moral character at

home? Our country will become the region of everlasting dis-
contents, reproaches, and animosities, and instead of finding
our independence a blessing, we shall soon become Capado-
cians enough to wish it done away.

Another dealt with fiscal integrity.

THE THIRTEEN STATES, in relation to the discharge of the
debts of Congress, must consider themselves as one body animated by one soul. The stability of our Confederation at
home, our reputation abroad, our power of defense, the confidence and affection of the people of one state toward those
of another, all depend upon it. Without a sacred regard to
public justice no society can exist; it is the only tie which can
unite men's minds and hearts in pursuit of the common interest.

A third letter dealt with the iniquities of European countries and
the danger which American ministers faced from their designing,
loose women.

MY APPREHENSIONS of the importance of our foreign affairs
have been much increased by a residence of five or six years
in Europe. I see so much enmity to the principle of our governments, to the purity of our morals, the simplicity of our
manners, the honest integrity and sincerity of our hearts, to
our contentment with poverty, our love of labor, our affection
for liberty and our country; I see so many proofs of their
hatred of all this and of their dread of it, both as a dangerous
example among their own corrupted, debauched subjects and
as a sure and certain source of power and grandeur; I see so
many artifices practiced to debase everybody you send or who
comes to Europe; so many practiced by them in America
itself, hidden, covered up, disguised under all shapes; and I
see they will ever have it in their power to practice so many

of these arts and to succeed to such a degree, that I am convinced no pains or expenses should be spared to defend ourselves.

But how shall we defend ourselves? . . . Shall we recall all
our own ministers from Europe? . . . I confess I am for the
affirmative, and would give my voice for recalling every one if
I could not secure two points. The first is, to send men of
independent minds who will not be tools, men of virtue and
conscience. The second is, to persuade Congress to support
them firmly. . . . You may depend upon this: the moment an
American minister gives a loose to his passion for women,
that moment he is undone; he is instantly at the mercy of the
spies of the court, and the tool of the most profligate of the
human race.

The most important letter of this interim period was one to
Livingston advising him about representation at the Court of St.
James. A minister there was desirable, in Adams' opinion, to help
foil French schemes; and he did not forget that he had once been
commissioned to negotiate a treaty of commerce with Great Britain, "by the voice of eleven states, in twelve present, and . . . it
will never be the department of any one by a greater majority."
This entitled him, said John:

. . . to add what is my idea of the qualifications necessary for
an American foreign minister in general, and particularly and
above all to the Court of St. James.

In the first place, he should have an education in classical
learning and in the knowledge of general history, ancient and
modern, and particularly the history of France, England, Holland, and America. He should be well versed in the principles
of ethics, of the law of nature and nations, of legislation and
government, of the civil Roman laws, of the laws of England and the United States, of the public law of Europe, and
in the letters, memoirs, and histories of those great men who

have heretofore shone in the diplomatic order and conducted the affairs of nations and the world. He should be of an age to possess a maturity of judgment, arising from experience in business. He should be active, attentive, and industrious, and, above all, he should possess an upright heart and an independent spirit, and should be one who decidedly makes the interest of his country, not the policy of any other nation nor his own private ambition or interest, or those of his family, friends, and connections, the rule of his conduct.

Despite Adams' repeated protestations that he wanted to go home to his simple life in Braintree, his beloved wife and family, this letter was a definite bid for the British post. The qualifications listed—classical learning, a knowledge of history and the laws of Rome, England, America, and Europe—were all Adams' strong points. He surely was attentive and industrious and had an upright heart and an independent spirit. This letter was also designed to disqualify Franklin, by far the most logical man for the job because of his many firm friendships in England. But Franklin had no college-taught classical learning, no knowledge of law, and was beyond the "age to possess a maturity of judgment." Even the final reference to the interest of family was a slap at Franklin, who was then trying to get a diplomatic post for his grandson, Temple.

In the fall of 1783 the final treaty was signed with Great Britain by the American commissioners. Adams wrote:

THE THIRD OF SEPTEMBER will be more remarkable for the signature of the definitive treaties than for the battle of Naseby or Worcester or the death of Oliver Cromwell. We could obtain no alteration from the provisional articles. We could obtain no explanation of the articles respecting the Tories, nor any limitation respecting the interest or execution for debts. I am, however, less anxious about these things than others.

Hard on the heels of the treaty signing came a commission from

Congress for Franklin, Jay, and Adams to negotiate a treaty of commerce with England. Adams replied that he could "attend to this business and at the same time have some care of your affairs in Holland." He also proposed that their authority might be extended to make a number of treaties:

IF THE PRINCIPLE OF ECONOMY should restrain Congress from sending ministers to Vienna, Petersburg, Copenhagen, and Lisbon, they will probably send a commission to Paris to negotiate treaties there, because I think it will appear to be of great importance, both in a political and commercial light, to have treaties with these powers.

He wrote Abby:

ALL THIS WILL DETAIN ME in Europe this winter. If this letter arrives in season that you can come to me this fall with Miss Abby, I shall be supremely happy to see you. But still things are so unsettled in Congress that you may expect to return with me in the spring. You may come to London, Amsterdam, or L'Orient, to either of which places I will soon go to receive you after hearing of your arrival.

When he heard that Abigail and eighteen-year-old Nabby (who preferred to be called Amelia) were coming he effused to his "Dearest Friend":

YOUR LETTER OF THE 23RD has made me the happiest man upon earth. I am twenty years younger than I was yesterday. It is a cruel mortification to me that I cannot go to meet you in London, but there are a variety of reasons decisive against it, which I will communicate to you here. Meantime, I send you a son [John Quincy] who is the greatest traveler of his age, and without partiality, I think, as promising and manly a youth as is in the whole world. He will purchase a coach, in which we four must travel to Paris. Let it be large and strong, with an imperial and accommodations for traveling. . . . You may come conveniently with your two children and your maid in the coach, and your man may ride on horseback or in the stagecoach.

The simple farmer of Braintree had been left far behind.

Another addition to the Paris scene shortly after Abby's arrival was Thomas Jefferson, come to replace Franklin, or, as the Virginian graciously put it, "to succeed him, nobody could replace him." Remarkably different as they were in appearance, manner, interests, and background, the little fat Puritan from Massachusetts and the tall, graceful deist from Virginia were drawn together by their common love of their country, her independence, and her people. At this point in time they were in complete agreement, and Adams threw himself into the relationship without reserve.

Since their first meeting in the second Continental Congress Jefferson had held a high opinion of Adams, and their association in Paris did nothing to becloud it, although the Virginian did see faults in the man from Massachusetts. James Madison had long been one of Adams' severest critics, and Jefferson now wrote him:

You know the opinion I formerly entertained of my friend Mr. Adams. Yourself and the governor were the first who shook that opinion. I afterward saw proofs which convicted him of a degree of vanity, and of a blindness to it, of which no germ had appeared in Congress. A seven months' intimacy with him here and as many weeks in London have given me opportunities of studying him closely. He is vain, irritable, and a bad calculator of the force and probable effect of the motives which govern men. He is as disinterested as the being which made him; he is profound in his views; and accurate in his judgment except where knowledge of the world is necessary to form a judgment. He is so amiable that I pronounce you will love him if ever you become acquainted with him. He would be, as he was, a great man in Congress.

In anticipation of his wife's arrival John had rented a large house in Auteuil, and Abigail described their settling in to her sister:

AUTEUIL IS A VILLAGE four miles distant from Paris, and one from Passy. The house we have taken is large, commodious, and agreeably situated, near the woods of Boulogne, which belong to the King, and which Mr. Adams calls his park, for he walks an hour or two every day in them. The house is much larger than we have need of; upon occasion, forty beds may be made in it. I fancy it must be very cold in winter. . . .

But, with an expense of thirty thousand livres in looking glasses, there is not a table in the house better than an oak board, nor a carpet belonging to the house. . . . These floors will by no means bear water, so that the method of cleaning them is to have them waxed, and then a man-servant with foot brushes drives round your room dancing here and there like a Merry Andrew. This is calculated to take from your foot every atom of dirt, and leave the room in a few moments as he found it. . . . The expense of living abroad, I always supposed to be high, but my ideas were nowise adequate to the thing. . . . For this house, garden, stables, etc., we give two hundred guineas a year. Wood is two guineas and a half per cord; coal, six livres the basket of about two bushels; this article of firing, we calculate at one hundred guineas a year. . . . For our coachman and horses alone (Mr. Adams purchased a coach in England), we give fifteen guineas a month.

It is the policy of this country to oblige you to a certain number of servants, and one will not touch what belongs to the business of another, though he or she has time enough to perform the whole. In the first place, there is a coachman who does not an individual thing but attend to the carriages and horses; then the gardener, who has business enough; then comes the cook; then *the mâitre d'hôtel,* his business is to purchase articles in the family, and oversee that nobody cheats but himself; a *valet de chambre*—John serves in this capacity; a *femme de chambre*—Esther serves in this line [John and Esther were American servants] and is worth a dozen others. A *coiffeuse;* for this place I have a French girl about nineteen whom I have been upon the point of turning away, because Madame will not brush a chamber; "it is not de fashion, it is not her business." I would not have kept her a day longer, but found, upon inquiry, that I could not better myself; and hairdressing here is very expensive, unless you keep such a madam in the house. She sews tolerably well, so I make her as useful as I can. . . . Thus, with seven servants and hiring a charwoman upon occasion of company, we may possibly make out to keep house; with less, we should be hooted at as ridiculous, and could not entertain any company. To tell this in our own country would be considered as extravagance; but would they send a person here in a public character to be a public jest?

Abigail had lingered a while in London before journeying on to Paris and wrote of her preference for England over France.

THE CULTIVATION is by no means equal to that of England; the villages look poor and mean, the houses all thatched, and rarely a glass window in them. . . . If I was agreeably disappointed in London, I am as much disappointed in Paris. It is the very dirtiest place I ever saw. . . . Boston cannot boast so elegant public buildings; but, in every other respect, it is as much superior in my eyes to Paris, as London is to Boston.

After attending the opera she reported:

THE FIRST DANCE which I saw upon the stage shocked me.

. . . No sooner did the dance commence than I felt my delicacy wounded, and I was ashamed to be seen to look at them.
Girls, clothed in the thinnest silk and gauze, with their petticoats short, springing two feet from the floor, poising themselves in the air with their feet flying and as perfectly showing
their garters and drawers as though no petticoat had been
worn, was a sight altogether new to me. . . . Shall I speak a
truth, and say that repeatedly seeing these dances has worn
off that disgust, which I at first felt, and that I see them now
with pleasure? Yet, when I consider the tendency of these
things, the passions they must excite, and the known character, even to a proverb, which is attached to an opera girl,
my abhorrence is not lessened, and neither my reason nor
judgment has accompanied my sensibility in acquiring any
degree of callousness. . . . As soon as a girl sets her foot upon
the floor of the opera she is excommunicated by the Church,
and denied burial in holy ground. She conceives nothing
worse can happen to her; all restraint is thrown off, and she
delivers herself to the first who bids high enough for her. But
let me turn from a picture of which the outlines are but just
sketched; I would willingly veil the rest, as it can only tend to
excite sentiments of horror.

Her condemnation of French women culminated in a wonderfully catty pen portrait of Franklin's friend, Madame Helvètius.

THIS LADY I dined with at Dr. Franklin's. She entered the
room with a careless, jaunty air. . . . "How I look!" said she,
taking hold of a chemise made of tiffany which she had on
over a blue lutestring, and which looked as much upon the
decay as her beauty, for she was once a handsome woman; her
hair was frizzled; over it she had a small straw hat, with a
dirty gauze half-handkerchief round it, and a bit of dirtier
gauze than ever my maids wore was bowed on behind. She
had a black gauze scarf thrown over her shoulders. . . . When

we went into the room to dine she was placed between the Doctor and Mr. Adams. She carried on the chief of the conversation at dinner, frequently locking her hand into the Doctor's, and sometimes spreading her arms upon the backs of both the gentlemen's chairs, then throwing her arm carelessly upon the Doctor's neck.

I should have been greatly astonished at this conduct if the good Doctor had not told me that in this lady I should see a genuine Frenchwoman, wholly free from affectation or stiffness of behavior, and one of the best women in the world. For this I must take the Doctor's word; but I should have set her down for a very bad one, although sixty years of age, and a widow. I own I was highly disgusted, and never wish for an acquaintance with any ladies of this cast. . . . Thus you see, my dear, that manners differ exceedingly in different countries. I hope, however, to find amongst the French ladies manners more consistent with my ideas of decency, or I shall be a mere recluse.

Still, the Auteuil interlude after the signing of the peace was one of Adams' happiest periods abroad. He was proud of a treaty he submitted to the King of Prussia and was "charmed to find the King do us the honor to agree to the platonic philosophy of some of our articles, which are at least a good lesson to mankind." He approached the knotty question of the Barbary pirates by disagreeing with Jefferson, who wanted to fight them. Adams wrote to Jay, who had replaced Livingston as Secretary of State:

SOME . . . think it humiliating to treat with such enemies of the human race, and that it would be more manly to fight them. . . . [They] have more spirit than prudence. As long as France, England, Holland, the Emperor, etc., will submit to be tributary to these robbers, and even encourage them, to what purpose should we make war upon them? The resolution might be heroic, but would not be wise. . . . If we take a vessel of theirs we get nothing but a bad vessel fit only to burn, a few guns and a few barbarians, whom we may hang. . . . When they take a vessel of ours, they not only get a rich prize, but they enslave the men. . . . Unless it were possible, then, to persuade the great maritime powers of Europe to unite in the suppression of these piracies, it would be very imprudent for us to entertain any thoughts of contending with them, and will only lay a foundation by irritating their passions and increasing their insolence and their demands, for long and severe repentance. I hope, therefore, we shall think of nothing but treating with them.

And John spent many pleasant evenings with John Quincy, helping him to cram for his entrance to Harvard.

WE WENT with some accuracy through the geometry in the Preceptor, the eight books of Simpson's Euclid in Latin, and compared it, problem by problem and theorem by theorem, with le père de Chales in French; we went through plane trigonometry and plain sailing, Fenning's algebra, and the decimal fractions, arithmetical and geometrical proportions, and the conic sections, in Ward's mathematics. I then attempted a sublime flight, and endeavored to give him some idea of the differential method of calculation of the Marquis de L'Hopital, and the method of fluxions and infinite series of Sir Isaac Newton; but alas! it is thirty years since I thought of mathematics, and I found I had lost the little I once knew, especially of these higher branches of geometry, so that he is as yet but a smatterer, like his father.

By May 1785, when John's commission as minister plenipotentiary to the Court of St. James arrived, the Adams family had some regret in leaving Auteuil. Abby was loath to quit her "delightful and blooming garden" and to part with Mr. Jefferson, "one of the choice ones of the earth." She wrote: "I think I have somewhere met with the observation that nobody ever leaves Paris but with a degree of tristesse."

John recorded one of the rare instances when he spoke like a diplomat:

AT VERSAILLES, the Count de Vergennes said he had many felicitations to give me upon my appointment to England. I answered that I did not know but it merited compassion more than felicitation. "Ay, why?" "Because, as you know, it is a species of degradation in the eyes of Europe, after having been accredited to the King of France, to be sent to any other court." "But permit me to say," replied the Count, "it is a great thing to be the first ambassador from your country to the country you sprang from. It is a mark." I told him that these points would not weigh much with me.

Adams immediate reception in England did naught to lessen the regret at leaving Auteuil. Prevalent British opinion was expressed by an editorial in the *Public Advertiser*. "An Ambassador from America! Good Heavens what a sound!—the Gazette surely never announced anything so extraordinary before, nor once on a day so little expected. This will be such a phenomenon in the Corps Diplomatique that 'tis hard to say which can excite indignation most, the insolence of those who appoint the character, or the meanness of those who receive it." But if George III shared this opinion he hid it well. Adams carefully prepared and memorized a speech to deliver on the occasion of his presentation to His Majesty, a speech which he hoped would be the first step in the reconciliation of the two countries. He reported the interview to Jay:

I WENT WITH HIS LORDSHIP through the levee room into the King's closet. The door was shut and I was left with His Majesty and the secretary of state alone. I made the three reverences—one at the door, another about halfway, and a third before the presence—according to the usage established at this and all the northern courts of Europe, and then addressed myself to His Majesty in the following words:

"Sir, The United States of America have appointed me their minister plenipotentiary to Your Majesty, and have directed me to deliver to Your Majesty this letter which contains the evidence of it. It is in obedience to their express commands that I have the honor to assure Your Majesty of their unanimous disposition and desire to cultivate the most friendly and liberal intercourse between Your Majesty's subjects and their citizens, and of their best wishes for Your Majesty's health and happiness, and for that of your royal family. The appointment of a minister from the United States to Your Majesty's court will form an epoch in the history of England and of America. I think myself more fortunate than all my fellow citizens in having the distinguished honor to be the first to stand in Your Majesty's royal presence in a diplomatic character; and I shall esteem myself the happiest of men if I can be instrumental in recommending my country more and more to Your Majesty's royal benevolence, and of restoring an entire esteem, confidence, and affection, or, in better words, the old good nature and the old good humor between people, who, though separated by an ocean, and under different governments, have the same language, a similar religion, and kindred blood.

"I beg your Majesty's permission to add that, although I have some time before been intrusted by my country, it was never in my whole life in a manner so agreeable to myself."

The King listened to every word I said, with dignity, but with an apparent emotion. Whether it was the nature of the interview or whether it was my visible agitation—for I felt more than I did or could express—that touched him, I cannot say. But he was much affected, and answered me with more tremor than I had spoken with, and said:

"Sir, The circumstances of this audience are so extraordinary, the language you have now held is so extremely proper, and the feelings you have discovered so justly adapted to the occasion, that I must say that I not only receive with pleasure the assurance of the friendly dispositions of the United States, but that I am very glad the choice has fallen upon you to be their minister. I wish you, sir, to believe, and that it may be understood in America, that I have done nothing in the late contest but what I thought myself indispensably bound to do by the duty which I owed to my people. I will be very frank with you. I was the last to consent to the separation; but the separation having been made, and having become inevitable, I have always said, as I say now, that I would be the first to meet the friendship of the United States as an independent power. The moment I see such sentiments and language as yours prevail, and a disposition to give to this country the preference, that moment I shall say, let the circumstances of language, religion, and blood have their natural and full effect."

The King then asked me whether I came last from France, and upon my answering in the affirmative, he put on an air of familiarity, and, smiling, or rather laughing, said: "There is an opinion among some people that you are not the most attached of all your countrymen to the manners of France." I was surprised at this because I thought it an indiscretion and a departure from dignity. I was a little embarrassed, but determined not to deny the truth, on one hand, nor leave him to infer from it any attachment to England, on the other. I threw off as much gravity as I could and assumed an air of gaiety and a tone of decision as far as was decent, and said: "That opinion, sir, is not mistaken; I must avow to Your Majesty I have no attachment but to my own country." The King replied, as quick as lightning: "An honest man will never have any other." . . .

There are a train of other ceremonies yet to go through, in presentations to the Queen, and visits to and from ministers and ambassadors, which will take up much time and interrupt me in my endeavors to obtain all that I have at heart—the objects of my instructions. It is thus the essence of things is lost in ceremony in every country of Europe. We must submit to what we cannot alter. Patience is the only remedy.

Adams had always held a higher opinion of George III—and kings in general—than most rebels; and it is well that his meeting with the monarch was so pleasant. It was one of the few pleasant things that happened during his three years in England.

Six weeks later he wrote Jay:

THE POPULAR PULSE seems to beat high against America. The people are deceived by numberless falsehoods industriously circulated by the gazettes and in conversation, so that there is too much reason to believe that, if this nation had another hundred millions to spend, they would soon force the ministry into a war against us. The court itself, whatever may be thought of it, appears at present to be the principal barrier against a war, and the best disposed toward us. . . .

Their determination to consider us as foreigners . . . is so fixed . . . that I despair of any equal treaty, and, therefore, of any treaty, until they shall be made to feel the necessity of it. It cannot, therefore, be too earnestly recommended to all the states to concur . . . in giving to Congress full power to make treaties of commerce, and, in short, to govern all our external commerce; for I really believe it must come to that. . . . You will easily infer, from all this, that I have no hopes of a treaty before next spring, nor then without the most unanimous concurrence of all our states in vigorous measures which shall put out of all doubt their power and their will to retaliate.

Adams had been instructed by Congress to insist "that the United States be put without further delay in possession of all the posts and territories . . . now held by British garrisons"; to remonstrate "against the infraction of the treaty of peace by the

exportation of Negroes and other American property"; to "represent in strong terms the losses which many of our and also of their
merchants will sustain if the former be unreasonable and immod-
erately pressed for the payment of debts contracted before the
war."

His first meeting with William Pitt indicated that he was unlikely
to accomplish most of this. To Jay, Adams quoted Pitt as saying:

... that the carrying off the Negroes was so clearly against the
treaty that they must take measures to satisfy that demand if
we could prove how many were carried off. . . . But, as to the
posts, says he, that is a point connected with some others, that
I think must be settled at the same time. I asked him, what
these points were. He said, the debts.

The letter continued for many pages about the inability of British creditors to get satisfaction in state courts; the question of navigation acts and free trade; more on the fisheries; and a treaty of
commerce was mentioned. The meeting ended in polite evasion:

HE OWNED he was for taking advantage of the present short
time of leisure, to mature some plan about these things. I told
him . . . that I was anxious for an answer concerning the posts,
as I was in duty bound to insist on their evacuation. He said
he thought that connected with several other points and
should be for settling all these together so that he must reserve
himself at entire liberty concerning them.

And there the matter rested throughout Adams' stay in England. The British blandly used the unpaid debts to their merchants as an excuse for violating the treaty by retaining their posts
in the Great Lakes area, posts which protected their participation
in the profitable fur trade.

By the end of six months Adams was writing Jay in this tenor:

I AM ANXIOUS to convey to you, if I can, in as strong a light as that in which I see it myself, the impossibility of our doing anything satisfactory with this nation, especially under this ministry, that the States may neither neglect nor delay any measure which they would judge necessary or expedient upon the certainty that England will not alter her conduct. . . . As they have now evidence, as they think, that their commerce flourishes, and their credit is established without a treaty with the United States, and without opening the West Indies or Canada, Nova Scotia and Newfoundland to us . . . they will not now think it necessary to do any of these things. . . .

The posts upon our frontier give me great uneasiness. The ministers and people are so assured of peace with all their neighbors in Europe that they hold all we can do in indifference . . . they rely upon it that we shall not raise an army to take the posts. The expense and difficulty they know will be great and, therefore, they think they may play with us as long as they please. . . . The resolutions of some of the United States, staying proceedings at law for old debts, and some other resolutions concerning the Tories, represented to have been in some instances contrary to the treaty, will be the pretense.

In short, sir, I am like to be as insignificant here as you can imagine. I shall be treated, as I have been, with all the civility that is shown to other foreign ministers, but shall do nothing. I shall not even be answered; at least, this is my opinion. . . . To borrow an expression from the late Governor Bernard, I find myself at the end of my tether; no step that I can take, no language I can hold, will do any good, or, indeed, much harm. It is Congress and the legislatures of the states who must deliberate and act at present.

All in all the Adams were not personally unhappy in the commodious house which they had rented in Grosvenor Square, adjacent to Hyde Park. There was little formal entertaining because, after the official calls, the Adamses were virtually ignored by the British officials. Nabby was deliriously happy in a romance with Adams' secretary, Colonel William Smith, whom she shortly married. There was a growing American colony in London which created some diversion, particularly the young artists Copley, Trumbull, Mather Brown, and West.

It was, perhaps, well that little entertaining was necessary because the niggardly American Congress refused to allow the country's ambassadors sufficient funds for this purpose. One London journal reported: "The American minister has not yet paid his way, that is, given a diplomatic dinner to the ministers, because Congress' paper [money] will not pass here." When Abigail, in an effort to economize, took over the food shopping herself, one paper said that she looked like a farmer's wife, "going in an old chaise to market with a little fresh butter."

Although Abigail retained her partiality for the English versus the French, her basic attitude was "a plague on both their houses." She wrote her sister:

I WOULD RECOMMEND to this nation a little more liberality and discernment; their contracted sentiments lead them to despise all other nations. Perhaps I should be chargeable with the same narrow sentiments if I give America the preference over these old European nations. In the cultivation of the arts and improvement in manufactures they greatly excel us; but we have native genius, capacity, and ingenuity equal to all their improvements, and much more general knowledge diffused amongst us. You can scarcely form an idea how much superior our common people, as they are termed, are to those of the same rank in this country. Neither have we that servility of manners which the distinction between nobility and citizens gives to the people of this country. We tremble not either at the sight of name of majesty. I own that I never felt myself in a more contemptible situation than when I stood four hours together for a gracious smile from majesty, a witness to the anxious solicitude of those around me for the same mighty boon.

And in another letter:

WERE YOU TO BE A WITNESS to the spectacles of wretchedness and misery which these old countries exhibit, crowded with inhabitants, loaded with taxes, you would shudder at the sight. I never set my foot out without encountering many objects whose tattered parti-colored garments hide not half their nakedness . . . covered with disease and starving with hunger they beg, with horror in their countenances. Besides these, what can be said of the wretched victims who are weekly sacrificed upon the gallows in numbers sufficient to astonish a civilized people? I have been credibly informed that hundreds of children from four years and upward sleep under the trees, fences, and hedges of Hyde Park nightly, having nowhere else to lay their heads; and they subsist by day upon the charity of the passengers . . . there must be some essential defect in the government and morals of a people, when punishments lose their efficacy and crimes abound. But I shall make you sick with my picture of wretchedness.

By the summer of 1786 John and Abigail were alone in their big house; Nabby had married and John Quincy was in Harvard. They were overjoyed to receive a short visit from Jefferson, and the two diplomats made a leisurely, pleasant tour of England. While Jefferson measured buildings and bridges and made copious notes on manure, Adams recorded his feelings on politics, people, and places. He noted that Edgehill and Worcester

. . . were curious and interesting to us as scenes where freemen had fought for their rights. The people in the neighborhood appeared so ignorant and careless at Worcester that I was provoked, and asked, "And do Englishmen so soon forget the ground where liberty was fought for? Tell your neighbors and your children that this is holy ground, much holier than that on which your churches stand. All England should come in pilgrimage to this hill once a year. . . ."

Stratford upon Avon is interesting, as it is the scene of the birth, death, and sepulcher of Shakespeare. Three doors from the inn is the house where he was born, as small and mean as you can conceive. They showed us an old wooden chair in the chimney corner where he sat. We cut off a chip according to custom. A mulberry tree that he planted has been cut down, and is carefully preserved for sale. The house where he died has been taken down, and the spot is now only yard or garden. The curse upon him who should remove his bones, which is written on his gravestone, alludes to a pile of some thousands of human bones which lie exposed in that church. There is nothing preserved of this great genius which is worth knowing, nothing which might inform us what education, what company, what accident, turned his mind to letters and the drama. His name is not even on his gravestone. An ill-sculptured head is set up by his wife, by the side of his grave in the church. But paintings and sculpture would be thrown away upon his fame. His wit, fancy, his taste and judgment, his knowledge of nature, of life and character, are immortal.

At Birmingham we only walked round the town, and viewed a manufactory of paintings upon paper. The gentlemen's seats were the highest entertainment we met with. Stowe, Hagley, and Blenheim are superb; Woburn, Caversham, and the Leasowes are beautiful. Wotton is both great and elegant, though neglected. Architecture, painting, statuary, poetry, are all employed in the embellishment of these residences of greatness and luxury. A national debt of two hundred and seventy-four millions sterling, accumulated by jobs, contracts, salaries, and pensions in the course of a century, might easily produce all this magnificence. The pillars, obelisks, etc., erected in honor of kings, queens, and princesses, might procure the

means. . . . It will be long, I hope, before ridings, parks, pleasure grounds, gardens, and ornamented farms grow so much in
fashion in America; but nature has done greater things and
furnished nobler materials there; the oceans, islands, rivers,
mountains, valleys, are all laid out upon a larger scale.

Characteristically, Adams inserted this little note in the midst of
his description of their holiday:

WEDNESDAY. This is the anniversary of the Battle of Lexington, and of my reception at the Hague by their High Mighti-
nesses. This last event is considered by the historians and other
writers and politicians of England and France as of no consequence; and Congress and the citizens of the United States
in general concur with them in sentiment.

Throughout 1786 scores of letters to Jay emphasized that nothing could be accomplished with England unless the states would
delegate to Congress power to deal as a national government for
the *united* states. The following is typical:

BY THE ANSWER of Lord Carmarthen [British Foreign Secre-
tary] . . . Congress will see that the detention of the posts is
attempted to be justified by the laws of certain states impeding
the course of law for the recovery of old debts, etc. Were another memorial to be now presented relative to the Negroes,
the same answer would undoubtedly be given, or, more probably, a reference only to that answer. It is my duty to be explicit with my country, and therefore I hope it will not be
taken amiss by any of my fellow citizens when they are told
that it is in vain to expect the evacuation of posts, or payment
for the Negroes, a treaty of commerce, or restoration of prizes
. . . compensation to the Boston merchants, or any other relief
of any kind, until these laws are repealed. . . .

What, then, is to be done? The states, it may be said, will

not repeal their laws. If they do not, then let them give up all expectation from this court and country, unless you can force them to do as you please by investing Congress with full power to regulate trade.

In January of 1788 Adams formally asked to be relieved of his duties upon the expiration of his commission, and followed this with a personal letter to Jay.

I WROTE TO YOU YESTERDAY, in your ministerial capacity as well as mine, my ultimate determination to revisit my country, this time twelve months. I now write to you this private letter to entreat you, as a friend, to promote, in every way in your power, an arrangement as early as possible, by which I may be permitted to return with decorum. . . . It would hurt me to come home in disobedience, but in all events I will come home. If Congress should send me a new commission, I shall certainly return it unaccepted. This is between you and me, and not intended to offend the feelings of any man whatever. My northern friends may wish me to remain longer in Europe, but I must be excused. I shall complete, with submission to Providence, my ten years in Europe, and then go home.

And to Jefferson he added:

FOR A MAN who has been for thirty years rolling like a stone, never three years in the same place, it is no very pleasant speculation to cross the seas, with a family, in a state of uncertainty what is to be his fate, what reception he shall meet at home, whether he shall settle down in private life to his plough, or push into the turbulent scenes of sedition and tumult; whether he be sent to Congress, or a convention, or God knows what. If it lay in my power, I would take a vow to retire to my little turnip-yard, and never again quit it.

Adams received word that his resignation had been accepted late in 1788, but Congress forgot to recall him formally from the Dutch court, to which he was still minister plenipotentiary, or to advise the British king of the change. Of this gaucherie Adams wrote:

HOME I MUST GO and leave all Europe to conjecture that I have given offense in Holland; and, in England, that I have misbehaved abroad, though my conduct has been approved at home. When the public shall hear that I have gone home without taking leave, there will be no end of criticism, conjectures, and reflections. . . . To a man who has taken the utmost pains to do his duty, and to fulfill every obligation to the smallest punctilio, nothing can be more disagreeable than such disappointments.

He finally decided to detour through Holland to explain his recall and recounted a coldly polite farewell audience with George III, which was far different from his pleasant reception three years before. The American thanked His Majesty "for the protection and civilities of the court" and offered

. . . good wishes of prosperity to His Majesty, his royal family, his subjects, and dominions. The King's answer to me was in these words. "Mr. Adams, you may, with great truth, assure the United States that, whenever they shall fulfill the treaty on their part, I, on my part, will fulfill it in all its particulars. As to yourself, I am sure I wish you a safe and pleasant voyage, and much comfort with your family and friends.

Shortly before he left he received a letter from Jefferson describing the confusion in France which would soon result in revolution. Adams' reply voiced his basic pessimism on the motivation of mankind:

NEITHER PHILOSOPHY, nor religion, nor morality, nor wisdom, nor interest, will ever govern nations or parties, against their vanity, their pride, their resentment or revenge, or their avarice or ambition. Nothing but force and power and strength can restrain them.

CHAPTER V

THE POLITICAL PHILOSOPHER

୫

If the reputation of John Adams rested solely on his accomplishments as a diplomat during his ten-year sojourn in Europe, he would be scarcely known to history. Although he attached considerable importance to his success in Holland, the Dutch treaty and loan do not loom large as a result of ten years work. He was no shining success as a diplomat, although he was not as bad as some and no worse than many in a group which contained no really capable diplomat except Franklin.

Adams has been called "the Father of the Revolution," and perhaps he deserves this appellation as much as Madison deserves the title of "Father of the Constitution." Both are catch phrases of no historical accuracy. Prior to 1776 Adams deserves fame as the leading responsible, well-informed man who supported independence for the colonies. There were others who shouted this cry—his cousin Samuel for one, and Patrick Henry. But neither of these was considered as wholly responsible. Their support of the cause was largely emotional; Adams based his case on a sound foundation of reason.

The outstanding aspect of Adams' public service was his ability as a scholar of government and an advocate of the type of republican system which was ultimately adopted by the United States. Few, if any, of the other Founding Fathers had Adams' deep knowledge of the history of government forms and theories. This was a lifelong interest with Adams. At the age of twenty-three he had resolved to "aim at an exact knowledge of the nature, end, and means of government, compare the different forms of it with each other, and each of them with their effects on public and private happiness." It is, perhaps, not entirely true to call him a political philosopher, in that he was not a prime mover in creating any school of thought on government. But his deep research and his able advocacy were important in bringing the subject into focus.

Adams' writings on government may be divided into three periods. The first lasted until about 1786, and during this time there was no basic conflict between his views and those of Jefferson, Madison, and several other leaders. This period embraces his *Dissertations on the Canon and Feudal Law, Novanglus,* and his *Thoughts on Government.* The second period started during his residence in England and continued throughout the rest of his public career. Early in this period his views were unquestionably influenced by his admiration for the British system of government. And, too, his position had changed. He was no longer a rebel; he had made a name for himself; he had a position in society. The third period came after his retirement, when he adopted a middle ground with a return to many of the more liberal ideas of his youth combined with some of the fixed concepts of his second period.

Adams never admitted this transition of ideas. He maintained that he had always been completely consistent. His detractors challenged this and were able to point to many instances in which he seemed to contradict himself. To quote one such case, in *Thoughts on Government* he had written: "Where annual elections end, there slavery begins." Later he said, on several occasions, that he saw nothing wrong in a chief executive serving for life. As an instance, in 1790 he wrote to Benjamin Rush that he hoped that "election at stated periods" would continue "until the people shall be convinced that fortune, providence, or chance, call it what you will, is better than election." In *Thoughts* Adams probably meant that it was vital that direct representatives of the people in the lower house of the legislature be elected at frequent intervals; but that is not what he said, and his seeming inconsistencies on this and several other points were fine fuel for his political opponents.

Adams' most pretentious work on government was written in London, starting in 1786, under the mouth-filling title, *A Defense of the Constitutions of Government of the United States of America against the attack of M. Turgot, in his letter to Dr. Price, dated the twenty-second of March, 1778,* hereafter called *Defense.* Adams explained his reason for writing *Defense* by recording:

IN 1780 when I arrived in France, I carried a printed copy of the report of the Grand Committee of the Massachusetts Convention, which I had drawn up; and this became an object of speculation. Mr. Turgot, the Duke de la Rochefoucauld, and Mr. Condorcet and others admired Mr. Franklin's constitution [for Pennsylvania] and reprobated mine. Mr. Turgot, in a letter to Dr. Price, printed in London, censured the American constitution as adopting three branches in imitation of the constitution of Great Britain. The intention was to celebrate Franklin's Constitution and condemn mine. I understood it, and undertook to defend my constitution, and it cost me three volumes.

In justice to myself, however, I ought to say that it was not the miserable vanity of justifying my own work or eclipsing the glory of Mr. Franklin's that induced me to write. I never thought of writing till the Assembly of Notables in France had commenced a revolution, with the Duke de la Rochefoucauld and Mr. Condorcet at their head, who I knew would establish a government in one assembly, and that I knew would involve France and all Europe in all the horrors we have seen, carnage and desolation, for fifty, perhaps for a hundred years.

At the same time, every western wind brought us news of

town and county meetings in Massachusetts adopting Mr. Turgot's ideas, condemning my constitution, reprobating the office of governor and the assembly of the Senate as expensive, useless, and pernicious, and not only proposing to toss them off, but rising in rebellion against them.

In this situation I was determined to wash my hands of the blood that was about to be shed in France, Europe, and America, and show to the world that neither my sentiments nor actions should have any share in countenancing or encouraging any such pernicious, destructive, and fatal schemes. In this view I wrote my defense of the American constitutions. I had only the Massachusetts constitution in view, and such others as agreed with it in the distribution of the legislative power into three branches, in separating the executive from the legislative power, and the judiciary power from both. These three volumes had no relation to the Constitution of the United States. That was not in existence, and I scarcely knew that such a thing was in contemplation till I received it at the moment my third volume was about to issue from the press.

Despite his protestations, wounded pride was undoubtedly part of the inspiration for *Defense;* his brainchild, the Massachusetts Constitution, had been attacked. Worse, Franklin's political theories had been supported in opposition to his, and praise for Franklin was a red flag to Adams. The turmoil in western Massachusetts to which he referred was Shays' Rebellion, in which agrarian debtors had risen in arms against courts that were enforcing hard money laws, for which the farmers blamed merchants in the Massachusetts Senate. All of these were factors, but the main reason for *Defense* may have been that Adams liked to write theses and briefs.

The three lengthy volmes with which he answered Turgot's letter actually constituted a legal brief in which he expounded his ideas for a certain type of government and supported his case with scores of historical precedents. Approximately 75 percent of the material consists of quotations from almost every renowned historian or political philosopher or analyst on every ancient and modern democratic, monarchical, and aristocratic republic. Adams wrote his treatise hurriedly, with scant regard for organization, consistency, or detailed accuracy. It apparently did not occur to him that there was anything reprehensible in quoting page after page from works of other authors, frequently without acknowledging the source or even using quotation marks. This makes for confusion in reading. He sometimes starts a paragraph with an opinion given in the first person and then goes into a lengthy quotation without indicating that it is a quotation; so that one may read several pages taken from Plato's *Republic* under the impression that these are the words of Adams. It is certain that this resulted from haste and carelessness and was not deliberate plagiarism.

M. Turgot had written, of the American state constitutions,

. . . that by most of them the customs of England are imitated, without any particular motive. Instead of collecting all authority into one center, that of the nation, they have established different bodies, a body of representatives, a council, and a governor, because there is in England a House of Commons, a House of Lords, and a king. They endeavor to balance these different powers as if this equilibrium, which in England may be a necessary check to the enormous influence of royalty, could be of any use in republics founded upon the equality of all the citizens, and as if establishing different orders of men was not a source of divisions and disputes.

In *Defense* Adams sought to refute this by proving that no government had ever succeeded without a built-in balance of power. On this concept he was always consistent. As far back as 1775 he had written Richard Henry Lee:

A LEGISLATIVE, an executive, and a judicial power comprehend the whole of what is meant and understood by government. It is by balancing each of these powers against the other two that the efforts in human nature toward tyranny can alone be checked and restrained and any degree of freedom preserved in the constitution.

Forty years later he wrote to Jefferson:

THE FUNDAMENTAL article of my political creed is that despotism, or unlimited sovereignty, or absolute power, is the same in a majority of a popular assembly, an aristocratical council, an oligarchical junto, and a single emperor. Equally arbitrary, cruel, bloody, and in every respect diabolical. Accordingly, arbitrary power, wherever it has resided, has never failed to . . . corrupt.

In *Defense,* in 1788, he pointed with pride to the American constitutions, particularly that of Massachusetts, which were based on this idea.

LET US COMPARE every constitution we have seen with those of the United States of America, and we shall have no reason to blush for our country. On the contrary, we shall feel the strongest motives to fall upon our knees in gratitude to heaven for having been graciously pleased to give us birth and education in that country and for having destined us to live under her laws! We shall have reason to exult if we make our comparison with England and the English constitution. Our people are undoubtedly sovereign; all the landed and other property is in the hands of the citizens; not only their representatives but their senators and governors are annually chosen; there are are no hereditary titles, honors, offices, or distinctions; the legislative, executive, and judicial powers are carefully separated from each other; the powers of the one, the few, and the many are nicely balanced in the legislatures; trials by jury are preserved in all their glory, and there is no standing army; the *habeas corpus* is in full force; the press is the most free in the world. Where all these circumstances take place, it is unnecessary to add that the laws alone can govern.

In the preamble of *Defense* he laid the foundation for his historical precedents by writing:

ACCORDING TO A STORY in Herodotus, the nature of monarchy, aristocracy, and democracy, and the advantages and inconveniences of each, were as well understood at the time of the neighing of the horse of Darius as they are at this hour. A variety of mixtures of these simple species were conceived and attempted with various success by the Greeks and Romans. Representations instead of collections of the people; a total separation of the executive from the legislative power, and of the judicial from both; and a balance in the legislature by three independent, equal branches are perhaps the only three discoveries in the constitution of a free government since the institution of Lycurgus. Even these have been so unfortunate that they have never spread; the first has been given up by all the nations, excepting one, which had once adopted it; and the other two, reduced to practice, if not invented, by the English nation, have never been imitated by any other except their own descendants in America. . . .

We shall learn to prize the checks and balances of a free government and even those of the modern aristocracies if we recollect the miseries of Greece, which arose from its ignorance of them. The only balance attempted against the ancient kings was a body of nobles; and the consequences were perpetual alternations of rebellion and tyranny and the butchery of thousands upon every revolution from one to the other. When kings were abolished, aristocracies tyrannized; and then no balance was attempted but between aristocracy and democracy. This, in the nature of things, could be no balance at all, and therefore the pendulum was forever on the swing.

America, said Adams, was in the best position to profit by the lessons of history.

THE PEOPLE IN AMERICA have now the best opportunity and the greatest trust in their hands that Providence ever committed to so small a number since the transgression of the first pair; if they betray their trust, their guilt will merit even greater punishment than other nations have suffered and the indignation of Heaven.

Adams' concept of a three-way balance of power was somewhat different from the division of authority between the three branches of government as we now know it—legislative, executive, and judicial. He was more concerned about a three-way balance within the first two branches; a lower house in the legislature which directly represented the people, an upper house which represented the elite, and a strong executive which would keep either from dominating the other while they, in turn, prevented the executive from becoming a despot. This balance of power was necessary because:

THOUGH WE ALLOW BENEVOLENCE and generous affections to exist in the human breast, yet every moral theorist will admit the selfish passions in the generality of men to be the strongest. There are few who love the public better than themselves, though all may have some affection for the public. We are not, indeed, commanded to love our neighbor better than ourselves. Self-interest, private avidity, ambition, and avarice will exist in every state of society, and under every form of government. A succession of powers and persons, by frequent elections, will not lessen these passions in any case in a governor, senator, or representative; nor will the apprehension of an approaching election restrain them from indulgence if they have the power. The only remedy is to take away the power; by controlling the selfish avidity of the governor by the senate and house; of the senate by the governor and house; and of the house by the governor and senate. Of all possible forms of government, a sovereignty in one assembly, successively chosen by the people, is perhaps the best calculated to facilitate the gratification of self-love, and the pursuit of the private interest of a few individuals.

Adams envisioned the Senate as representing the rich, or upper class. This did not seem to conform to the concept of "all men are created equal." Of this he wrote:

LET US NOW RETURN to M. Turgot's idea of a government consisting in a single assembly. He tells us our republics are "founded on the equality of all the citizens, and, therefore, 'orders' and 'equilibriums' are unnecessary and occasion disputes." But what are we to understand here by equality? . . . Was there, or will there ever be, a nation whose individuals were all equal in natural and acquired qualities, in virtues, talents, and riches? The answer of all mankind must be in the negative. It must then be acknowledged that . . . there are in-equalities which God and nature have planted there, and which no human legislator ever can eradicate. . . .

In this society of Massachusettensians then there is, it is true, a moral and political equality of rights and duties among all the individuals and as yet no appearance of artificial inequalities of conditions. . . . There are, nevertheless, inequalities of great moment . . . because they have a natural and inevitable influence in society. Let us enumerate some of them: 1. There is an inequality of wealth. . . . 2. Birth. Let no man be surprised that this species of inequality is introduced here. Let the page in history be quoted where any nation, ancient or modern, civilized or savage, is mentioned, among whom no difference was made between the citizens on account of their extraction. . . .

It will be readily admitted there are great inequalities of merit, or talents, virtues, services, and what is of more moment, very often of reputation. . . .

These sources of inequality, which are common to every people and can never be altered by any because they are founded in the constitution of nature—this natural aristocracy among mankind has been dilated on because it is a fact essential to be considered in the institution of a government. It forms a body of men which contains the greatest collection of virtues and abilities in a free government, is the brightest ornament and glory of the nation, and may always be made the greatest blessing of society if it be judiciously managed in the constitution. But if this be not done it is always the most dangerous; nay, it may be added, it never fails to be the destruction of the commonwealth.

Elsewhere in *Defense* Adams correlates his aristocracy with a college education:

THE PEOPLE, in all nations, are naturally divided into two sorts, the gentlemen and the simplemen, a word which is here chosen to signify the common people. By gentlemen are not meant the rich or the poor, the high-born or the low-born, the industrious or the idle; but all those who have received a liberal education, an ordinary degree of erudition in liberal arts and sciences, whether by birth they be descended from magistrates and officers of government or from husbandmen, merchants, mechanics, or laborers; or whether they be rich or poor. We must, nevertheless, remember that generally those who are rich, and descended from families in public life, will have the best education in arts and sciences, and therefore the gentlemen will ordinarily, notwithstanding some exceptions to the rule, be the richer and born of more noted families. By the common people we mean laborers, husbandmen, mechanics, and merchants in general, who pursue their occupations and industry without any knowledge in liberal arts or sciences or in anything but their own trades or pursuits; though there may be exceptions to this rule, and individuals may be found in each of these classes who may really be gentlemen.

Now it seems to be clear that the gentlemen in every country are, and ever must be, few in number, in comparison of the simplemen. If you please, then, by the democratical portion of society we will understand the common people, as before explained; by the aristocratical part of the community we will understand the gentlemen. The distinctions which have been introduced among the gentlemen, into nobility greater or lesser, are perfectly immaterial to our present purpose; knights, barons, earls, viscounts, marquises, dukes, and even princes and kings are still but gentlemen, and the word noble signifies no more than knowable or conspicuous. But the gentlemen are more intelligent and skillful as well as generally richer and better connected, and therefore have more influence and power than an equal number of the common people.

What does this do to democracy? Adams undertook to prove that, "No democracy ever did or can exist." He reasoned:

No SUCH PASSION as a love of democracy, stronger than self-love, or superior to the love of private interest, ever did, or ever can, prevail in the minds of the citizens in general, or of a majority of them. . . . No love of equality, at least since Adam's fall, ever existed in human nature, any otherwise than as a desire of bringing others down to our own level, which implies a desire of raising ourselves above them, or depressing them below us. . . .

Therefore, the democracy of Montesquieu, and its principle of virtue, equality, frugality, etc., according to his definitions of them, are all mere figments of the brain, and delusive imaginations. His passion of love of the democracy would be, in the members of the majority, only a love of the majority; in those of the minority, only a love of the minority. . . . In reality, the word democracy signifies nothing more nor less than a nation of people without any government at all, and before any constitution is instituted.

What would happen if a pure democracy on the basis of total equality were attempted? Adams painted a dark picture:

SUPPOSE A NATION, rich and poor, high and low, ten millions in number, all assembled together. Not more than one or two millions will have lands, houses, or personal property; if we take into the account the women and children, or even if we leave them out of the question, a great majority of every nation is destitute of property, except a small quantity of clothes, and a few trifles or other movables. . . . Property is surely a right of mankind as really as liberty.

Perhaps, at first, prejudice, habit, shame or fear, principle or religion, would restrain the poor from attacking the rich, and the idle from usurping on the industrous; but the time would not be long before courage and enterprise would come, and pretexts be invented by degrees to countenance the majority in dividing all the property among them, or at least, in sharing it equally with the present possessors. Debts would be abolished first; taxes laid heavy on the rich, and not at all on the others; and at last a downright equal division of everything be demanded and voted.

What would be the consequence of this? The idle, the vicious, the intemperate, would rush into the utmost extravagance of debauchery, sell and spend all their share, and then demand a new division of those who purchased from them. The moment the idea is admitted into society that property is not as sacred as the laws of God, and that there is not a force of law and public justice to protect it, anarchy and tyranny commence. If "THOU SHALT NOT COVET" and "THOU SHALT NOT STEAL" were not commandments of Heaven, they must be made inviolable precepts in every society before it can be organized or made free.

Adams realized that his talented aristocracy represented a threat to the liberties of the people. By ability or corruption they might dominate the legislature. He queried, "What shall be done to guard against it?" and answered:

THERE IS BUT ONE expedient yet discovered to avail the society of all the benefits from this body of men which they are capable of affording, and at the same time to prevent them from undermining or invading the public liberty; and that is to throw them all, or at least the most remarkable of them, into one assembly together, in the legislature; to keep all the executive power entirely out of their hands as a body; to erect a first magistrate over them invested with the whole executive authority; to make them dependent on that executive magistrate for all public executive employments; to give that first magistrate a negative on the legislature, by which he may defend both himself and the people from all their enterprises in the legislature.

A strong executive would be impartial in his relations with both the democratic and aristocratic bodies in the legislature, but he would provide the greatest protection for the common people if he controlled all appointments and had an absolute veto on both houses.

IF ANY BODY OF GENTLEMEN have the gift of offices, they will dispose of them among their own families, friends, and connections; they will also make use of their votes in disposing of offices, to procure themselves votes in popular elections to the senate or other council, or to procure themselves appoint-

ments in the executive department. It is the true policy of the
common people to place the whole executive power in one
man, to make him a distinct order in the state, from whence
arises an inevitable jealousy between him and the gentlemen;
this forces him to become a father and protector of the common people, and to endeavor always to humble every proud,
aspiring senator, or other officer in the state, who is in danger
of acquiring an influence too great for the law or the spirit of
the constitution. This influences him to look for merit among
the common people, and to promote from among them such as
are capable of public employments; so that the road to preferment is open to the common people much more generally and
equitably in such a government than in an aristocracy, or one
in which the gentlemen have any share in appointments to
office.

Although he admitted that the contemporary English government was corrupt, Adams made no secret of his admiration for the
British system.

IF THE PEOPLE are not equitably represented in the House of
Commons, this is a departure in practice from the theory. If
the lords return members of the House of Commons, this is an
additional disturbance of the balance. . . . I only contend that
the English constitution is, in theory, both for the adjustment
of the balance and the prevention of its vibrations, the most
stupendous fabric of human invention; and that the Americans ought to be applauded instead of censured for imitating
it as far as they have done. Not the formation of languages,
not the whole art of navigation and shipbuilding, does more
honor to the human understanding than this system of government. . . . In future ages, if the present states become great
nations, rich, powerful, and luxurious, as well as numerous,
their own feelings and good sense will dictate to them what to

do; they may make transitions to a nearer resemblance of the British constitution.

Adams had nothing against kings, as such. In his mind a limited monarchy could be the perfect type of republican government—as, he believed, it would be under George III if the system was not corrupted by the aristocracy. In 1782 he had written La Fayette:

I HAVE THE HONOR and consolation to be a republican on principle; that is to say, I esteem that form of government the best of which human nature is capable. . . . I am not, however, an enthusiast who wishes to overturn empires and monarchies for the sake of introducing republican forms of government, and, therefore, I am no king-killer, king-hater, or king-despiser.

In *Defense* he challenged political philosopher Marchamont Nedham on the subject of kings by tracing the corruption of Rome when her ancient kings were dethroned.

NEDHAM TALKS OF "senate and people feeling the burdens of the fury of the kings." But as we cannot accuse this writer of ignorance, this must have been either artifice or inadvertence. There is not in the whole Roman history so happy a period as this under their kings. . . . As soon as the monarchy was abolished and an ambitious republic of haughty, aspiring aristocratics was erected, they were seized with the ambition of conquest and became a torment to themselves and the world. . . . The only change made by the revolution was to take off a little awe which the name king inspired. The office, with all its dignities, authorities, and powers, was in fact continued under the title of consul; it was made annually elective it is true, and became accordingly a mere tool of the senate.

Adams' willingness to accept a limited monarchy—perhaps his preference for some aspects of it—would later be the basis for rabid opposition. Anyone who reads Adams' writings fully must know that he was not a monarchist in the accepted sense of the term. He saw the chief executive as a man who must be above party and faction. To assure this he had no objection to the executive, like a king, holding office for life, regardless of what he was called. In a later work he wrote:

IN ELECTIVE GOVERNMENTS something very like this always takes place toward the first character. His person, countenance, character, and actions are made the daily contemplation and conversation of the whole people. Hence arises the danger of a division of this attention. Where there are rivals for the first place, the national attention and passions are divided and thwart each other; the collision enkindles fires; the conflicting passions interest all ranks; they produce slanders and libels first, mobs and sedition next, and civil war, with all her hissing snakes, burning torches, and haggard horrors at last.

This is the true reason why all civilized free nations have found, by experience, the necessity of separating from the body of the people, and even from the legislature, the distribution of honors, and conferring it on the executive authority of government. When the emulation of all the citizens looks up to one point, like the rays of a circle from all parts of the circumference, meeting and uniting in the center, you may hope for uniformity, consistency, and subordination; but when they look up to different individuals, or assemblies, or councils, you may expect all the deformities, eccentricities, and confusion of the Ptolemaic system.

Adams' most forthright statement on monarchy was made in a letter to Dr. Benjamin Rush in 1789 in which he opined that the United States must someday adopt this form of government.

THAT EVERY PART of the conduct and feelings of the Americans tends to that species of republic called a limited monarchy I agree. They were born and brought up in it. Their habits are fixed in it; but their heads are most miserably bewildered about it. There is not a more ridiculous spectacle in the universe than the politics of our country exhibits: bawling about republicanism which they understand not, and acting a farce of monarchy. We will have as you say "but one great man," yet even he shall not be a great man.

I also am as much a republican as I was in 1775. I do not "consider hereditary monarchy or aristocracy as rebellion against nature." On the contrary I esteem them both as institutions of admirable wisdom and exemplary virtue in a certain stage of society in a great nation—the only institutions that can possibly preserve the laws and liberties of the people—and I am clear that America must resort to them as an asylum against discord, seditions, and civil war, and that at no very distant period of time. I shall not live to see it—but you may. I think it therefore impolitic to cherish prejudices against institutions which must be kept in view as the hope of our posterity. I am by no means for attempting any such thing at present. Our country is not ripe for it in many respects, and it is not yet necessary, but our ship must ultimately land on that shore or be cast away.

In this same letter Adams stated his belief in the trappings of monarchy.

I DO NOT "abhor titles, nor the pageantry of government." If I did I should abhor government itself; for there never was, and never will be, because there never can be, any government without titles and pageantry. There is not a Quaker family in Pennsylvania governed without titles and pageantry: not a school, not a college, not a club can be governed without them.

And in another letter to Rush he said that the outward symbols of monarchical courts were necessary:

. . . to make offices and laws respected; and not so much by the virtuous part of the community, as by the profligate, the criminal and abandoned who have little reverence for reason, right or law, divine or human. These are overawed by titles frequently when laws and punishments cannot restrain them.

A year later, when Rush sent him some notes for a book he was planning, Adams denounced his earlier letters.

HOW MANY FOLLIES and indiscreet speeches do your minutes in your notebook bring to my recollection, which I had forgotten forever! Alas! I fear I am not yet much more prudent. . . . I deny an attachment to monarchy, and I deny that I have changed my principles since 1776. . . .

My friend Dr. Rush will excuse me if I caution him against a fraudulent use of the words *monarchy* and *republic*. I am a mortal and irreconcilable enemy to monarchy. I am no friend to hereditary limited monarchy in America. This I know can never be admitted without a hereditary Senate to control it, and a hereditary nobility or Senate in America I know to be unattainable and impracticable. I should scarcely be for it, if it were. Do not, therefore, my friend, misunderstand me and misrepresent me to posterity. I am for a balance between the legislative and executive powers, and I am for enabling the executive to be at all times capable of maintaining the balance between the Senate and House, or in other words, between the aristocratical and democratical interests. Yet I am for having all three branches elected at stated periods, and these elections, I hope, will continue until the people shall be convinced that fortune, providence, or chance, call it which you will, is better than election. If the time should come when corruption shall be added to intrigue and maneuver in elections, and produce civil war, then, in my opinion, chance will be better than choice for all but the House of Representatives.

Accusations of monarchical leanings were not limited to Adams' enemies. When Mercy Warren published a history of the Revolution in 1805 she said that Adams, during his stay in England, "became so enamored with the British constitution and the government, manners, and laws of the nation, that a partiality for monarchy appeared, which was inconsistent with his former professions of republicanism." Thomas Jefferson capsuled Adams' political philosophy, as he saw it, by recording a conversation between him and Alexander Hamilton:

THE . . . conversation . . . by some circumstance, was led to the British constitution, on which Mr. Adams observed: "Purge that constitution of its corruption and give to its popular branch equality of representation, and it would be the most perfect constitution ever devised by the wit of man." Hamilton paused and said: "Purge it of its corruption, and give to its popular branch equality, and it would become impracticable government: as it stands at present, with all its supposed defects, it is the most perfect government which ever existed." And this was assuredly the exact line which separated the political creeds of these two gentlemen. The one [Adams] was for two hereditary branches and an honest elective one; and the other, for a hereditary king, with a House of Lords and Commons corrupt to his will, and standing between him and the people.

Adams concluded the first volume of *Defense* with what may have been a "weasel." When he wrote it he was an agent of a government consisting of a single legislative body such as he condemned. His system, if applied to the United States, would make the existing Congress a Senate of limited power, subject to the negative of an executive—a body which, in fact, would not have the power to appoint him to the position he was holding. But Adams did not seek to apply his system of government to the United States. He summarized his "balance of power" plan and then said:

THIS IS APPLICABLE to every state in America, in its individual capacity; but is it equally applicable to the United States in their federal capacity? The people of America and their delegates in Congress were of opinion that a single assembly was every way adequate to the management of all their federal concerns; and with very good reason, because Congress is not a legislative assembly, nor a representative assembly, but only a diplomatic assembly. A single council has been found to answer the purposes of confederacies very well.

This view of the American Congress as solely a diplomatic body representing a confederation of sovereign states is not wholly consistent with his many statements, in previous letters to Jay, that the Congress should have power to do such things as force the states to repeal internal laws covering debts, control the issuance of money, etc.

The first volume of *Defense* reached America a few months before the meeting of the Constitutional Convention. Adams had first speculated on the probable reception of his work in America by writing:

I DOUBT whether my sentiments of government are agreeable to the majority of our state, and I am not enough of an accommodating disposition to give up or conceal sentiments that I think of consequence, for the sake of places. The commotions in New England alarmed me so much that I have thrown together some hasty speculations upon the subject of government, which you will soon see. If the general spirit of those papers is not approved in our country, my career in political life will be very short.

Later he wrote, of the reception of *Defense* in America:

A NUMEROUS EDITION of it was soon abroad in Philadelphia, another in New York and a third in Boston, and the public voice was so decidedly in favor of it that it revived the hopes and strengthened the hands of the convention. It soon dissipated the vapors of Franklin's foggy system, demolished Hamilton's airy castles, and united the convention in the plan they finally adopted, and Franklin himself thought fit at last to yield in his assent. It contributed also to unite the assemblies of the several states in the acceptance and adoption of it.

Whether or not the book had the influence on the adoption of the United States Constitution which Adams claimed, there is no doubt that its influence back home was considerable. It was a minor best-seller which went into several editions. It had the field to itself as the only exhaustive work on the history and theory of government. It was quoted by friends to prove that Adams was a stanch democrat and by enemies to support the charge that he was a monarchist. At the convention it was used principally as a reference book, although Madison quoted from it in four speeches, Hamilton in three, and King, Morris, and Patterson each quoted it once.

The second volume of *Defense* was a tedious and dull record of the Italian republics of the Middle Ages, mostly quotations from Italian historians. The third volume was entirely given to a criticism of "The Excellency of a Free State," by Marchamont Nedham. Adams tore into the poor Marchamont's thesis on the superiority of the simple democracy with his best lawyer-like reasoning, denunciation, sarcasm, and quoting of precedents, as follows:

MARCHAMONT NEDHAM lays it down as a fundamental principle and an undeniable rule, "that the people, that is, such as shall be successively chosen to represent the people, are the best keepers of their own liberties, and that for many reasons.

First, because they never think of usurping over other men's rights, but mind which way to preserve their own."

Our first attention should be turned to the proposition itself —"The people are the best keepers of their own liberties."

But who are the people?

"Such as shall be successively chosen to represent them."

Here is a confusion both of words and ideas, which, though it may pass with the generality of readers in a fugitive pamphlet or with a majority of auditors in a popular harangue, ought, for that very reason, to be as carefully avoided in politics as it is in philosophy or mathematics. If by "the people" is meant the whole body of a great nation, it should never be forgotten that they can never act, consult, or reason together because they cannot march five hundred miles, nor spare the time, nor find a space to meet; and, therefore, the proposition that they are the best keepers of their own liberties is not true. They are the worst conceivable; they are no keepers at all. They can neither act, judge, think, or will, as a body politic or corporation. . . .

If it is meant by "the people," as our author explains himself, a representative assembly, "such as shall be successively chosen to represent the people," still they are not the best keepers of the people's liberties or their own if you give them all the power—legislative, executive, and judicial. They would invade the liberties of the people, at least the majority of them would invade the liberties of the minority, sooner and oftener than an absolute monarchy such as that of France, Spain, or Russia, or than a well-checked aristocracy like Venice, Bern, or Holland.

An excellent writer has said, somewhat incautiously, that "a people will never oppress themselves or invade their own rights." This compliment, if applied to human nature, or to mankind . . . is more than has been merited. . . . All kinds of experience show that great numbers of individuals do oppress great numbers of other individuals; that parties often, if not always, oppress other parties; and majorities almost universally minorities. . . .

"The people never think of usurping over other men's rights." . . . If the people never, jointly nor severally, think of usurping the rights of others, what occasion can there be for any government at all? Are there no robberies, burglaries, murders, adulteries, thefts, nor cheats? Is not every crime a usurpation over other men's rights? Is not a great part, I will not say the greatest part, of men detected every day in some disposition or other, stronger or weaker, more or less, to usurp over other men's rights? If a majority are capable of preferring their own private interest or that of their families, counties, and party to that of the nation collectively, some provision must be made in the constitution in favor of justice to compel all to respect the common right, the public good, the universal law, in preference to all private and partial considerations. The proposition of our author, then, should be reversed, and it should have been said that they mind so much their own that they never think enough of others.

It was in the third volume that Adams deflated democracy and, in criticizing Montesquieu's *Spirit of Laws,* sought to prove that law rather than virtue must be the foundation of government.

LET US PROCEED to the inquiry, what is virtue? It is not that classical virtue which we see personified in the choice of Hercules, and which the ancient philosophers summed up in four words—prudence, justice, temperance, and fortitude. It is not Christian virtue, so much more sublime, which is summarily comprehended in universal benevolence. What is it then? . . .

Montesquieu tells us virtue in a republic is a love of the republic; virtue in a democracy is a love of the democracy; and why might he not have said that virtue in a monarchy is a love of the monarchy; in a despotism, of the despot; in a mixed government, of the mixture? Men in general love their country and its government. Can it be proved that Athenians loved Athens, or Romans Rome, more than Frenchmen love France, or Englishmen their island? . . .

It may be well questioned whether love of the body politic is precisely moral or Christian virtue, which requires justice and benevolence to enemies as well as friends and to other nations as well as our own. It is not true, in fact, that any people ever existed who loved the public better than themselves, their private friends, neighbors, etc., and therefore this kind of virtue, this sort of love, is as precarious a foundation for liberty as honor or fear; it is the laws alone that really love the country, the public, the whole better than any part; and that form of government which unites all the virtue, honor, and fear of the citizens in a reverence and obedience to the laws is the only one in which liberty can be secure, and all orders, and ranks, and parties, compelled to prefer the public good before their own; that is the government for which we plead . . .

Montesquieu adds, "a love of democracy is that of equality." But what passion is this? Every man hates to have a superior, but no man is willing to have an equal; every man desires to be superior to all others. If the meaning is that every citizen loves to have every other brought down to a level with himself, this is so far true, but is not the whole truth. When every man is brought down to his level, he wishes them depressed below him; and no man will ever acknowledge himself to be upon a level or equality with others till they are brought down lower than him.

A copy of the new Constitution of the United States reached Adams in London just as he was finishing the third volume of *Defense* and he was able to conclude his work with a prideful, though somewhat qualified, praise for a document that basically followed his balance of power concept:

THE FORMER CONFEDERATION of the United States was
formed upon the model and example of all the confederacies,
ancient and modern, in which the federal council was only a
diplomatic body. . . . The magnitude of territory, the population, the wealth and commerce, and especially the rapid
growth of the United States, have shown such a government to
be inadequate to their wants; and the new system, which seems
admirably calculated to unite their interests and affections,
and bring them to an uniformity of principles and sentiments,
is equally well combined to unite their wills and forces as a
single nation. A result of accommodation cannot be supposed
to reach the ideas of perfection of any one; but the conception
of such an idea, and the deliberate union of so great and various a people in such a plan, is, without all partiality or prejudice, if not the greatest exertion of human understanding, the
greatest single effort of national deliberation that the world
has ever seen.

Scholars have often commented on the coincidence that two
Americans who might have made great contributions to the drafting of a charter of government—Jefferson and Adams—were absent when the Constitution was created, and some have speculated
what might have happened had they been present. It is not unlikely
that, had Adams been in Philadelphia during that hot summer,
there would have been no Constitution from that convention. The
Constitution was a bundle of compromises; and Adams was no
compromiser—particularly when the compromises were proposed,
as some were at Philadelphia, by Benjamin Franklin.

His first reaction to the Constitution was contained in an exchange of letters with Jefferson. The latter wrote: "How do you
like our new constitution? I confess there are things in it which
stagger all my dispositions to subscribe to what such an assembly
has proposed. The house of federal representatives will not be adequate to the management of affairs either foreign or federal. Their
President seems a bad edition of a Polish king. He may be re-

elected from four years to four years for life. Reason and experience prove to us that a chief magistrate, so continuable, is an officer for life." To which Adams replied:

YOU ARE AFRAID OF THE ONE—I, of the few. We agree perfectly that the many should have a full fair and perfect representation. You are apprehensive of monarchy; I, of aristocracy. I would therefore have given more power to the President and less to the Senate. The nominations and appointments of all officers I would have given to the President, assisted only by a privy council of his own creation, but not a vote or voice would I have given to the Senate or any senator, unless he were of the privy council. Faction and distraction are the sure and certain consequence of giving to a Senate a vote in the distribution of offices.

You are apprehensive the President when once chosen will be chosen again and again as long as he lives. So much the better as it appears to me. You are apprehensive of foreign interference, intrigue, influence. So am I. But, as often as elections happen, the danger of foreign influence recurs. The less frequently they happen the less danger. And if the same man may be chosen again . . . the danger of foreign influence will be less. Foreigners, seeing little prospect, will have less courage for enterprise.

Elections, my dear sir, elections to offices which are great objects of ambition, I look at with terror. Experiments of this kind have been so often tried, and so universally found productive of horrors, that there is great reason to dread them.

It is generally said that these letters are the first signals of the political rift that would later develop between Adams and Jefferson. Actually, their basic difference is apparent in a previous exchange of letters on Shays' Rebellion, which Jefferson considered a justifiable reaction of the farmers occasioned by ignorance and Adams looked on as a thoroughly reprehensible disregard for law and proper government.

The Constitution, in general, met with Adams' approval, but it had faults which, in his opinion, would lead to its subversion if they were not corrected by amendment. Principal of these was that it did not give enough power to the President. He summarized his views on this in three letters to Roger Sherman in which he said:

LET US . . . consider what our Constitution is, and see whether any other name can with propriety be given it than that of a monarchical republic, or if you will, a limited monarchy. The duration of our President is neither perpetual nor for life; it is only for four years; but his power during those four years is much greater than that of an avoyer, a consul, a podestà, a doge, a stadtholder; nay, than a king of Poland; nay, than a king of Sparta. . . .

That these powers are necessary, I readily admit. That the laws cannot be executed without them; that the lives, liberties, properties, and characters of the citizens cannot be secure without their protection, is most clear. But it is equally certain, I think, that they ought to have been still greater, or much less. The limitations upon them in cases of war, treaties, and appointments to office, and especially the limitations on the President's independence as a branch of the legislative, will be the destruction of this Constitution, and involve us in anarchy, if not amended. . . . A divided sovereignty without a balance, or in other words, where the division is unequal, is always at war, and consequently has no laws. In our Constitution the sovereignty—that is the legislative power—is divided into three branches. The House and Senate are equal, but the third branch, though essential, is not equal. The President must pass judgment upon every law; but in some cases his judgment may be overruled. These cases will be such as attack his constitutional power; it is, therefore, certain he has not equal power to defend himself, or the Constitution, or the judicial power, as the Senate and House have.

Power naturally grows. Why? Because human passions are insatiable. But that power alone can grow which already is too great; that which is unchecked; that which has no equal power to control it. The legislative power, in our Constitution, is greater than the executive; it will, therefore, encroach, because both aristocratical and democratical passions are insatiable. The legislative power will increase, the executive will diminish. In the legislature, the monarchical power is not equal either to the aristocratical or democratical; it will, therefore, decrease, while the other will increase. Indeed, I think the aristocratical power is greater than either the monarchical or democratical. That will, therefore, swallow up the other two. . . .

It is . . . possible that more than two thirds of the nation, the Senate and House may, in times of calamity, distress, misfortune, and ill success of the measures of government, from the momentary passion and enthusiasm, demand a law which will wholly subvert the Constitution. . . . The Constitution should guard against a possibility of its subversion; but we may take stronger ground and assert that it is probable such cases will happen, and that the Constitution will, in fact, be subverted, in this way. Nay, I go further and say that from the constitution of human nature, and the constant course of human affairs, it is certain that our Constitution will be subverted, if not amended, and that in a very short time, merely for want of a decisive negative in the executive.

Adams also believed that the President should not be limited by the legislature in making treaties, declaring war, and making appointments. Of the latter he wrote:

IT WILL WEAKEN the hands of the executive by lessening the obligation, gratitude, and attachment between the executive and legislative, which are natural enemies. Officers of government, instead of having a single eye and undivided attachment to the executive branch, as they ought to have, consistent with law and the Constitution, will be constantly tempted to be factious with their factious patrons in the Senate. The President's own officers, in a thousand instances, will oppose his just and constitutional exertions and screen themselves under the wings of their patrons and party in the legislature.

After he returned to the United States, and inspired by the course of the revolution in France, Adams wrote a sequel to *Defense* in a series of thirty-two articles for the *Gazette of the United States,* which were later published in book form under the title *Discourses on Davila.* Enrico Caterino Davila was an Italian historian of the seventeenth century who had written a *Histoire des guerres civiles de France.* The sad result of this upheaval of government under four French monarchs between 1560 and 1598 would, Adams believed, be paralleled by the contemporary French Revolution because the French were now aiming at a simple democracy rather than his "balance of power" republicanism.

The title of *Discourses* is misleading in that it indicates that they are a commentary on the Italian's history. Adams' grandson, in editing his papers, speaks of the book as "an analysis" of Davila's work. It is not. Eighteen of Adams' papers are merely translations of Davila. The remaining fourteen are essays on human nature based on the premise that man is not perfectible and that no such thing as real equality exists. Any government founded on the hope that man will become virtuous in a society of equals is doomed. There will always be an aristocracy, says Adams; it is good and should be preserved, but controlled.

The ideas that he propounds in *Discourses* parallel those presented in *Defense* except that in the former they are based on a moral philosophy rather than political or historical precedent. One is impressed with this aspect of Adams as a "moral writer"— until his essays are compared with the writings of Adam Smith. Then it is discovered that much of this section of *Discourses* is paraphrased or quoted verbatim, without credit, from a single chapter of Adam Smith's *Theory of Moral Sentiments.* However, where John paraphrased, his penchant for strings of epithets and metaphors produced more sprightly writing. A comparison of a section of the third paper in *Discourses* indicates this:

ADAM SMITH

To what purpose is all the toil and bustle of this world? What is the end of avarice and ambition, of the pursuit of wealth, of power, and pre-eminence? Is it to supply the necessities of nature? The wages of the meanest laborer can supply them. We see that they afford him food and clothing, the comfort of a house, and of a family. . . .

The poor man is ashamed of his poverty. He feels that it places him out of the sight of mankind. . . . He goes out and comes in unheeded, and when in the midst of a crowd is in the same obscurity as if shut up in his own hovel. . . .

To become the natural object of the joyous con-

JOHN ADAMS

The labor and anxiety, the enterprises and adventures, that are voluntarily undertaken in pursuit of gain are out of all proportion to the utility, convenience, or pleasure of riches. A competence to satisfy the wants of nature, food and clothes, a shelter from the seasons, and the comforts of a family, may be had for very little. The daily toil of the million, and of millions of millions, is adequate to a complete supply of these necessities and conveniences. . . .

The poor man's conscience is clear; yet he is ashamed. . . . Mankind takes no notice of him. He rambles and wanders unheeded. In the midst of a crowd, at church, in the market, at a play, at an execution or coronation, he is in as much obscurity as he would be in a garret or a cellar. . . .

Every personal quality, and every blessing of fortune, is

gratulations and sympathetic attentions of mankind is the circumstance which gives to prosperity all its dazzling splendor. cherished in proportion to its capacity of gratifying this universal affection for the esteem, the sympathy, admiration, and congratulations of the public.

This desire to be a man of distinction was a motivating force in human nature that could not be ignored. Adams played several variations on this theme throughout his essays.

MEN, in their primitive conditions, however savage, were undoubtedly gregarious; and they continue to be social, not only in every stage of civilization, but in every possible situation in which they can be placed. As nature intended them for society, she has furnished them with passions, appetites, and propensities, as well as a variety of faculties calculated both for their individual enjoyment and to render them useful to each other in their social connections. There is none among them more essential or remarkable than the *passion for distinction.* A desire to be observed, considered, esteemed, praised, beloved, and admired by his fellows is one of the earliest, as well as keenest, dispositions discovered in the heart of man. If anyone should doubt the existence of this propensity, let him go and attentively observe the journeyman and apprentices in the first workshop or the oarsmen in a cockboat, a family or a neighborhood, the inhabitants of a house or the crew of a ship, a school or a college, a city or a village, a savage or civilized people, a hospital or a church, the bar or the exchange, a camp or a court. Wherever men, women, or children are to be found, whether they be old or young, rich or poor, high or low, wise or foolish, ignorant or learned, every individual is seen to be strongly actuated by a desire to be seen, heard, talked of, approved, and respected, by the people about him, and within his knowledge.

Another variation of this idea read:

THERE IS IN HUMAN NATURE, it is true, simple *benevolence,* or
an affection for the good of others; but alone it is not a balance for the selfish affections. Nature then has kindly added to
benevolence the desire of reputation, in order to make us good
members of society. . . . Nature has sanctioned the law of
self-preservation by rewards and punishments. The rewards of
selfish activity are life and health; the punishments of negli-
gence and indolence are want, disease, and death. . . . The
same nature . . . has imposed another law, that of promoting
the good, as well as respecting the rights of mankind, and has
sanctioned it by other rewards and punishments. The rewards
in this case, in this life, are *esteem* and *admiration* of others;
the punishments are *neglect* and *contempt;* nor may anyone
imagine that these are not as real as the others. The desire of
the esteem of others is as real a want of nature as hunger; and
the neglect and contempt of the world as severe a pain as the
gout or stone. . . . It is a principal end of government to regulate this passion, which in its turn becomes a principal means
of government.

It has been remarked that Adams was cataloguing his own
weaknesses as basic faults of human nature; that the moral essays
in *Discourses* were subconscious confessions. Certain it is, from his
diary and much of his correspondence, that Adams felt a need for
recognition and acclaim that was almost psychopathic and which
has been characterized as an overweening vanity.

Adams pointed out that this competition for distinction had led
to the rise of leading families, which he endorsed.

IS THERE ANYTHING IN BIRTH, however illustrious or splendid,
which should make a difference between one man and another? If, from a common ancestor, the whole human race is
descended, they are all of the same family. . . . What founda-

tion has the whole science of genealogy and heraldry? Are there differences in the breeds of men, as there are in those of horses? If there are not, these sciences have no foundation in reason; in prejudice they have a very solid one. All that philosophy can say is that there is a general presumption that a man has had some advantages of education if he is of a family of note. . . .

The mighty secret lies in this: An illustrious descent attracts the notice of mankind. . . . Why? Because, although it excites the indignation of many, and the envy of more, it still attracts the *attention* of the world. Noble blood, whether the nobility be hereditary or elective, and, indeed, more in republican governments than in monarchies, least of all in despotisms, is held in estimation for the same reason. It is a name and a race that a nation has been interested in, and is in the habit of respecting. Benevolence, sympathy, congratulation, have been so long associated to those names in the minds of the people, that they are become national habits. . . . When the names of a certain family are read in all the gazettes, chronicles, records, and histories of a country for five hundred years, they become known, respected, and delighted in by everybody. . . . A wise man will lament that any other distinction than that of merit should be made. A good man will neither be proud nor vain of his birth, but will earnestly improve every advantage he has for the public good. A cunning man will carefully conceal his pride; but will indulge it in secret the more effectually, and improve his advantage to greater profit. But was any man ever known so wise, or so good, as really to despise birth or wealth? Did you ever read of a man rising to public notice, from obscure beginnings, who was not reflected on? Although, with every liberal mind, it is an honor and a proof of merit, yet it is a disgrace with mankind in general.

He summarized this by writing:

EQUAL LAWS may be ordained and executed; great families, as well as little ones, may be restrained. And . . . such families . . . are sent to be blessings; and they are blessings, until, by our own obstinate ignorance and imprudence, in refusing to establish such institutions as will make them always blessings, we turn them into curses.

Knowledge would not eradicate class distinction, said Adams, and asked:

HAS THE PROGRESS OF SCIENCE, arts, and letters yet discovered that there are no passions in human nature—no ambition, avarice, or desire for fame? . . . On the contrary, the more knowledge is diffused, the more the passions are extended, and the more furious they grow. . . .

The increase and dissemination of knowledge, instead of rendering unnecessary the checks of emulation and the balances of rivalry in the orders of society and constitution of government, augment the necessity of both. It becomes the more indispensable that every man should know his place and be made to keep it. Bad men increase in knowledge as fast as good men; and science, arts, taste, sense, and letters are employed for the purposes of injustice and tyranny as well as those of law and liberty, for corruption as well as for virtue.

The French passion for *égalité* was foolish, since man was neither perfect nor perfectible. Instead of beheading its aristocracy France should preserve and control it. He entreated;

FRENCHMEN! Act and think like yourselves! confessing human nature, be magnanimous and wise. Acknowledging and boasting yourselves to be men, avow the feelings of men. The affectation of being exempted from passions is inhuman. The grave pretention to such singularity is solemn hypocrisy. Both are unworthy of your frank and generous natures. Consider that government is intended to set bounds to passions which nature has not limited; and to assist reason, conscience, justice, and truth in controlling interest which without it would be as unjust as uncontrollable.

He admitted that the prospect of the French struggle for liberty was "enchanting," but added:

. . . amidst our enthusiasm there is great reason to pause and preserve our sobriety. It is true that the first empire of the world is breaking the fetters of human reason and exerting the energies of redeemed liberty. In the glowing ardor of her zeal she condescends, Americans, to pay the most scrupulous attention to your maxims, principles and example. There is reason to fear she has copied from you errors which have cost you very dear. . . . Amidst all their exultations Americans and Frenchmen should remember that the perfectibility of man is only human and terrestrial perfectibility. Cold will still freeze, and fire will never cease to burn; disease and vice will continue to disorder, and death to terrify mankind.

Of the proposed French system he said:

IF THE COMMON PEOPLE are advised to aim at collecting the whole sovereignty in single national assemblies . . . they will fail of their desired liberty, as certainly as emulation and rivalry are founded in human nature, and inseparable from civil affairs. It is not to flatter the passions of the people, to be sure, nor is it the way to obtain a present enthusiastic popularity, to tell them that in a single assembly they will act as arbitrarily and tyranically as any despot, but it is a sacred truth, and as demonstrable as any proposition whatever, that a sovereignty in a single assembly must necessarily and will certainly be exercised by a majority, as tyrannically as any sovereignty was ever exercised by kings or nobles. And if a balance of passions and interests is not scientifically concerted, the present struggle in Europe will be little beneficial to mankind, and produce nothing but another thousand years of feudal fanaticism, under new and strange names.

Adams summed up all of this moralizing by reiterating his theme that the only hope of mankind was a balanced government.

IT HAS BEEN SAID that it is extremely difficult to preserve a balance. This is no more than to say that it is extremely difficult to preserve liberty. To this truth all ages and nations attest. It is so difficult that the very appearance of it is lost over the whole earth, excepting one island [England] and North America. How long it will be before she returns to her native skies, and leaves the whole human race in slavery, will depend on the intelligence and virtue of the people. A balance, with all its difficulty, must be preserved, or liberty is lost forever. Perhaps a perfect balance, if it ever existed, has not been long maintained in its perfection; yet, such a balance as has been sufficient to liberty has been supported in some nations for many centuries together; and we must come as near as we can to a perfect equilibrium, or all is lost. When it is once widely departed from, the departure increases rapidly, till the while is lost. If the people have not understanding and public virtue enough, and will not be persuaded of the necessity of supporting an independent executive authority, an independent Senate, and an independent judiciary power, as well as an independent House of Representatives, all pretensions to a balance are lost, and with them all hopes of security to our dearest interests, all hopes of liberty.

In the last of the *Discourse* papers Adams started by saying that the surrender of all sovereign power to an individual and his descendants was "the most irrational and ridiculous idea imaginable," and then continued, with characteristic inconsistency, to fervently defend hereditary succession. This contained so much dynamite that the *Gazette* refused to continue the series. Adams recorded: ". . . the rage and fury of the Jacobinical journals against these discourses increased as they proceeded, intimidated the printer, John Fenno, and convinced me that to proceed would do more hurt than good. I therefore broke off abruptly." In later life, as with *Defense,* he would write numerous commentaries to support *Discourses.*

Politically, the best that can be said for *Discourses* is that their publication in 1790, by a man holding political office, was ill advised. A college professor, propounding such theories from his ivory tower, might have been excused. But the people of America were universally sympathetic to the people of France, who had been oppressed by these aristocrats whom Adams seemed to support. And, if Adams did not actually condone hereditary monarchy, his words could easily be twisted by anti-Federalist pamphleteers to support the charge that he and the Federalists whom he represented were iniquitous monarchists intent on enslaving the common people.

At the time, he was dismayed at the furor that *Discourses* aroused and brooded about his countrymen's low regard for his services and sacrifices. No one would ever appreciate his efforts, he wrote to Benjamin Rush.

THE HISTORY OF OUR REVOLUTION will be one continued lie from one end to the other. The essence of the whole will be *that Dr. Franklin's electrical rod smote the earth and out sprung General Washington. That Franklin electrized him with his rod—and henceforward these two conducted all the policy, negotiation, legislation, and war.* These lines contain the whole fable, plot, and catastrophe. If this letter should be preserved and read a hundred years hence, the reader will say, "The envy of . . . JA could not bear to think of the truth." He ventured to scribble to Rush, as envious as himself, blasphemy that he dared not speak when he lived.

CHAPTER VI

THE VICE-PRESIDENT

When the *Lucretia,* bearing John and Abigail, sailed into Boston harbor on June 17, 1788, the ex-diplomat had no cause to complain that he was without honor in his own country—or at least in his own state. Cannon boomed in salute from the Castle. The coach of Governor John Hancock waited on the Long Wharf to bear him to the executive mansion as thousands of proper Bostonians lowered their dignity to shout loud huzzas. He modestly refused an escort of cavalry to accompany him to Braintree; but he did not refrain from sending the eulogies published in the press to Jefferson and was pleased with the clippings he later received of their translations in French and Dutch papers.

He looked forward to retiring to private life in the new and larger home which he had purchased in Quincy; or so he said in some letters. But to Nabby he was soon repeating his usual complaint that he was not appreciated. He wrote that he did not "stand very high in the esteem, admiration, or respect of his country," and that others were already holding every public office which he could "accept of with consistency or honor or reputation." He had already been elected to the House of Representatives in *absentia,* where a resolution had been passed: "That a chair be assigned to

John Adams painted by Charles Willson Peale.

the Honorable John Adams, whenever he may please to attend the debates of the House." There was talk of appointing him to the new Senate, but he had no interest in becoming one of the rank and file of this elite body. He squelched this by writing to a supporter:

I HAVE LONG REVOLVED, in an anxious mind, the duties of the man and the citizen; and, without entering into details at present, the result of all my reflections on the place of a senator in the new government is an unchangeable determination to refuse it.

As the election neared, it was a foregone conclusion that Washington would be the first President. With a Virginian as Chief Executive, the Vice-President should be a New Englander. John Hancock was now governor, Samuel Adams lieutenant governor, and neither was a strong supporter of the new Constitution, although Hancock had given it his blessing at the ratification convention in return, it is said, for a promise that he would be the first Vice-President. John Adams was unquestionably the leading available man in the eastern states.

Political parties were already forming. The Federalists were well organized, with New Yorker Alexander Hamilton as their nominal head. The anti-Federalists, although probably more numerous, had no concerted leadership; in fact, they did not even have a positive name. Hamilton was not enthusiastic about Adams, who was far too righteous and independent to permit himself to be controlled for the good of the party. But the New England Federalists were too strong to risk opposing their favorite son. Hamilton wrote to Madison that he was backing Adams, "not without apprehensions."

Under the complex system adopted in the Constitution each presidential elector was to vote for two men without specifying which would be President and which Vice-President. The man with the most votes would have the first post; the next man the second. While Adams awaited the decision of the electors he wrote to Abigail, who was visiting Nabby, this philosophical reflection:

MY MIND HAD BALANCED all circumstances, and all are reducible to two articles—vanity and comfort. I have the alternative in my own power. If they mortify my vanity, they give me comfort. They cannot deprive me of comfort without gratifying my vanity.

Washington would surely be elected unanimously, so at least one vote must be cast away from Adams to prevent a tie. Hamilton did not want Adams to seem to be a near-unanimous choice. To weaken John's political position he advised Federalist leaders in several states to throw away a few votes in each state. As a result the final tally gave all sixty-nine votes to Washington but only thirty-four to Adams.

This infuriated John, and he moaned to Benjamin Rush:

IS NOT MY ELECTION to this office, in the scurvy manner in which it was done, a curse rather than a blessing? Is this justice? Is there common sense or decency in this business? Is it not an indelible stain on our Country, Countrymen, and Constitution? I assure you I think it so, and nothing but an apprehension of great mischief, and final failure of the government from my refusal and assigning my reasons for it, prevented me from spurning it.

Having decided to save the country by not resigning, John journeyed to the temporary capital in New York. Again, he had no cause for complaint at his distinguished treatment. He wrote Abby:

AT HARTFORD, the manufacturers presented me with a piece of broadcloth for a suit of clothes. At New Haven, the corporation presented me with the freedom of the city. At both

these towns the gentlemen came out to meet us, and went out
with us. At Horseneck we were met by Major Pintard and
Captain Mandeville with a party of horse from the state of
New York, and there is to be much parade on Monday.

In New York, Fenno's *Gazette*, which called him "the great
Adams," published a poem which lauded him as the father of
independence:

> Lo! Adams rose! a giant in debate
> And turned the vote which fix'd our empire's fate.

Another versifier credited him with the treaty which "Gave us
rank as a nation," and described him as "Columbia's Safeguard,
Glory, Boast, and Pride."

In John's acceptance speech to the Senate, which he had prepared with care, all was sweetness and light. He started by saying:

INVITED TO THIS RESPECTABLE SITUATION by the suffrages of
our fellow citizens, according to the Constitution, I have
thought it my duty cheerfully and readily to accept it. Unac-
customed to refuse any public service, however dangerous to
my reputation, or disproportioned to my talents, it would have
been inconsistent to have adopted another maxim of conduct
at this time when the prosperity of the country and the liberties of the people require, perhaps as much as ever, the attention of those who possess any share of the public confidence.

He lauded his colleagues in the upper house:

. . . those celebrated defenders of the liberties of this country,
whom menaces could not intimidate, corruption seduce, nor
flattery allure; those intrepid asserters of the rights of mankind
whose philosophy and policy have enlightened the world, in
twenty years, more than it was ever before enlightened in
many centuries.

He praised the Constitution without qualification:

IT IS WITH SATISFACTION that I congratulate the people of America on the formation of a national Constitution, and the fair prospect of a consistent administration of a government of laws; on the acquisition of a House of Representatives, chosen by themselves; of a Senate, thus composed by their own state legislatures; and on the prospect of an executive authority, in the hands of one whose portrait I shall not presume to draw.

Of Washington he asked:

. . . if we look over the catalogue of the first magistrates of nations, whether they have been denominated presidents or consuls, kings or princes, where shall we find one whose commanding talents . . . have so completely united all hearts and voices in his favor, who enjoyed the esteem and admiration of foreign nations and fellow citizens with equal unanimity?

And he closed with a meek avowal of his unworthiness.

IT IS ONLY NECESSARY to make an apology for myself. Not wholly without experience in public assemblies, I have been more accustomed to take a share in their debates than to preside in their deliberations. It shall be my constant endeavor to behave toward every member of this most honorable body with all that consideration, delicacy, and decorum which becomes the dignity of his station and character. But if, from inexperience or inadvertency, anything should ever escape me, inconsistent with propriety, I must entreat you, by imputing it to its true cause, and not to any want of respect, to pardon and excuse it.

At the capital Adams accepted an invitation to stay with John Jay. But he missed his own creature comforts and his Abigail. He had been there but four weeks when he wrote his "Dearest Friend," telling her to put their son Thomas in college:

. . . but I pray you to come on with Charles as soon as possible. As to the place, let my brother plough and plant as he will, as much as he will. He may send me my half of the butter, cheese, etc., here. As to money to bear your expenses, you must, if you can, borrow of some friend, enough to bring you here. If you cannot borrow enough, you must sell horses, oxen, sheep, cows, anything at any rate rather than not come on. If no one will take the place, leave it to the birds of the air and beasts of the field, but at all events break up that establishment and that household. . . . I have as many difficulties here, as you can have, public and private; but my life from my cradle has been a series of difficulties, and that series will continue to the grave.

The initial difficulties which John was having as President of the Senate had to do with his attachment to the titles and trappings of royal courts. When the Senate had to address the Speaker of the lower house, John wanted to call him Honorable, and lectured the body on this subject. He was roundly defeated and Senator William Maclay, a rugged democrat from Pennsylvania, recorded: "From this omen, I think our President [Adams] may go and dream about titles, for he will get none." Then John was concerned with how he should act when Washington visited the Senate. He declared:

I DO NOT KNOW whether the framers of the Constitution had in view the two kings of Sparta or the two consuls of Rome, when they formed it; one to have all the power while he held it, and the other to be nothing. I am possessed of two separate powers: the one in *esse* and the other in *posse*. I am Vice-President. In this I am nothing, but I may be everything. . . .

When the President comes into the Senate, what shall I be? I wish, gentlemen, to think what I shall be.

But the great problem on which the Senate wrangled for days was a title for the President. The democrats in the Senate wanted to call him simply that, President. But, Adams pointed out, there were all kinds of presidents; there were presidents of fire companies, presidents of cricket clubs. The President of the United States must have a more impressive title. He continued, speaking, out of order, from the chair:

Suppose the president to have the appointment of Mr. Jefferson at the court of France. Mr. Jefferson is, in virtue of that appointment, the most illustrious, the most powerful, and what not. But the President himself must be something that includes all the dignities of the diplomatic corps, and something greater still. What will the common people of foreign countries—what will the sailors and soldiers say, "George Washington, President of the United States"? They will despise him.

The "Committee on Titles" finally proposed the mouth-filling appellation: "His Highness the President of the United States and Protector of the Rights of the Same." Adams was satisfied with this, although he seemed to prefer the more simple, "His Majesty the President." The Senate would have neither, and the subject was postponed and died. On all of this Maclay recorded: "Ye Gods, with what indignation do I review the late attempt of some creatures among us to revive the vile machinery! O, Adams, Adams, what a wretch art thou!" Maclay's journal is one of the best records of what transpired in the first Senate, but it must be remembered that the Pennsylvanian was a stanch champion of the common man and a states'-righter who opposed most of Adams' political concepts.

Adams did get a title. He was contemptuously called "His Rotundity." And his insistence on pomp and pageantry convinced some that he had monarchical leanings, even before *Discourses* was published. Also it was said that he had his eye on the presidential office for himself and would seek to induce Washington to resign in his favor. Of this there is no evidence; but he could not help but think of himself in relation to the highest office. He wrote to James Lovell:

YOU MUST INSINUATE that I am accused "of deciding in favor of the power of the prime, because I look up to that goal." That I look up to that goal sometimes is very probable, because it is not far above me, only one step, and it is directly before my eyes, so that I must be blind not to see it. I am forced to look up to it, and bound by duty to do so, because there is only the breath of one mortal between me and it.

The chair of the first Senate would have been a difficult position for any man because there were no precedents to guide him. The Senate had no rules—and did not get any, formally, until Thomas Jefferson became its President eight years later and wrote a rule book. The Vice-Presidency had been an afterthought at the Constitutional Convention. When it was decided that each presidential elector should vote for two men it was accepted without debate that the man with the second highest number of votes should succeed the President in the event of his death. Since he should have something to do in the interim he was put on ice, so to speak, in the chair of the Senate where, so long as the President lived, he would be a nonentity.

Temperamentally, Adams was totally unsuited for such a position. In his acceptance speech he admitted that his forte was debating in, rather than presiding over, a legislative body, and debate he did, despite the fact that accepted parliamentary procedure limited the presiding officer to keeping order and voting in cases of a tie. He wrote to Abigail, "It is, to be sure, a punishment to hear other men talk five hours every day and not be at liberty to talk at all myself, especially as more than half I hear appears to me very young, inconsiderate, and inexperienced."

On one occasion Adams ended a debate with Senator Pierce Butler by sharply calling the South Carolinian to order. He later apologized privately, but this did not entirely mollify Butler, who sent him a note saying that he would overlook this instance, "But if anything similar to it takes place again I shall in justification of my own feelings . . . be under a necessity of personally resenting it." Under the code of the fiery Southerner that meant a duel.

Ex-schoolmaster Adams could not refrain from lecturing the Senate on many occasions, a practice which infuriated many members of the body. Maclay recorded that, in a debate on the question of the jurisdiction of the Supreme Court over ambassadors of foreign nations, the Vice-President fidgeted in his chair until he could stand it no longer. Then, said the Pennsylvanian, "up he got to tell us all about ambassadors, other ministers, and consuls; and what he did with His Majesty here, and His Majesty there; and how he got an answer in this, and how he never got an answer in that." Senator Robert Morris wryly remarked that Adams had been made Vice-President to keep him quiet, but the experiment seemed to have failed. Adams did not have total respect for his colleagues, most of whom knew nothing about "everything in human nature by which mankind ever were or ever will be governed." In general they were "a wise, mild, and noble body of men," but few of them were lawyers; and Adams said he "never knew a great statesman in my sense of the word who was not a lawyer."

In the small Senate, Adams had many opportunities to cast a tie-breaking vote. The first occasion arose on the question of whether the President could remove an appointee from office without the consent of the Senate. The Constitution required such consent for appointment but said nothing about removal. Adams recorded copious notes of the debate on this subject.

William Grayson of Virginia said, "There will be every endeavor to increase the consolidatory powers; to weaken the Senate and strengthen the President. No evil in the Senate's participating with the President in removal." George Read of Delaware said, "The President is to take care that the laws be faithfully executed. He is responsible. How can he do his duty or be responsible, if he cannot remove his instruments?" Charles Carrol of Maryland said, "The same power which creates must annihilate." Oliver Ellsworth of Connecticut said, "The President, not the Senate, appoints; they only consent and advise. The Senate is not an executive council; has no executive power." And Richard Henry Lee of Virginia said, "The danger to liberty is greater from the disunited opinions and jarring plans of many than from the energetic operations of one. Marius, Sulla, Caesar, Cromwell trampled on liberty with armies." Adams noted in his characteristically cryptic manner that Grayson also said, "Bowstring. General Lally. Brutus's power to put his sons to death," but did not explain what this had to do with the subject.

Apparently Adams said nothing from the chair on this matter, although he considered the issue a very important one in terms of the greater powers which he advocated for the executive branch of the government. By a masterful job of buttonholing individual senators in what would later be known as cloakroom politics, he engineered a nine-to-nine tie and gleefully cast the deciding vote to give the President sole power of removal.

One aspect of his new position which he detested throughout the remainder of his public life was the flood of applications for jobs. He had no power of appointment, but most of his friends and many strangers believed that he might have influence with Washington, and they petitioned him to use his good offices. He wrote many letters such as this:

THE PARTICULAR OFFICE you solicit by that letter will be sought by numbers, and among them probably will be men advanced in life, encumbered with large families, in necessitous circumstances perhaps occasioned by public services, by depreciated public promises, etc. The President will, as he ought, weigh all these particulars, and give the preference upon the whole as justice, humanity, and wisdom shall dictate. . . . I must caution you, my dear sir, against having any dependence on my influence or that of any other person. No man, I believe, has influence with the President. He seeks information from all quarters and judges more independently than any man I ever knew.

Throughout his first term as Vice-President, Adams was, in a sense, a whipping-boy for Washington. No one dared criticize the great first President, and many unjustly vented their displeasure on the second in command. When he voted to increase Washington's powers in the matter of removals, some saw this as, an attempt to augment his own position. A poem in the Massachusetts *Sentinel* is typical of the many aspersions of Adams for his supposed pretentions.

> Be grateful then, YE CHOSEN! mod'rate wise,
> Nor stretch your claims to such preposterous size,
> Lest your too partial country—wiser grown—
> Should on your native dunghills set you down.
> Ape not the fashions of the foreign great,
> Nor make your betters at your *levees* wait—
> Resign your awkward pomp, parade and pride,
> And lay that useless *etiquette* aside;
> The unthinking laugh, but all the thinking hate
> Such vile, abortive mimicry of State;
> Those idle lackeys, saunt'ring at your door,
> But ill become *poor servants* of the POOR.

Adams made no comment on this except to say that it was good verse. Abigail was disposed to argue. She pointed out to her sister that they were living quite simply; it was Washington who had the "idle lackeys" at the door.

The Adams had to live simply. It was some time before the Congress got around to voting John a salary, and when they did it was so small—$5,000—that he called it "a curiosity." Abigail had found a large, somewhat run-down house at Richmond Hill, about a mile and a half from the city proper, of which she wrote:

THE HOUSE in which we reside is situated upon a hill, the avenue to which is interspersed with forest trees, under which a shrubbery rather too luxuriant and wild has taken shelter. . . . In front of the house, the noble Hudson rolls his majestic waves, bearing upon his bosom innumerable small vessels, which are constantly forwarding the rich products of the neighboring soil to the busy hand of a more extensive commerce. Beyond the Hudson rises to our view the fertile country of the Jerseys, covered with a golden harvest, and pouring forth plenty like the cornucopiae of Ceres. On the right hand, an extensive plain presents us with a view of fields covered with verdure, and pastures full of cattle. On the left, the city opens upon us, intercepted only by clumps of trees, and some rising ground, which serves to heighten the beauty of the scene by appearing to conceal a part. . . . If my days of fancy and romance were not past, I could find here an ample field for indulgence.

Abigail's domestic arrangements were complicated by problems with servants. The only trained ones in New York were Negro slaves, whom, on principle, she would not hire from their masters. White immigrants of this class were an ignorant and drunken lot. She finally imported good, reliable New Englanders.

John was, perhaps, as happy here as he could be—all things considered. He was distressed by what he considered a general lack of understanding of the principles of good government and, more particularly, by the growing spirit of factionalism. He felt that New England was going too far in compromising, that she mortified herself "in compliance to southern pride." He was disturbed by the increasing trend toward political parties. In his position he should have been the head of the Federalist party; but if he was he did not know it; nor did he want to be.

The Adamses were hardly settled in Richmond Hill before they again had to move to Philadelphia, which Congress had selected as the second temporary capital. Again Abigail penned a description of a suburban dwelling at

... Bush Hill, as it is called, though by the way there remains neither bush nor shrub upon it, and very few trees, except the pine grove behind it—yet Bush Hill is a very beautiful place. But the grand and sublime I left at Richmond Hill. The cultivation in sight and prospect are superior, but the Schuylkill is not more like the Hudson than I to Hercules. . . . We are only two miles from town, yet . . . the road from hence to the pavement is one mile and a half, the soil a brick clay, so that, when there has been heavy rain . . . you must wallow to the city through a bed of mortar without a bottom, the horses sinking to their knees.

Immediately upon the opening of the first session of the Second Congress Adams had a chore that, for him, was not amusing. When Franklin died the French National Assembly went into mourning, and many members read eulogies. Then they bundled these up and sent them to the American Congress, where Adams had to read them to the Senate. This he did with poor grace, after commenting sarcastically on the number of titles appended to the name of a man who claimed to abhor titles. Maclay said that he read with "coldness and apathy," and commented that, while the National Assembly had sent fraternal greetings to their fellow legislators in America, "we, cold as clay, care not a fig about them, Franklin or freedom."

In 1791 what seemed to be a trifling incident, which had its roots in London and Paris, placed considerable strain on the friendship of Adams and Thomas Jefferson, a step on the road that would lead to total estrangement. By this time the French Revolution had progressed to the point where Louis XVI had accepted the assembly as a legislative body. In London, Edmund Burke, a professed Whig who was secretly in the pay of the Crown, wrote his *Reflections of the Revolution in France,* which upheld the "divine right of kings" and referred to the French legislators as an ignorant rabble. Thomas Paine replied with the *Rights of Man,* his great defense of simple democracy, which he dedicated to Washington.

An early copy of *Rights* was loaned to Jefferson, with instructions to forward it to a printer for publication in America after he had read it. This Jefferson did with a note, in which he said that he was "extremely pleased to find it will be reprinted here and that something is at length to be publicly said against the political heresies which have sprung up among us." He later said that he had written this merely to "take off a little of the dryness of the note." Without Jefferson's permission, and over his title as Secretary of State, the printer published the note as a preface to the book.

Everybody knew, or thought they knew, that Jefferson's reference to "political heresies" meant Adams' *Discourses on Davila,* which had just been published. Anti-Federalists widely quoted Jefferson, as well as Paine, in refuting the aristocratic principles of the "Duke of Braintree." To explain this embarrassing difference within the executive branch, Jefferson wrote to Washington:

I AM AFRAID the indiscretion of a printer had committed me with my friend, Mr. Adams, for whom, as one of the most honest and disinterested men alive, I have a cordial esteem, increased by long habits of concurrence in opinion in the days of his republicanism; and even since his apostasy to hereditary monarchy and nobility, though we differ, we differ as friends should. . . . Mr. Adams will unquestionably take to himself the charge of political heresy, as conscious of his own views of drawing the present government to the form of the English constitution, and, I fear, will consider me as meaning to injure him in the public eye.

At this juncture a new series of articles appeared, signed "Publicola," defending *Discourses* and attacking Paine and Jefferson. These, too, were attributed to Adams, which was only half right. John now realized that such squabbling in the press about the principles of government was not proper conduct for a Vice-President and had rising young lawyer John Quincy Adams write these articles. His grandson, Charles Francis Adams, later said that they were written "without any communication with his father." This may be taken with a grain of salt. In any event, at the time, everybody attributed them to the older Adams.

Appalled by the furor which he had unwittingly created, Jefferson wrote his friend, saying, "I have a dozen times taken up my pen to write to you, and as often laid it down again, suspended between opposing considerations. I determine, however, to write from a conviction that truth between candid minds can never do harm." After a detailed explanation of how the unfortunate preface came into being, Jefferson continued:

THUS WERE OUR NAMES thrown on the public stage, as public antagonists. That you and I differ in our ideas of the best form of government is well known to us both; but we have differed as friends should do, respecting the purity of each other's motives, and confining our difference of opinion to private conversation; and I can declare with truth, in the presence of the Almighty, that nothing was further from my intention or expectation than to have had either my own or your name brought before the public on this occasion. The friendship and confidence which has so long existed between us required this explanation from me, and I know you too well to fear any misconstruction of the motives of it."

Adams replied:

I GIVE FULL CREDIT to your relation of the manner in which your note was written and prefixed to the Philadephia edition of Mr. Paine's pamphlet on the *Rights of Man;* but . . . the pamphlet, with your name to so striking a recommendation of it . . . was generally considered as a direct and open personal attack upon me, by countenancing the false interpretation of my writings, as favoring the introduction of hereditary monarchy and aristocracy into this country. The question everywhere was, what heresies are intended by the Secretary of State? The answer in the newspapers was, "The Vice-President's notions of a limited monarchy, an hereditary government of King and Lords, with only elective Commons."

Adams continued to lament that his cousin Samuel had made a speech "holding up the idea of hereditary powers"; that John Hancock showed "neglect" of him; and that "all together served as a hue and cry to all my enemies and rivals . . . to hunt me down like a hare, if they could." He disavowed Publicola, saying, "The writer, in the composition of his pieces, followed his own judgment, information, and discretion, without any assistance from me." And he righteously denied any monarchical taint:

IF YOU SUPPOSE that I have, or ever had, a design or desire of attempting to introduce a government of Kings, Lords, and Commons, or in other words, an hereditary executive, or an hereditary Senate, either into the government of the United States or that of any individual state, you are wholly mistaken. There is not such a thought expressed or intimated in any public writing or private letter, and I may safely challenge all mankind to produce such a passage, and quote the chapter and verse. If you have ever put such a construction on anything of mine, I beg you would mention it to me, and I will undertake to convince you that it has no such meaning.

Upon this occasion I will venture to say that my unpolished writings, although they have been read by a sufficient number of persons to have assisted in crushing the insurrection of the Massachusetts [farmers], in the formation of the new constitutions of Pennsylvania, Georgia, and South Carolina, and in procuring the assent of all the states to the new national Constitution, yet have not been read by great numbers. Of the few who have taken the pains to read them, some have misunderstood them, and others have willfully misrepresented them, and these misunderstandings and misrepresentations have been made the pretense for overwhelming me with floods and whirlwinds of tempestuous abuse, unexampled in the history of this country.

He concluded by saying:

I THANK YOU, SIR, very sincerely for writing to me upon this occasion. It was high time that you and I should come to an explanation with each other. The friendship that has subsisted for fifteen years without the smallest interruption, and until this occasion without the slightest suspicion, ever has been and still is very dear to my heart. There is no office which I would not resign rather than give a just occasion to one friend to forsake me. Your motives for writing to me I have not a doubt were the most pure and the most friendly; and I have no suspicion that you will not receive this explanation from me in the same friendly light.

Jefferson terminated the correspondence, a little coolly, by blaming the whole thing on Publicola:

YOU WILL PERCEIVE . . . my dear sir, that my note contributed nothing to the production of these disagreeable pieces. As long as Paine's pamphlet stood on its own feet and on my note, it was unnoticed. As soon as Publicola attacked Paine, swarms appeared in his defense. To Publicola, then, and not in the least degree to my note, this whole contest is to be ascribed, and all its consequences.

A rather strange by-product of the controversy was an increase in Hamilton's distrust of Adams. The Secretary of the Treasury, who was a more ardent supporter of the British form of government than Adams, told Jefferson that he believed "that the present government is not that which will answer the ends of society, by giving stability and protection to its rights, and that it will probably be found expedient to go into the British form." But this was not the time for a change. "Therefore, whoever by his writings disturbs the present order of things, is really blameable, however pure his intentions may be, and he was sure Mr. Adams were pure."

Adams was certainly justified in claiming that his writings were either misunderstood or deliberately misinterpreted. He was writing objectively about government forms and theories at a time when few of his readers could understand objectivity. Emotions were running high, and a man was either one thing or another. If he was a patriot he believed in equality and liberty for the common man and his right to self-government. Otherwise he was a monarchist; and any man who even talked about titles, an aristocracy, and heredity was condemned with that label.

As the second election loomed, the anti-Federalists made much of the monarchist charge. This time they had a candidate, General George Clinton, of New York, although they were still poorly organized. Their New York paper listed John Adams last in a list that included, besides Clinton, Samuel Adams, John Jay, Thomas Mifflin, and James Madison. Adams himself, with his usual pessimism, believed that Jefferson might be the choice. Before the votes were opened he wrote to Abigail: "I received yesterday the votes from Kentucky. They are said to be all for Mr. Jefferson. Let us, my dear, prepare our minds, and as well as we can, our circumstances, to get out of this miserable scramble."

Whether they liked it or not the extreme Federalists believed Adams to be their strongest candidate and gave him uniform support. He was surely helped to victory by the apathy toward the presidential election in the solidly anti-Federalist back country. In Pennsylvania, forty thousand voted in the congressional election but only four thousand in the presidential election.

Congress and the country had little interest in domestic issues during Washington's second term. The French Revolution and relations with France and England became the principal bones of contention between the Federalists and the Republicans, as the anti-Federalists were now called. Francophile Republicans built miniature guillotines, seemingly hoping that they could someday use the real thing on America's aristocrats. Jefferson said of the French Revolution:

THE LIBERTY OF THE WHOLE EARTH was depending on the issue of the contest . . . rather than it should have failed, I would have seen half the earth desolated; were there but an Adam and Eve left in every country, and left free, it would be better than as it now is.

During the early stages of the French struggle Adams wrote:

I KNOW NOT WHAT to make of a republic of thirty million atheists. The Constitution is but an experiment, and must and will be altered. I know it to be impossible that France should be long governed by it. . . . Too many Frenchmen, after the example of too many Americans, pant for equality of persons and property. The impracticability of this God Almighty has decreed, and the advocates for liberty who attempt it will surely suffer for it.

And, again in another letter:

THERE IS SUCH A COMPLICATION of tragedy, comedy and farce in all the accounts from France, that it is to me to the last degree disgusting to attend to them in detail. I read over the accounts in general and then endeavor to direct my own attention from any very serious, which must be very melancholy, reflections upon them.

To Abigail he confided:

I EXPECT, ere long, to hear that Paine is split and sliced for an aristocrat; perhaps roasted, or broiled, or fried. He is too lean to make a good pie, but he is now in company with a number who are admirable qualified and disposed to feed upon each other. The foolish vote of the constituting assembly in favor of a rotation and excluding themselves from being re-elected has cost every man of weight and talents among them his life, or his country and his fortune. All are murdered, banished, and confiscated. Danton, Robespierre, Marat, etc., are furies. Dragon's teeth have been sown in France and come up monsters. . . . We have our Robespierres and Marats, whose wills are good to do mischief, but the flesh is weak. They cannot yet persuade the people to follow them. If the National Assembly can subdue the mutinous rabble at Paris . . . they may be free, and do something, but what, I know not.

As the Terror spread he queried:

WHAT THINK THE CLERGY of New England? . . . Do they still admire the French republicans? Do they think them virtuous? Do they wish to see them imitated by all nations? Do they wish to resign all their salaries, and to have their churches all turned into riding houses, the Sabbath abolished, and one day in ten substituted to sing songs to the manes of Marat? O, my soul, come not thou into the secrets of such republicans! The guillotine itself would not make me a sincere republican upon such conditions.

Generally, Adams' second term as Vice-President was more serene. He wrote nothing that was controversial and the Republican editors had become sufficiently bold to switch their thunder directly at Washington. Adams noted:

OUR ANTI-FEDERALIST SCRIBBLERS are so fond of rotations that they seem disposed to remove their abuse from me to the

President. Bache's paper, which is nearly as bad as Freneau's, begins to join in concert with it to maul the President for his drawing rooms, levees, declining to accept of invitations to dinners and tea parties, his birthday odes, visits, compliments, etc. I may be expected to be an advocate for a rotation of objects of abuse and for equality in this particular. I have held the office of Libellee General long enough. The burden of it ought to be participated and equalized according to modern republican principles.

Benjamin Bache was Franklin's grandson; Phillip Freneau was another Republican editor who was supported by Jefferson through a salaried job in the State Department.

Abigail was more distressed by the scribblers and replied:

THE PRESIDENT has been openly abused in the *National Gazette*—abused for his levees as an ape of royalty; Mrs. Washington abused for her drawing-rooms; their celebration of birthdays sneered at; himself insulted because he has not come forward and exerted his influence in favor of a further compensation to the army. They even tell him that a greater misfortune cannot befall a people than for their President to have no competitor; that it infuses into him a supercilious spirit, renders him self-important, and creates an idea that one man only is competent to govern. They compare him to a hyena and a crocodile; charge him with duplicity and deception. The President has not been accustomed to such language, and his feelings will be wounded, I presume.

It has been a subject of no small satisfaction to me that the bitterest party-writer has never dared to impeach either the honor, the honesty, or the integrity of the Vice-President, or fix a blemish upon his private character. Though they have not been so honest as Robert R. Livingston of New York, who said, nothing vexed him so much in all the French Revolution and the horrid cruelties they committed, as to see the fools by their conduct playing the game into the hands of that Mr. Adams, and proving the truth of his books. Why, said Benson, to whom the observation was made, "Mr. Adams reads the Scriptures, and he reads there that man is as stupid as the wild ass's colt. Mr. Adams does not write the Scriptures; he only reads and believes."

When France declared war on England, Washington issued a proclamation of neutrality which the French considered a repudiation of the treaty of 1777. The Republican-dominated lower house promptly passed anti-British commercial bills, and Adams' tie-breaking vote was instrumental in preventing two from passing the Senate. Of this he wrote Abby:

THIS DAY the senators were equally divided upon a question which seemed to me to involve nothing less than peace and war, and I was obliged to decide it, to the no small chagrin of a number. If this country is involved in war it shall not be by my fault; but if it comes either from the malice of our enemies or the imprudence of our own people, it may perhaps be found that I shall not shrink from its difficulties sooner than some who now seek it in disguise.

He told his wife:

THE MAJORITY OF THE HOUSE is certainly for mischief, and there is no doubt they represent the people in the southern states and a large number in the northern. *Vox populi, vox Dei,* they say, and so it is, sometimes; but it is sometimes the voice of Mahomet, of Caesar, of Catiline, the Pope and the Devil.

And in another letter:

YOU CANNOT IMAGINE what horror some persons are in lest peace should continue. The prospect of peace throws them

into distress. Their countenances lengthen at the least opening
of an appearance of it. Glancing gleams of joy beam from
their faces whenever all possibility of it seems to be cut off.

However, said John, with seeming resignation, there was not
much that he could do about the dangerous situation.

I KNOW NOT HOW IT IS, but in proportion as danger threatens
I grow calm. I am very apprehensive that a desperate anti-
Federal party will provoke all Europe by their insolence. But
my country has, in its wisdom, contrived for me the most insignificant office that ever the invention of man contrived or
his imagination conceived; and as I can do neither good nor
evil, I must be borne away by others and meet the common
fate.

Although reading Franklin's eulogies to the Senate had been an
unpleasant chore, Adams soon had a consolation when he read to
that body a message from the President nominating "John Quincy
Adams of Massachusetts to be resident minister of the United
States at The Hague."

Late in 1794 the Republicans switched their fire to Chief Justice
John Jay when he was sent by Washington to negotiate a treaty
with Great Britain, although Adams was not forgotten in their
vilification. Maclay noted that, when an effigy of Jay was pilloried
in Philadelphia, "Hung from the neck by a hemp string was a copy
of the 'Defense of the Constitutions.' " Adams wrote his wife:

THE OPPOSITION to Mr. Jay has been quickened by motives
which always influence everything in an elective government.
. . . If Jay should succeed it will recommend to the choice of
the people for President, as soon as a vacancy shall happen.
This will weaken the hopes of the southern states for Jefferson.
This I believe to be the secret motive of the opposition to him,
though other things were alleged as ostensible reasons.

Jay brought back a treaty which was decidedly pro-British. The Federalist Senate approved it, and Washington signed it, although Adams said that he "wavered about signing the treaty, which he ought not to have done one moment."

The Republican lower house at first refused to pass the appropriations to implement the treaty. In Adams' words they "fastened with their teeth and all their nails," and seemed determined to "bite like savages and tear like lions." There was nothing he could do about it, he wrote Abby:

I HAVE NO VOICE and although the fate of the treaty will not be justly imputable to me in any degree, yet there is reason to expect that many will suspect me and others charge me with a greater share of it than would belong to me if I had a voice. All these things terrify me little.

Still, he could not come home. "There are so many wild projects and motions," he wrote, "and so many to support them, that I am become of more importance than usual, in the opinion of the soundest part of the community." When the treaty appropriation was finally approved, Adams ruminated:

IT IS A MORTIFYING CONSIDERATION that five months have been wasted upon a question whether national faith is binding on a nation. Nothing but the ignorance and inexperience of this people can excuse them. Really, we have not a right sense of moral or national obligation. We have no national pride, no national sense of honor.

Most of what John was doing during this period is known only from letters to Abby. He was doing more reading in the classics than writing. Repetitiously he bemoaned his obligation to stay in his tedious job.

I MUST REMAIN HERE, because my friends say I must not go.

Those whose principles are the same with mine, whose views of public good coincide with mine, say that if we keep together we shall succeed to the end of the sessions as we have hitherto done in keeping off all the most pernicious projects.

And in another letter: "We go on as usual, Congress resolving one thing and the democratical societies resolving the contrary; the President doing what is right, and clubs and mobs resolving it to be all wrong."

The clubs to which he referred were the Democratic clubs, on the Jacobin pattern, which had been formed by the Republicans to propagandize against Federalist measures adopted by the administration. They infuriated Washington, who considered them treasonable. Adams saw no reason why they should not exist, and wrote: "I take it for granted that political clubs must and ought to be lawful in every free country. I belonged to several in my youth, and I wish I could belong to one now." But he considered their criticism of the laws as wrong and their denunciation of personalities as libelous. Of such groups he wrote:

AFFILIATIONS, combinations, correspondences, corporate acts of such societies must be prohibited. A snake with one head at each end, crawling opposite ways, must split the snake in two, unless one head is so much stronger than the other as to drag it along over thorns and stones till it loses its headship. . . . A man drawn between two horses is a neat image of a nation drawn between its government and self-created societies acting as corporations and combining together.

In these days of bitterly fought political campaigns it is amusing to contemplate that some of the Founding Fathers considered organized political opposition as seditious.

During the latter part of Washington's administration some felt that the executive branch seemed to be falling apart. Jefferson resigned as Secretary of State early in the second term, to be followed a year later by Hamilton from the Treasury and Knox as Secretary of War. Jefferson's successor, Edmund Randolph, left under a cloud based on the charge that he had taken a bribe from France. Washington found it difficult to replace him. Wrote Adams:

THERE SEEMS TO BE a necessity of distributing the offices about the states in some proportion to their numbers; but, in the southern part of the Union, false politics have struck their roots so deep that it is very difficult to find gentlemen who are willing to accept of public trusts, and, at the same time, capable of discharging them. The President offered the office of State to several gentlemen who declined: to Mr. Patterson, Mr. King, Mr. Henry of Virginia, Mr. Charles Cotesworth Pinckney of South Carolina, and three others whose names I don't recollect. He has not been able to find anyone to accept the War office. The expenses of living at the seat of government are so exorbitant, so far beyond all proportion to the salaries, and the sure reward of integrity in the discharge of public functions is such obloquy, contempt, and insult, that no man of any feeling is willing to renounce his home, forsake his properties and profession, for the sake of removing to Philadelphia, where he is almost sure of disgrace and ruin.

When Washington finally secured second-rate men for the posts, Adams commented, "The offices are once more full. But how differently filled than when Jefferson, Hamilton, Jay, etc., were here!"

John continued to complain to Abigail. "Tedious days and lonesome nights! I am weary of ye!" "It is painful to feel an impulse to write where there is nothing to say." "We are wasting our time in the most insipid manner, waiting for the treaty" "Business in Congress as languid, as gaping and yawning as if Morpheus had poured out all his soporifics upon the two houses. The voice of faction, even, is scarcely heard." He longed to come home, he told Abby:

CONGRESS HAVE BEEN TOGETHER more than two months, and have done nothing, and will continue sitting two months longer, and do little. I, for my part, am wearied to death with *ennui*. Obliged to be punctual by my habits, confined to my seat, as in a prison, to see nothing done, hear nothing said, and to say and do nothing. O, that my rocks were here within a mile or two, and my little habitation, and pretty little wife above all. Ah, I fear that some fault unknown has brought upon me such punishments, to be separated both when we were too young and when we are too old.

But if he came home he would be

... charged with deserting the President, forsaking the Secretary of State, betraying my friend Jay, abandoning my post, and sacrificing my country to a weak attachment to a woman, and a weaker fondness for my farm, if I quit at this moment. So, be thou thankful alone, that thou hast a good husband here, that thy children are safe and in honor in Europe, and that thy daughter has given thee a fine grand-daughter, besides innumerable blessings to thy country. I will be thankful and joyous here all alone.

As the end of the term approached, Washington's prospective retirement and its consequences became a prime subject of speculation with John. He wrote his wife:

IN PERFECT SECRECY between you and me, I must tell you that I now believe the President will retire. The consequence to me is very serious, and I am not able as yet to see what my duty will demand of me. I shall take my resolutions with cool deliberation. I shall watch the course of events with more critical attention than I have done for some time, and what Providence shall point out to be my duty, I shall pursue with patience and decision.

It is no light thing to resolve upon retirement. My country has claims, my children have claims, and my own character has claims upon me; but all these claims forbid me to serve the public in disgrace. Whatever anyone may think, I love my country too well to shrink from danger in her service, provided I have a reasonable prospect of being able to serve her to her honor and advantage. But if I have reason to think that I have either a want of abilities or of public confidence to such a degree as to be unable to support the government in a higher station, I ought to decline it. But in that case I ought not to serve in my present place under another, especially if that other should entertain sentiments so opposite to mine as to endanger the peace of the nation. It will be a dangerous crisis in public affairs if the President and Vice-President should be in opposite boxes. These lucubrations must be confined to your own bosom. But I think, upon the whole, the probability is strong that I shall make a voluntary retreat and spend the rest of my days, in a very humble style, with you. Of one thing I am very sure it would be to me the happiest portion of my whole life.

John's reference to his duty to his family had become such a formula with him that he apparently used it without think that the children were grown up and on their own. And he had no real intention of retiring. A few weeks later he speculated:

I SOMETIMES THINK that if I were in the House of Representatives, and could make speeches there, I could throw some light upon these things. If Mr. Jefferson should be President, I believe I must put up as a candidate for the House. But this is my vanity. I feel sometimes as if I could speechify among them, but, alas, alas! I am too old. It would soon destroy my health. I declare, however, if I were in that House, I would drive out of it some demons that haunt it. There are false doc-

trines and false jealousies predominant there at times that it
would be easy to exorcise.

The House, with its Republican majority of representatives of
the common people, presented a danger to balanced government,
he avowed:

AS THE PEOPLE OF ROME scrambled for power against the
Senate; as the people of Athens scrambled for more power
than was reserved for them by the laws of Solon; as the people
of Carthage scrambled for power against their Senate; as the
people of England scrambled for power against the king and
lords, and set up Oliver; as the people of France scrambled for
power against every majority and set up Robespierre; so the
House of Representatives of the United States will scramble
for power against the President and Senate. And the fre-
quency of popular elections will corrupt all before them. May
God of his infinite mercy grant that some remedy may be
found before it is too late.

But Adams' sights were definitely set on the presidency. He gave
himself away when he said that he was "too old" to continue
"more than one, or, at most, more than two years," and a single
term was "scarcely time enough to form conduct, and complete
any very useful system." He seemed to take pleasure in the fact
that he was being courted in some quarters when he wrote:

I AM AS YOU SAY, quite a favorite. I am to dine today again. I
am heir apparent, you know, and a succession is soon to take
place. But, whatever may be the wish or the judgment of the
present occupant, the French and the demagogues intend, I
presume, to set aside the descent. All these hints must be
secrets. It is not a subject of conversation as yet. I have a pious
and a philosophical resignation to the voice of the people in
this case, which is the voice of God. I have no very ardent

desire to be the butt of party malevolence. Having tasted of that cup, I find it bitter, nauseous, and unwholesome.

In one letter to Abby, John saw no cause for alarm in the change of chief executive and then speculated on what the result of the upcoming election might be.

IN MY OPINION there is no more danger in the change than there would be in changing a member of the Senate, and whoever lives to see it will own me to be a prophet. If Jay or even Jefferson (and one or the other it certainly will be, if the succession should be passed over) should be the man, the government will go on as well as ever. Jefferson could not stir a step in any other system than that which is begun. Jay would not wish it. The votes will run for three persons. Two I have mentioned; the third, being the heir apparent [himself] will not probably be wholly overlooked. If Jefferson and Jay are President and Vice-President, as is not improbable, the other retires without noise, or cries, or tears to his farm. . . . If this other should be President and Jefferson or Jay Vice-President, four years more, if life last, of residence in Philadelphia will be his and your portion, after which we shall probably be desirous of imitating the example of the present pair; or if, by reason of strength and fortitude, eight years should be accomplished, that is the utmost limit of time that I will ever continue in public life at any rate.

Be of good courage therefore, and tremble not. I see nothing to appall me, and I feel no ill forebodings or faint misgivings. I have not the smallest dread of private life nor of public. If private life is to be my portion, my farm and my pen shall employ the rest of my days.

Jefferson and Adams still maintained at least a surface friendship at this time. From his retreat atop Monticello the Virginian wrote that, although the papers had placed them "in a point of opposition to each other," he hoped that their personal relations would not be affected. He then warned his friend against Alexander Hamilton.

IT IS POSSIBLE that you may be cheated of your succession by a trick worthy the subtlety of your arch-friend of New York who has been able to make of your real friends tools to defeat their and your just wishes. Most probably he will be disappointed as to you; and my inclinations place me out of his reach.

Adams was convinced that his old friend had become a political heretic whose mind was "poisoned with passion, prejudice, and faction." To John Quincy his father confided that Jefferson's retirement was a shrewd step to create for himself "a reputation of an humble, modest, meek man, wholly without ambition or vanity," but that he was really "as ambitious as Cromwell." To Abby he wrote, "I hear frequent reflections which indicate that Jefferson, although in good hands he might do very well, yet in such hands as will hold him he would endanger too much."

Jefferson had no competition as the white hope of the Republicans. Adams was the only candidate on which moderate Federalists and the extremists led by Hamilton could agree. During the somewhat bitter campaign both candidates stayed in seclusion. The old charges on monarchy were brought against John, and his *Defense* and *Discourses* were rehashed line by line. The French minister, Pierre Adet, supported Jefferson with a message which intimated that the election of Adams would mean war with France. Adams commented mildly: "John Adams must be an intrepid to encounter the open assaults of France, and the secret plots of England, in concert with all his treacherous friends and open enemies in his own country. Yet, I assure you, he never felt more serene in his life."

Abigail was not so mild in a long letter to John Quincy reciting his father's tribulations.

AT THIS EVENTFUL PERIOD, I can judge of your solicitude to learn, through a channel upon which you could depend, whatever affects the interests of our country. In a quotation from the *Chronicle* you cannot expect truth. Falsehood and malevolence are its strongest features. It is the offspring of faction, and nursed by sedition, the adopted bantling of party. It has been crying monarchy and aristocracy, and vociferating anathemas against the "Defense" as favoring monarchy; and making quotations of detached sentences, as the atheist endeavored to prove from Scripture that "there is no God," by omitting, "the fool hath said in his heart."

One writer asserts that "Mr. Adams has immortalized himself as an advocate for hereditary government, as much as Mr. Jefferson has distinguished himself, in and out of office, as a true republican. Mr. Adams has sons placed in high offices, and who are, no doubt, understood to be what he calls the well-born and who, following his own principle, may, as he hopes, one time become the seigneurs or lords of this country." . . .

By such false and glaring absurdities do these miserable beings endeavor to deceive and delude the people into a distrust of their most disinterested friends, the real guardians of their liberties and defenders of their privileges. . . .

I feel perhaps too keenly the abuse of party. Washington endured it; but he had the support of the people and their undiminished confidence to the hour of his resignation, and a combination of circumstances which no other man can look for. . . . Take his character all together, and we shall not look upon his like again; notwithstanding which, he was reviled and abused, his administration perplexed, and his measures impeded. What is the expected lot of a successor? He must be armed as Washington was with integrity, with firmness, with intrepidity. These must be his shield and his wall of brass; and religion too, or he never will be able to stand sure and steadfast.

Adams was on tenterhooks while he awaited the outcome of the election. He speculated on how friends among the electors had voted:

THE FEELING OF FRIENDSHIP excites a curiosity to know how McKean will vote. . . . But I have seen friendships of S. Quincy, Jonathan Sewall, Daniel Leonard, General Brattle, Treasurer Gray and fifty others go away like a vapor before political winds; and a constant succession of others go the same way from that time to this that I cannot depend upon any judgment I can form. . . . But McKean and Adams can never believe the lies that are told. If they could vote against me, it must be because they think I should not be supple enough to the French.

Regardless of all other considerations, Adams needed this job. Almost toothless and palsied he could not go back to private law practice. His pittance from the vice-presidency had sufficed only to permit him to live in lodgings during most of his stay in Philadelphia, but, with his farm income, it had supported his comfortable home in Quincy. The President's salary would permit him to live in some style. Even before the votes were counted he speculated on this to Abby:

I HAVE MADE some inquiry concerning horses and carriages and find that a common chariot of the plainest sort cannot be had under twelve hundred dollars, and if you go to a little more ornament and elegance, you must have fifteen hundred. The President has a pair of horses to sell . . . for which he asks a thousand dollars, and there is no probability of procuring a decent span for less than six hundred dollars. House rent, another indispensable article, will be extravagantly high. The plenty of paper has unsettled everything. Nothing has a price. Everyone asks and everyone cheats as much as he can, I think. I wish I knew what would be asked for a chariot in Boston.

John Adams at the age of ninety. Portrait by Gilbert Stuart in the Adams Clement Collection, National Collection of Fine Arts.

On the eighth of February, 1797, Adams had the honor to announce to the Senate the result of his own election as President. The result had been close: seventy-one electoral votes for Adams to sixty-eight for Jefferson. Under the strange system then in use this made his political opponent his Vice-President. The election of Jefferson was aided by one of Hamilton's Machiavellian plans which backfired. Thomas Pinckney of North Carolina was the Federalist vice-presidential candidate. Knowing that the southerner would undoubtedly run ahead of Adams in his home territory, Hamilton sought to induce the Federalist electors from New England to vote for both Adams and Pinckney, thereby, he hoped, assuring Pinckney the first place, due to his plurality in the South. His scheme was too obvious, and New Englanders deflected so many votes from Pinckney that he failed even to secure the vice-presidency.

Adams surely knew of this plot of Hamilton's, but his reaction was surprisingly mild. He wrote to Elbridge Gerry that there was a plan

. . . by surprise to bring in Pinckney. I believe they honestly meant to bring in me; but they were frightened into a belief that I should fail, and they, in their agony, thought it better to bring in Pinckney than Jefferson, and some, I believe, preferred bringing in Pinckney President rather than Jefferson should be Vice-President.

To Abby he wrote:

IF COLONEL HAMILTON'S PERSONAL DISLIKE of Jefferson does not obtain too much influence with Massachusetts electors, neither Jefferson will be President, nor Pinckney Vice-President. I am not enough of an Englishman, nor little enough of a Frenchman, for some people. These would be willing that Pinckney should come in chief. But they will be disappointed. . . . There have been maneuvers and combinations in this election that would surprise you. I may one day or other develop them to you.

There is an active spirit, in the Union, who will fill it with his politics wherever he is [Hamilton]. He must be attended to, not suffered to do too much.

He also commented on the scheme to favor Pinckney in a letter to Henry Knox:

IT IS A DELICATE THING for me to speak of the late election. To myself, personally, "my election" might be a matter of indifference or rather of aversion. Had Mr. Jay or some others, been in question, it might have less mortified my vanity, and infinitely less alarmed my apprehensions for the public. But to see such a character as Jefferson, and much more such an unknown being as Pinckney, brought over my head, and trampling on the bellies of hundreds of other men infinitely his superiors in talents, services, and reputation, filled me with apprehensions for the safety of us all. It demonstrated to me that, if the project succeeded, our Constitution could not have lasted four years. We should have been set afloat, and landed, the Lord knows where. That must be a sordid people, indeed —a people destitute of a sense of honor, equity, and character, that could submit to be governed, and see hundreds of its most meritorious public men governed, by a Pinckney, under an elective government. Hereditary government, when it imposes young, new, inexperienced men upon the public, has its compensations and equivalent, but elective government has none. I mean by this no disrespect to Mr. Pinckney. I believe him to be a worthy man. I speak only by comparison with others.

Adams bid farewell to his colleagues in the Senate in a short speech which was reminiscent, in its polite prevarications, of the address with which he had first greeted them. He said:

I OUGHT NOT TO DECLARE for the last time your adjournment
before I have presented to every senator present, and to every
citizen who has ever been a senator of the United States, my
thanks for the candor and favor invariably received from
them all. It is a recollection of which nothing can ever deprive
me; and it will be a source of comfort to me through the
remainder of my life that . . . I have never had the smallest
misunderstanding with any member of the Senate. In all the
abstruse questions, difficult conjunctures, dangerous emergen-
cies, and animated debates upon the great interests of the
country, which have so often and so deeply impressed all our
minds, and interested the strongest feelings of the heart, I have
experienced a uniform politeness and respect from every quarter of the house. When questions of no less importance than
difficulty have produced a difference of sentiment (and differences of opinion will always be found in free assemblies of
men, and probably the greatest diversities upon the greatest
questions), when the Senators have been equally divided, and
my opinion has been demanded, according to the Constitution, I have constantly found in that moiety of the senators
from whose judgment I have been obliged to dissent a disposition to allow me the same freedom of deliberation and independence of judgment which they asserted for themselves.

The threat of a duel from Pierce and the heckling of Maclay and
others were long since forgotten.

On the same day on which he announced his victory, Abigail,
in Quincy, penned him a heartfelt letter:

The sun is dressed in brightest beams
To give thy honors to the day.

And may it prove an auspicious prelude to each ensuing
season. You have this day to declare yourself head of a nation.
"And now, O Lord, my God, Thou hast made Thy servant

ruler over the people. Give unto him an understanding heart, that he may know how to go out and come in before this great people; that he may discern between good and bad. For who is able to judge this Thy so great a people?" were the words of a royal sovereign; and not less applicable to him who is invested with the chief magistracy of a nation, though he wear not the crown, nor the robes of royalty.

My thoughts and my meditations are with you, though personally absent; and my petitions to Heaven are that "the things which make for peace may not be hidden from your eyes." My feelings are not those of pride or ostentation upon the occasion. They are solemnized by a sense of the obligations, the important trusts and numerous duties connected with it. That you may be enabled to discharge them with honor to yourself, with justice and impartiality to your country, and with satisfaction to this great people, shall be the daily prayer of your

AA.

CHAPTER VII

CHAPTER VII

THE PRESIDENT

 જ

YOUR DEAREST FRIEND never had a more trying day than yesterday. A solemn scene it was, indeed; and it was made more affecting to me by the presence of the General [Washington], whose countenance was as serene and unclouded as the day. He seemed to me to enjoy a triumph over me. Methought I heard him say: "Ay! I am fairly out, and you fairly in! See which of us will be happiest." When the ceremony was over he came and made me a visit and cordially congratulated me and wished my administration might be happy, successful, and honorable.

In the chamber of the House of Representatives was a multitude as great as the space could contain, and I believe scarcely a dry eye but Washington's. The sight of the sun setting full orbed, and another rising, though less splendid, was a novelty. Chief Justice Ellsworth administered the oath, and with great energy. . . . I had not slept well the night before, and did not sleep well the night after. I was unwell, and did not know whether I should get through or not. I did, however. How the business was received, I know not, only I have been told that Mason, the treaty publisher, said we should lose nothing by the change, for he never heard such a speech in public in his life.

All agree that, taken altogether, it was the sublimest thing ever exhibited in America.

So John Adams described to his wife his inauguration as President of the United States. It is not quite clear whether the "sublimest thing" to which he refers was the entire ceremony or his inaugural address. This latter was primarily a declaration of republican faith, devoid of his usual theorizing on government forms and designed to squelch decisively the accusations that he was a monarchist. It was generally well received and commended more highly by his political opponents than by the Anglophile extremists of his own party, who resented what they considered a conciliatory attitude toward the Republicans and toward France.

He started by tracing the political history of his country during the preceding twenty-five years, the creation and subsequent decline of the Confederacy. Then he added:

IN THIS DANGEROUS CRISIS the people of America were not abandoned by their usual good sense, presence of mind, resolution, or integrity. Measures were pursued to concert a plan to form a more perfect union, establish justice, ensure domestic tranquillity, provide for the common defense, promote the general welfare, and secure the blessings of liberty. The public disquisitions, discussions, and deliberations issued in the present happy Constitution of government. . . .

Claiming a right of suffrage in common with my fellow citizens, in the adoption or rejection of a Constitution, which was to rule me and my posterity as well as them and theirs, I did not hesitate to express my approbation of it on all occasions, in public and private. It was not then nor has been since any objection to it, in my mind, that the executive and Senate were not more permanent. Nor have I entertained a thought of promoting any alteration in it but such as the people them-

selves, in the course of their experience, should see and feel
to be necessary or expedient, and by their representatives in
Congress and the state legislatures, according to the Constitution itself, adopt and ordain.

There can be nothing, he said, "more pleasing, more noble, majestic or august" than a government of which all officers were, "by
citizens selected at regular periods by their neighbors, to make
and execute laws for the general good. Can anything essential,
anything more than mere ornament and decoration, be added to
this by robes or diamonds?" But there was danger:

. . . if anything partial or extraneous should infect the purity
of our free, fair, virtuous, and independent elections. If an
election is to be determined by a majority of a single vote, and
that can be procured by a party through artifice or corruption,
the government may be the choice of a party for its own ends,
not of the nation for the national good. If that solitary suffrage
can be obtained by foreign nations, by flattery or menaces; by
fraud or violence; by terror, intrigue, or venality; the government may not be the choice of the American people, but of
foreign nations. It may be foreign nations who govern us, and
not we, the people who govern ourselves."

There followed a tribute to Washington and a single sentence of
almost a thousand words in which he promised to execute the laws
in terms of the "rights, interest, honor, and happiness of all the
states in the Union, without preference or regard to a northern or
southern, an eastern or western, position." He hoped to reconcile
"various political opinions . . . and virtuous men of all parties
and denominations," and to support

. . . every rational effort to encourage schools, colleges, universities, academies and every institution for propagating knowledge, virtue, and religion among all classes of the people, not

only for their benign influence on the happiness of life in all its stages and classes and of society in all its forms, but as the only means of preserving our Constitution from its natural enemies—the spirit of sophistry, the spirit of party, the spirit of intrigue, the profligacy of corruption, and the pestilence of foreign influence which is the angel of destruction to elective governments.

He expressed "an inflexible determination to maintain peace and inviolable faith with all nations, and that system of neutrality and impartiality among the belligerent powers of Europe which has been adopted by the government."

He said that he had "a personal esteem for the French nation, formed in a residence of seven years chiefly among them, and a sincere desire to preserve the friendship which has been so much for the honor and interest of both nations." He concluded:

... with the sense and spirit, the faith and honor, the duty and interest of the same American people pledged to support the Constitution of the United States, I entertain no doubt of its continuance in all its energy; and my mind is prepared without hesitation to lay myself under the most solemn obligations to support it to the utmost of my power. And may that Being, who is supreme over all, the patron of order, the fountain of justice, and the protector, in all ages of the world, of virtuous liberty, continue his blessing upon this nation and its government and give it all possible success and duration consistent with the ends of His providence!

John was pleasantly surprised when his speech brought none of the brickbats to which he had become accustomed. He wrote to Abby:

THE STILLNESS AND SILENCE astonishes me. . . . Two or three persons have ventured to whisper in my ear that my speech made an agreeable impression. I have ventured to say things, both in that speech and in my farewell address to the Senate, so open to scoffs and sarcasms that I expected them in abundance. I have not yet seen any. The more may come. I have been so strangely used in this country, so belied and so undefended, that I was determined to say some things as an appeal to posterity.

He was suspicious of this calm. A week later he wrote his wife:

AND NOW, the world is as silent as the grave. All the Federalists seem to be afraid to approve anybody but Washington. The Jacobin papers damn with faint praise, and undermine with misrepresentation and insinuation. If the Federalists go to playing pranks I will resign the office and let Jefferson lead them to peace, wealth, and power if he will.

From the situation where I now am, I see a scene of ambition beyond all my former suspicions or imaginations, an emulation which will turn our government topsy-turvy. Jealousies and rivalries have been my theme, and checks and balances as their antidotes till I am ashamed to repeat the words; but they never stared me in the face in such horrid forms as at present. I see how the thing is going. At the next election England will set up Jay or Hamilton, and France, Jefferson, and all the corruption of Poland will be introduced, unless the American spirit should rise and say, we will have neither John Bull nor Louis Baboon.

If Adams considered the Republican reception of his speech damning with faint praise, he was surely hard to please. The most rabid of the Republican editors was Benjamin Bache, who wrote in his *Aurora:*

HOW GRATEFUL to every Republican to hear their new President so highly estimating "institutions which spring from the

hearts and judgments of an honest and enlightened people."
. . . Not less pleasing must it be to hear him place in a light
bordering on ridicule the "diamonds, robes, and other orna-
ments and decorations" of royalty. . . . How will the anti-
Republicans foam at finding him also determined not to attempt or support any amendments to the Constitution of the
United States but in the mode prescribed therein. He has
thought proper to announce . . . that he will "love virtuous
men of all parties and denominations." . . . May he persevere
in it uninfluenced by the menaces or machinations of artful
and designing men. . . . Nor ought Mr. Jefferson's extempore
speech to the Senate pass unnoticed. The terms in which he
speaks of Mr. Adams . . . do credit to his head and heart. How
satisfactory . . . to know from Mr. Jefferson, himself, that the
strictest friendship subsists between the two first officers in
government.

Adams made no change in the cabinet which he inherited from
Washington, and this was probably the gravest error of his administration. Three of the four men in it were Alexander Hamilton's
creatures. Historian Claude Bowers described the situation by
writing: "Ali Baba among his Forty Thieves is no more deserving
of sympathy than John Adams shut up within the seclusion of his
cabinet room with his official family of secret enemies." Secretary
of War James McHenry made no bones about taking orders from
Hamilton. Secretary of State Timothy Pickering was scarcely less
docile. Treasury Secretary Oliver Wolcott maintained a pose of independence—Hamilton gave him suggestions rather than orders.
Only Attorney General Charles Lee was not a Hamilton man, and
he was completely without initiative. It is amazing that Adams,
who knew that Hamilton was no friend, did not understand the
danger of keeping Hamilton's men as department heads; but he
wrote, confidently: "Pickering and all his colleagues are as much
attached to me as I desire. I have no jealousies from that quarter."
The Washingtons left for Mount Vernon immediately after the

inauguration, taking much of the furniture of the executive mansion. Ten days later John wrote his wife:

I HOPE TO GET INTO THE HOUSE on Monday next, but shall purchase no nice furniture till you come. I shall make a little establishment for myself and keep bachelors' hall for some time. I have procured some horses and a carriage, and ride on horseback as often as the weather will permit.

It was late in May before Abby arrived to settle in their new home.

Relations with France were tense. That nation considered the Jay treaty and the Neutrality Proclamation as definite violations of their treaty with America. James Monroe, a minister to France whom the French liked and trusted, had mollified them for a time. Then Washington had peremptorily recalled Monroe and sought to replace him with Federalist Charles Cotesworth Pinckney, whom the French refused to receive. Joel Barlow, writing from Paris shortly after the election, said:

THE FRENCH SAW that the character of the new President would be a criterion by which the friendship or enmity of the United States for France could clearly be seen. . . . The candidates were Adams and Jefferson; the one a reputed royalist . . . the other an eminent Republican. . . . When the election of Adams was announced here it produced the order of the 2nd March, which was meant to be little short of a declaration of war.

The act to which he referred called for the seizure of American shipping and the treatment as pirates of American seamen found on British ships.

Adams was basically pro-British, but he sincerely tried to maintain neutrality. To John Quincy he wrote:

My ENTRANCE INTO OFFICE is marked by a misunderstanding with France, which I shall endeavor to reconcile, provided that no violation of faith, no stain upon honor, is exacted. But if infidelity, dishonor, or too much humiliation is demanded, France shall do as she pleases, and take her own course. America is *not scared.*

When word came of the French Directory's refusal to receive Pinckney, he addressed a questionnaire to his cabinet, asking their advice on fourteen points.

Were "the refusal to receive Mr. Pinckney, and the rude orders to quit Paris . . . bars to all further measures of negotiation. Or, in other words, will a fresh mission to Paris be too great a humiliation of the American people in their own sense and that of the world?" If another mission were sent, "what parts or articles of the treaty of amity and commerce with Great Britain be offered to France?" And, "What articles of the treaty of alliance, and of the treaty of commerce with France, should be proposed to be abolished?" How should America remonstrate against "capture of vessels, imprisonment of masters and mariners, cruelties, insults, and abuses of every kind to our citizens?" And should a project of "a new treaty, abolishing the old treaties and consular convention, be proposed to France?"

Three of the cabinet officers promptly consulted Hamilton. The New Yorker advised further attempts at negotiation. McHenry submitted Hamilton's reply verbatim over his own name. Meanwhile, Adams had approached Jefferson with a suggestion that the Vice-President might go to France. When Jefferson refused, Adams asked him to sound out Madison, who also rejected the post. For the first few weeks of the administration a bipartisan rapport between Adams and Jefferson seemed possible, based on their old friendship. Jefferson's letters were conciliatory, and Adams expressed hopes of closer ties in his correspondence. He said that he had never lost faith in his old friend's honor and integrity, but Jefferson's support of such characters as Freneau and Tom Paine had long "been a source of . . . anxiety to me. . . . But I hope and believe that his advancement and his situation in the Senate, an excellent school, will correct him. He will have too many friends about him to flatter him, but I have hope we can keep him steady." This *entente cordiale* lasted but ten weeks; it terminated abruptly when Adams called a special session of Congress and made a speech that was a bombshell to the Republicans.

After an introduction in which he thanked "the Supreme Dispenser of national blessings for general health and promising seasons; for domestic and social happiness; for the rapid progress and ample acquisitions of industry through extensive territories; for civil, political, and religious liberty," he added that "It is with extreme regret that I shall be obliged to turn your thoughts to other circumstances, which admonish us that some of these felicities may not be lasting." These other circumstances arose from the French refusal to receive a minister who had been directed "faithfully to represent the disposition of the government and people of the United States . . . to remove jealousies and obvious complaints . . . to restore that mutual confidence which had been so unfortunately and injuriously impaired and to explain the relative interests of both countries and the real sentiments of his own." Not only had the French refused to receive Pinckney but he had been ordered "to quit the territories of the Republic. . . . During his residence at Paris, cards of hospitality were refused him and he was threatened with being subjected to the jurisdiction of the minister of police." This refusal to receive our minister, "until we have acceded to their demands without discussion and without investigation, is to treat us neither as allies, nor as friends, nor as a sovereign State."

Adams then harked back to what he considered a further insult from the French when Monroe had left.

WITH THIS CONDUCT of the French government it will be proper to take into view the public audience given to the late minister of the United States on his taking leave of the execu-

tive Directory. The speech of the President discloses sentiments more alarming than the refusal of a minister, because
more dangerous to our independence and union, and at the
same time studiously marked with indignities toward the government of the United States. It evinces a disposition to separate the people of the United States from the government; to
persuade them that they have different affections, principles,
and interests, from those of their fellow citizens whom they
themselves have chosen to manage their common concerns;
and thus to produce divisions fatal to our peace. Such attempts ought to be repelled with a decision which shall convince France and the world that we are not a degraded people,
humiliated under a colonial spirit of fear and sense of inferi-
ority, fitted to be the miserable instruments of foreign influence, and regardless of national honor, character, and interest.

I should have been happy to have thrown a veil over these
transactions if it had been possible to conceal them; but they
have passed on the great theatre of the world, in the face of
all Europe and America, and with such circumstances of
publicity and solemnity that they cannot be disguised, and
will not soon be forgotten. They have inflicted a wound in the
American breast. It is my sincere desire, however, that it may
be healed. It is my desire to preserve peace and friendship
with all nations; and believing that neither the honor nor the
interest of the United States absolutely forbids the repetition
of advances for securing these desirable objects with France,
I shall institute a fresh attempt at negotiation, and shall not
fail to promote and accelerate an accommodation on terms
compatible with the rights, duties, interests, and honor of the
nation.

To this point, the speech was, except for some rather harsh
words about France, conciliatory. But the President then continued
in a different vein.

WHILE WE ARE ENDEAVORING to adjust all our differences

with France by amicable negotiation, the progress of the war
in Europe, the depredations on our commerce, the personal
injuries to our citizens, and the general complexion of affairs,
render it my indispensable duty to recommend to your consideration effectual measures of defense. . . .

A naval power, next to the militia, is the natural defense of
the United States. . . . Our seacoasts, from their great extent,
are more easily annoyed, and more easily defended by a naval
force than any other. With all the materials our country
abounds; in skill our naval architects and navigators are equal
to any; and commanders and seamen will not be wanting. . . .

But besides a protection of our commerce on the seas, I
think it highly necessary to protect it at home, where it is col-
lected in our most important ports . . . to guard against sudden and predatory incursions. . . . You will seriously deliberate whether the means of general defense ought not to be
increased by an addition to the regular artillery and cavalry,
and by arrangements for forming a provisional army.

With the same view, and as a measure which, even in a time
of universal peace, ought not to be neglected, I recommend to
your consideration a revision of the laws for organizing, arm-
ing, and disciplining the militia, to render that natural and
safe defense of the country efficacious.

This was the end of the honeymoon with the Republicans, who
were sure that Adams was back under Hamilton's thumb. Bache's
Aurora sneered:

WHATEVER MAY BE SAID of the President by *three votes,* he
has certainly one characteristic feature, that of dissimulation.
From the time of his appointment until the present moment he
has completely deceived the people, who were led by his inaugural speech and other circumstances to believe . . . that
he was under no *extraneous influence.* [And, added Bache:]
. . . we are unavoidably led to believe that his men Timothy
and Oliver have fed him upon pepperpot these three weeks

past in order to bring his nerves to a proper anti-Gallican tone. The effects which aromatics on high-seasoned food produce upon a cold northern constitution every quack can tell.

Another result of the warlike speech was an irrevocable break between Adams and Jefferson. The latter wrote that he approved of defense measures, but that "I do not think the speech and addresses of Congress as conciliatory as the preceding irritations on both sides would have rendered wise." When Uriah Forrest sent Adams a copy of a critical Jefferson letter, the President replied:

I RECEIVED YESTERDAY your favor of the 23rd, and am very much obliged to you for it. The paper inclosed in it is a serious thing. It will be a motive, in addition to many others, for me to be upon my guard. It is evidence of a mind, soured, yet seeking for popularity, and eaten to a honeycomb with ambition, yet weak, confused, uninformed, and ignorant. I have been long convinced that this ambition is so inconsiderate as to be capable of going great lengths.

To John Quincy he write that he was loath to give up his friend but, "I am obliged to look upon him as a man whose mind is warped by prejudice and so blinded by ignorance as to be unfit for the office he holds."

Two aspects of the policy inaugurated by Adams' speech did not at first sit well with the public. One was what amounted to a standing army, which had always been considered a threat to American liberty. The other was the unfortunate name chosen for the revenue bill passed to support the enlarged military establishment—a Stamp Tax. This bill gave Adams some minor qualms as to a possible interference with his prerogatives. He wrote Treasury Secretary Wolcott:

THE ORGANIZATION OF THE STAMP TAX suggests a vexation to me. The bill was worth money, and money was so much

wanted for the public service that I would not put it at risk;
otherwise I would have negatived that bill; not from personal
feelings, for I care not a farthing for all the personal power in
the world. But the office of the Secretary of the Treasury is, in
that bill, premeditatedly set up as a rival to that of the President; and that policy will be pursued, if we are not on our
guard, till we have a quintuple or a centuple executive directory, with all the Babylonish dialect which modern pedants
most affect.

This refers to the then unusual procedure, established when
Hamilton was Secretary, of the Treasury head reporting directly to
the Congress, not through the President.

To negotiate with France, Adams appointed a three-man commission. Pinckney was retained and flanked by arch-Federalist
John Marshall and Elbridge Gerry, a friend of Adams' and a rather
temperate Republican. To the latter he wrote:

IT IS MY SINCERE DESIRE that an accommodation may take
place; but our national faith and the honor of our government
cannot be sacrificed. You have known enough of the unpleasant effects of disunion among ministers to convince you of the
necessity of avoiding it like a rock or quicksand. . . .

It is probable there will be maneuvers practiced to excite
jealousies among you, both by Americans, English, Dutch,
and French; this should not produce too much irritation, but
should press you closer together. You will hear a great deal of
affected contempt, as well as a great deal of affected esteem
and admiration of America. Neither should affect you much.
But I cannot enlarge. I wish . . . that you may acquire glory
enough to compensate for all your cares.

N.B. I must give you a hint about economy. I would be as
plain and cheap as possible in dress, equipage, lodgings, livery, and everything. I would not give many feasts to Ameri-

cans. Decorum must be observed. You will be surrounded with projectors and swindlers. You will not be deceived by them.

After a brief respite in Quincy during the summer of 1797 the President returned in November to make a second address to Congress. Nothing much had happened since his previous message.

OUR ENVOYS EXTRAORDINARY to the French Republic embarked, one in July, the other early in August, to join their colleague in Holland. . . . Whatever may be the result of this mission, I trust that nothing will have been omitted on my part to conduct the negotiation to a successful conclusion, on such equitable terms as may be compatible with the safety, honor, and interests of the United States.

However, while negotiations were going on, "nothing has occurred . . . which renders inexpedient those precautionary measures recommended by me . . . at the opening of your late extraordinary session. If that system was then prudent, it is more so now, as increasing depredations strengthen the reasons for its adoption." The President enlarged on this, based on his usual pessimistic views of human nature.

INDEED, whatever may be the issue of the negotiation with France, and whether the war in Europe is or is not to continue, I hold it most certain that perfect tranquillity and order will not soon be obtained. The state of society has so long been disturbed, the sense of moral and religious obligation so much weakened, public faith and national honor have been so impaired, respect to treaties has been so diminished, and the law of nations has lost so much of its force, while pride, ambition, avarice, and violence have been so long unrestrained, there remains no reasonable ground on which to raise an expectation that a commerce, without protection or defense, will not be plundered.

In a country that was still predominantly agricultural, Adams said not a word about farming and commodities; except that they depended on commerce. He was talking for New England rather than America when he said:

THE COMMERCE of the United States is essential, if not to their existence, at least to their comfort, their growth, prosperity, and happiness. The genius, character, and habits of the people are highly commercial. Their cities have been formed and exist upon commerce. Our agriculture, fisheries, arts, and manufactures are connected with and depend upon it. In short, commerce has made this country what it is; and it cannot be destroyed or neglected without involving the people in poverty and distress. Great numbers are directly and solely supported by navigation. The faith of society is pledged for the preservation of the rights of commercial and seafaring, no less than of the other citizens. Under this view of our affairs, I should hold myself guilty of a neglect of duty if I forbore to recommend that we should make every exertion to protect our commerce, and to place our country in a suitable posture of defense as the only sure means of preserving both.

It was March 1798 before formal dispatches were received from the commissioners in France, but Adams had much earlier received word that all was not going well. In January he sent another questionnaire to his cabinet soliciting their advice on what should be done "if our envoys extraordinary should be refused an audience, or, after an audience, be ordered to depart without accomplishing the objects of their mission." Should the commissioners go to Holland or come home?

WHAT MEASURES should be recommended to Congress? Shall an immediate declaration of war be recommended or suggested? If not, what other system shall be recommended more than a repetition of the recommendations heretofore repeatedly made to both houses? Will it in any case, and in what cases, be advisable to recommend an embargo?

McHenry replied that there was "a general aversion to war in the minds of the people of the United States, and a particular dislike, on the part of a portion of them, to a war with France." He recommended "a vigorous defensive plan." Lee called for an immediate declaration of war, and Pickering an offensive and defensive alliance with England. Adams did nothing until the full story was unfolded in the commissioners' dispatches.

It was a singular and sordid story. After a brief and rather vague interview with Talleyrand, the new French Minister, the Americans had been approached by three of Talleyrand's agents with demands for a loan from America, an apology by Adams for the harsh words in his speech to the special session, and, particularly, a substantial bribe. This was accompanied by a threat emphasizing the danger of a breach with France and a reference to her power, which "nothing could resist."

Adams' first reaction was to write: "A Message Referring to a Decree of the Directory," which was little short of a demand for a declaration of war. Then he cooled down and sent a short message relative to the envoys to Congress in which he said:

WHILE I FEEL A SATISFACTION in informing you that their exertions for the adjustment of the differences between the two nations have been sincere and unremitted, it is incumbent on me to declare that I perceive no ground of expectation that the objects of their mission can be accomplished on terms compatible with the safety, honor, or the essential interests of the nation. . . . Under these circumstances I cannot forbear to reiterate the recommendations which have been formerly made and to exhort you to adopt, with promptitude, decision, and unanimity, such measures as the ample resources of the country afford for the protection of our seafaring and commercial citizens, for the defense of any exposed portions of our territory, for replenishing our arsenals, establishing founderies and military manufactories, and to provide such efficient revenue as will be necessary to defray extraordinary expenses, and supply the deficiencies which may be occasioned by depredations on our commerce.

The present state of things is so essentially different from that in which instructions were given to collectors to restrain vessels of the United States from sailing in an armed condition that the principle on which those orders were issued has ceased to exist. I therefore deem it proper to inform Congress that I no longer conceive myself justifiable in continuing them.

Fearing for the safety of the commissioners, who were still in France, he did not forward their dispatches to Congress.

The House of Representatives promptly demanded to see the dispatches, and Adams sent them, "omitting only some names and a few expressions descriptive of the persons." For the names of the French agents he substituted the letters X,Y,Z, and the matter has since been known as the "XYZ Affair."

The corruption of the French cut the ground out from under the Republicans, although Jefferson tried to minimize the importance of the affair and place the blame on the commissioners and Adams. He pointed out: "Mr. Adams' speech to Congress in May is deemed such a national affront that no explanation on other topics can be entered on till that, as a preliminary, is wiped away." If this were done negotiations might go on:

No DIFFICULTY was expressed toward an adjustment of all differences and misunderstandings, or even ultimately a payment for spoliations, if the insult from our Executive should be first wiped away. . . . The little slanderous imputation before mentioned [the bribe] has been the bait which hurried the opposite party into this publication [of the dispatches]. . . . It is evident, however, on reflection, that these papers do not offer one motive the more for our going to war.

The general public quickly turned against the French and their Republican supporters. Popular opinion was evident in the toast offered at a dinner for Marshall when he returned from France: "Millions for defense but not one cent for tribute." In Congress, Republican moderates and independents swung into the Federalist camp. There was pressure on Adams to call for a declaration of war. He resisted this, but in his answers to many addresses received from cities and towns he took a belligerent stand.

To the people of Province he wrote:

THE HONOR OF OUR NATION is now universally seen to be at stake, and its independence in question, and all America appears to declare, with one heart and one voice, a manly determination to vindicate both.

To the citizens of Bridgetown, New Jersey, he said:

IT WAS, however, no part of the system of my predecessor, nor is it any article of my creed, that neutrality should be purchased with bribes, by the sacrifice of our sovereignty and the abandonment of our independence, by the surrender of our moral character, by tarnishing our honor, by violations of public faith, or by any means humiliating to our own national pride or disgraceful in the eyes of the world; nor will I be the instrument of procuring it on such terms.

To Lancaster, Pennsylvania, he reported:

THE OBSERVATIONS made by me were mild and moderate in a degree far beyond what the provocation would have justified; and if the American people or their government could have borne it without resentment, offered as it was in the face of all the world, they must have been fit to be the tributary dupes they have since been so coolly invited to become.

And to his home base in Boston he cried:

THE STATE OF THE WORLD is such, the situation of all the nations of Europe with which we have relation is so critical, that vicissitudes must be expected, from whose deleterious influences nothing but arms and energy can protect us. To arms, then, my young friends—to arms, especially by sea, to be used as the laws shall direct, let us resort. For safety against dangers, which we now see and feel, cannot be averted by truth, reason, or justice.

When the provisional army that Adams had asked for was approved by the Congress it was necessary to have officers, and this led to disagreement and unpleasantness far greater than the subject merited. On July 6, 1798, Adams wrote to McHenry:

IT IS MY DESIRE that you embrace the first opportunity to set out on your journey to Mount Vernon and wait on General Washington with the commission of Lieutenant General and Commander-in-Chief of the armies of the United States, which, by the advice and consent of the Senate, has been signed by me.

The reasons and motives which prevailed with me to venture on such a step as the nomination of this great and illustrious character . . . are too obvious and important to escape the observation of any part of America or Europe; but, as it is a movement of great delicacy, it will require all your address to communicate the subject in a manner that shall be inoffensive to his feelings, and consistent with all the respect that is due from me to him.

If the General should decline the appointment, all the world will be silent and respectfully acquiesce. If he should accept, all the world, except the enemies of this country, will rejoice. If he should come to no decisive determination, but take the subject into consideration, I shall not appoint any other Lieutenant General until his conclusion is known.

His advice in the formation of a list of officers would be extremely desirable to me. The names of Lincoln, Morgan, Knox, Hamilton, Gates, Pinckney, Lee, Carrington, Hand, Muhlenberg, Dayton, Burr, Brooks, Cobb, Smith may be mentioned to him, and any others that occur to you. Particularly, I wish to have his opinion of the man most suitable for Inspector General, and Adjutant General, and Quartermaster General.

According to McHenry, Washington accepted command on condition that he would not be called on active service unless he was absolutely needed and that he be allowed to name his confidential officers, "and without whom, I think, he would not serve."

Washington nominated Hamilton for Inspector General and Charles Cotesworth Pinckney and Henry Knox, all to rank as Major Generals. Since Washington would probably not be an active Commander-in-Chief, the precedence of the subordinate commissions was important to determine who would be second in command and, in effect, actual commander. In terms of seniority in the service Knox and Pinckney ranked Hamilton; they had been Generals when he was a Captain. But State Secretary Pickering, and Hamilton himself, connived to get the job through secret letters to Washington. In all, thirteen lengthy documents changed hands on this during the summer of 1798, when Adams was in Quincy.

Washington had proposed the names in the order of Hamilton, Pinckney, and Knox; and McHenry was convinced that this indicated his preference for Hamilton in second place, although he had mentioned him only as Inspector General. In Adams' longest letter on the subject he said:

MY OPINION IS and has always been clear that as the law now stands the order of nomination or of recording has no weight, or effect, but that officers appointed on the same day, in whatever order, have a right to rank according to antecedent services. I made the nomination according to the list presented to me by you, from General Washington, in hopes that rank might be settled among them by agreement or acquiescence, believing at the time, and expressing to you that belief, that the nomination and appointment would give Hamilton no command at all, nor any rank before any Major General. This is my opinion still. I am willing to settle all decisively at present (and have no fear of the consequences), by dating the commissions, Knox on the first day, Pinckney on the second, and Hamilton on the third. . . .

You speak to me of the expediency of attempting an alteration in the rank of the gentlemen in question. You know, sir, that no rank has ever been settled by me. You know my opinion has always been, as it is now, that the order of names in the nomination and record was of no consequence.

General Washington has, through the whole, conducted with perfect honor and consistency. I said, and I say now, if I could resign to him the office of President, I would do it instantly, and with the highest pleasure; but I never said I would hold the office, and be responsible for its exercise, while he should execute it. Nor has he ever intimated a desire of the kind. He has always in all his letters said that these points must ultimately depend on the President.

The power and authority are in the President. I am willing to exert this authority at this moment, and to be responsible for the exercise of it. All difficulties will in this way be avoided. But if it is to be referred to General Washington, or to mutual and amicable accommodation among the gentlemen themselves, I foresee it will come to me at last after much altercation and exasperation of passions, and I shall then determine it exactly as I should now—Knox, Pinckney, and Hamilton.

There has been too much intrigue in this business with General Washington and me; if I shall ultimately be the dupe of it, I am much mistaken in myself.

The Hamiltonians in the cabinet bombarded both Washington and Adams with letters protesting this decision. McHenry quoted a letter from Washington in which the General said:

I CAN PERCEIVE pretty clearly that the matter is or very soon will be brought to the alternative of submitting to the President's forgetfulness of what I considered a compact or a condition of acceptance of the appointment . . . or to return him my commission. . . . You will recollect too that, my acceptance being conditional, I requested you to take the commission back, that it might be restored or annulled according to the President's determination to accept or reject the terms on which I had offered to serve.

Washington now was apparently saying that a condition of his acceptance was Hamilton as second in command. Adams reluctantly backed down and wrote to Washington:

YOU REQUEST to be informed whether my determination to preserve the order of the three Major Generals is final; and whether I mean to appoint another Adjutant General without your concurrence. I presume that before this day you have received information from the Secretary of War that I some time ago signed the three commissions and dated them on the same day, in hopes, similar to yours, that an amicable adjustment, or acquiescence, might take place among the gentlemen themselves. But, if these hopes should be disappointed and controversies should arise, they will, of course, be submitted to you as Commander-in-Chief, and if, after all, anyone should be so obstinate as to appeal to me from the judgment of the Commander-in-Chief, I was determined to confirm that judgment.

Meanwhile, McHenry had taken offense at Adams' reference to "intrigues" and the President wrote him:

YOUR REQUEST to be informed whether I attach any portion of the intrigues . . . to you is reasonable; and I have no scruple to acknowledge that your conduct through the whole toward me has been candid. I have suspected, however, that extraordinary pains were taken with you to impress upon your mind that the public opinion and the unanimous wish of the Federalists was that General Hamilton might be first, and even Commander-in-Chief; that you might express this opinion to General Washington more forcibly than I should have done; and that this determined him to make the arrangement as he did. If this suspicion was well founded, I doubt not you made the representation with integrity. I am not and never was of the opinion that the public opinion demanded General Hamilton for the first, and I am now clear that it never expected nor desired any such thing.

This whole matter seems like a tempest in a teapot, but it may have had far-reaching conclusions. That summer seemed to mark a turning point in Adams' relations with his cabinet and the dawn of a new independence which would lead to a dismissal of two of Hamilton's creatures and steps to effect a reconciliation with France.

Meanwhile a more significant storm was brewing which would be the most controversial of Adams' administration. Early in the summer of 1798 Congress had passed four pieces of legislation which became known as the Alien and Sedition Acts. The first bill increased to fourteen years "the length of time necessary for an alien to reside here before he can be admitted a citizen." The next two gave the President power to seize, restrain, secure, or remove enemy aliens and their possessions and provided special penalties for treason by an alien. The final bill, the famous Sedition Act, proclaimed a sort of martial law under which anyone could be fined or imprisoned, "who shall by writing, printing, or speaking, threaten any person holding an office under the government, with damage to his character, person, or estate." Subject to similar punishment was "any libelous attack by writing, printing, publishing, or speaking against the legislature of the United States or the President of the United States, or any court or judge thereof."

The Alien Acts were ostensibly directed toward the many French emigrants, particularly in Philadelphia, who might have a greater allegiance to their homeland than to their new haven, although most of them were refugees from the French government in power. Actually, in passing the Alien Acts, the Federalists were aiming at the hordes of Irish and dissident English emigrants who were swelling the Republican ranks. The Sedition Act would make it possible for the Federalists to curb the Republican clubs and the rabid Republican press.

Adams did not write the Alien and Sedition Acts and had no direct hand in their passage. He did sign them and approved of their strict enforcement. It was a wartime witch hunt in which, although he did not lead, he willingly participated. On one occasion, when asked what a particular alien was charged with, he replied, "Nothing in particular, but he's too French." In several of his replies to addresses from cities and counties he made such statements as, "Until lately licentiousness has been too little restrained." To the citizens of Boston he said that "the profligate spirit of falsehood and malignity, which has appeared in some, and the unguarded disposition in others to encourage it, are serious evils, and bear a threatening aspect upon the union of the state, their constitution of government, and the moral character of the nation." And to New York he reported, "If we glory in making our country an asylum for virtue in distress and for innocent industry, it behooves us to beware that under this pretext it is not made a receptacle of malevolence and turbulence for the outcasts of the universe."

In view of the later contribution of the Du Pont family to the economic growth of America, a letter from Adams to State Secretary Pickering is of special interest.

I SHALL NOT BE GUILTY of so much affection of regard to science as to be very willing to grant passports to Du Pont de Nemours or any other French philosophers, in the present situations of our country. We have had too many French philosophers already, and I really begin to think, or rather suspect, that learned academies, not under immediate inspection and control of government, have disorganized the world and are incompatible with social order.

Under the Sedition Act ten Republican editors were convicted; the number one target of the Federalists, Franklin's grandson Benny Bache, thwarted them by dying of yellow fever after he was indicted. Pickering was the main witch hunter here, but Adams did nothing to temper the political persecution which was practiced in the name of national security. Jefferson led the opposition to the iniquitous acts and practiced sedition himself by secretly writing resolutions for the legislatures of Kentucky and Virginia which implied a threat of secession and put forward for the first time the principle of nullification—the idea that a state might reject acts of the Congress which it considered unconstitutional.

When Adams left Quincy for Philadelphia in November 1798 the Federalists were still riding high, but the President was not their actual leader, nor did he want to be. He was certain, more than ever, that he was President of the United States, not of the Federalists. He abhorred partisan factions, even his own; and he had new thoughts on the French situation, which he had intimated in a letter to Pickering, in which he said:

ANOTHER INQUIRY IS, whether any further proposals of negotiation can be made with safety; and whether there will be any use or advantage, in Europe or America, by uniting minds more in our favor by any such measure. In a message to both houses of Congress, on the 21st day of July last, the President expressed his opinion of the impropriety of sending any ministers to France without assurances that they shall be received. In this opinion he perseveres. But the question is, whether, in the speech, the President may not say that in order to keep open the channels of negotiation, it is his intention to nominate a minister to the French Republic who may be ready to embark for France as soon as he, or the President, shall receive from the Directory satisfactory assurances that he shall be received and entitled to all the prerogatives and privileges of the general law of nations, and that a minister of equal rank and powers shall be appointed and commissioned to treat with him.

Hamilton and the cabinet conferred on this in some consternation and drafted a reply to Adams in which they said that, while a declaration of war would be "inexpedient and ought not to be recommended," the government should not give the opposition a "rallying point." To send another minister "to make a new attempt at negotiation would be an act of humiliation to which the United States ought not to submit without extreme necessity; no such necessity exists." In short, the war fever, short of actual war, was politically advantageous to the Federalists, and Hamilton did not want the *status quo* disturbed.

In his message to Congress Adams accepted the recommendations of his cabinet. In fact his speech was written by Wolcott at Hamilton's direction. Some of it reiterated the policy of armed neutrality which had already led to an undeclared war at sea with France.

HITHERTO, therefore, nothing is discoverable in the conduct of France which ought to change or relax our measures of defense. On the contrary, to extend and invigorate them is our true policy. We have no reason to regret that these measures have been thus far adopted and pursued; and in proportion as we enlarge our view of the portentious incalculable situation of Europe, we shall discover new and cogent motives for the full development of our energies and resources. But in demonstrating by our conduct that we do not fear war in the necessary protection of our rights and honor, we shall give no room to infer that we abandon the desire of peace. An efficient preparation for war can alone ensure peace. It is peace that we have uniformly and perseveringly cultivated; and harmony between us and France may be restored at her option.

Adams made one slight but subsequently significant change in Wolcott's draft. The Treasury Secretary had written: "the sending [of] another minister to make a new attempt at negotiation would be an act of humiliation to which the United States ought not to submit without extreme necessity." The President changed this to: "But to send another minister without more determinate assurances that he would be received, would be an act of humiliation to which the United States ought not to submit. It must, therefore, be left to France, if she is indeed desirous of accommodation, to take the requisite steps." He ended with a sentence which might be construed as an invitation to the French to send a mission to America: "The United States will steadily observe the maxims by which they have hitherto been governed. They will respect the sacred rights of embassy."

Early in 1799 Adams' son Thomas Boylston returned from Europe. He had been serving as secretary to his older brother, John Quincy, who had moved to Berlin from The Hague, where he had been replaced by William Vans Murray. Thomas brought private letters from both his brother and Murray in which they expressed the opinion that France was now ready to treat for peace. Murray told of several meetings with a mysterious French agent named Pichon who had assured him of this, saying, ". . . the President has as much as said that if Talleyrand gave him the assurances he would treat, and we have anticipated this and given the assurances." Murray added, "Rest assured of it, France is impotent toward U.S.—or she would not have knuckled of late." He advised—and John Quincy concurred—that America be prepared to meet France halfway.

Based on all this, the President sent Pickering an abrupt order:

THE PRESIDENT of the United States requests the Secretary of State to prepare the draft of a project of a treaty and a consular convention such as in his opinion might at this day be acceded to by the United States, if proposed by France. It is his desire that the Secretary of State would avail himself of the advice and assistance of all the heads of department in the formation of this composition, to be completed as soon as the pressure of other business of more immediate necessity will permit. The necessity of inviolable confidence will be obvious.

This was shortly followed by a message to the Senate, which Jefferson read to that body with some surprise:

ALWAYS DISPOSED and ready to embrace every plausible appearance of probability of preserving or restoring tranquillity, I nominate William Vans Murray, our minister resident at The Hague, to be minister plentipotentiary of the United States to the French Republic.

If the Senate shall advise and consent to his appointment, effectual care shall be taken in his instructions that he shall not go to France without direct and unequivocal assurances from the French government, signified by their minister of foreign relations, that he shall be received in character, shall enjoy the privileges attached to his character by the law of nations, and that a minister of equal rank, title, and powers shall be appointed to treat with him, to discuss and conclude all controversies between the two republics by a new treaty.

Adams had, at long last, acted without consulting anyone, in or out of his cabinet. His move threw down the gauntlet to the Hamiltonians and took the wind out of the sails of the Republicans. He explained his decision in a letter to Washington.

I YESTERDAY DETERMINED to nominate Mr. Murray to be minister plenipotentiary to the French Republic. This I ventured to do upon the strength of a letter from Talleyrand himself, giving declarations, in the name of his government, that any minister plenipotentiary from the United States shall be received according to the condition at the close of my message to Congress of the 21st of June last. As there may be some reserves for chicane, however, Murray is not to remove from his station at The Hague until he shall have received formal assurances that he shall be received and treated in character. . . .

Tranquillity upon just and honorable terms is undoubtedly the ardent desire of the friends of this country, and I wish the babyish and womanly blubbering for peace may not necessitate the conclusion of a treaty that will not be just nor very honorable. I do not intend, however, that they shall. There is not much sincerity in the cant about peace; those who snivel for it now were hot for war against Britain a few months ago, and would be now, if they saw a chance. In elective governments, peace or war are alike embraced by parties when they think they can employ either for electioneering purposes.

Federalist wrath burst on Adams. Hamilton called him "a mere old woman and unfit for a President." Some Federalist congressmen threatened to resign. One wrote, "I have sacrificed as much as most men . . . to support this government and root out democracy and French principles, but . . . I feel it to be lost and worse. . . . I can and will resign if all must be given up to France." One anonymous correspondent who signed himself, "a ruined merchant, alas, with ten children made beggars by the French," proclaimed, "Assassination shall be your lot." Jefferson smugly observed that the Federalist senators were "graveled and divided; some were for opposing, others know not what to do."

When the Federalist senators shifted their attack from the mission to the appointee, Murray, on the grounds of youth and inexperience, Adams did agree to a three-man commission, but beyond this he would not go. He wrote to Attorney General Lee:

THE NOMINATION OF MURRAY has had one good effect, at least. . . . It has also produced a display of the real spirit of the parties in this country, and the objects they have in view. To me, it has laid open characters. Some of these will do well to study a little more maturely the spirit of their stations. But vanity has no limits; arrogance shall be made to feel a curb. If anyone entertains the idea that, because I am a President of three votes only, I am in the power of a party, they shall find that I am no more so than the Constitution forces upon me. If combinations of senators, generals, and heads of department shall be formed, such as I cannot resist, and measures are demanded of me that I cannot adopt, my remedy is plain and certain. I will try my own strength at resistance first, however.

Abigail had been ill in Quincy. When Congress adjourned early in the spring Adams hastened to her bedside, against the advice of several, like Uriah Forrest, who wrote, "I speak the truth when I say that your real friends wish you to be with your officers, because the public impression is that the government will be better conducted." But Adams was adamant that he would be with his wife. He replied:

THE PEOPLE ELECTED ME to administer the government, it is true, and I do administer it here at Quincy, as really as I could do at Philadelphia. The Secretaries of State, Treasury, War, Navy, and the Attorney General transmit me daily by the post all the business of consequence, and nothing is done without my advice and direction, when I am here, more than when I am in the same city with them. The post goes very rapidly, and I answer by the return of it, so that nothing suffers or is lost. . . .

Mrs. Adams, it is true, is better; but she is still in a state so delicate, and has such returns of that dreadful disorder which kept her on the brink of the grave almost all the last summer, that it would be a presumptuous imprudence, little less criminal than deliberate suicide, for her to attempt to go one hundred miles south of this latitude before the violent heat of summer shall be passed.

With Adams absent, the Hamiltonians in the cabinet delayed the dispatch of the other two envoys to France, and Pickering sought to interpret dispatches from Murray, with a letter from Talleyrand, as indicating a renewed French animosity. He pointed out that Talleyrand "does not forget the common practice of his government, to drop a reproach or insult while making amicable professions. It was certainly not necessary for him to insinuate that the President of the United States was wasting many months of precious time." To this Adams replied:

IT IS FAR BELOW THE DIGNITY of the President of the United States to take any notice of Talleyrand's impertinent regrets and insinuations of superfluities. You or Mr. Murray may answer them as you please in your correspondence with one another, or with the French minister. . . . Meantime, I dread no longer their diplomatic skill. I have seen it, and felt it, and been the victim of it these twenty-one years. But the charm is dissolved. Their magic is at an end in America. Still, they shall find, as long as I am in office, candor, integrity, and, as far as there can be any confidence or safety, a pacific and friendly disposition. If the spirit of exterminating vengeance ever arises, it shall be conjured up by them, not me. In this spirit I shall pursue the negotiation, and I expect the cooperation of the heads of departments. . . . I pray you to lose no time in conveying to Governor Davie his commission, and to the Chief Justice and his Excellency copies of these letters from Mr. Murray and Talleyrand, with a request that, laying aside all other employments, they make immediate preparations for embarking. . . .

The principal points, indeed, all the points of the negotiation, were so minutely considered and approved by me and all

the heads of department, before I left Philadelphia, that nothing remains but to put them into form and dress. This service
I pray you to perform as promptly as possible.

The summer passed with no decisive action. The cabinet had
moved to Trenton to avoid a yellow fever epidemic in Philadelphia.
Late in the season Hamilton arrived there. Newly appointed Navy
Secretary, Benjamin Stoddert, no Hamilton man, urged the President to come for

. . . both public considerations, and those which relate more
immediately to yourself . . . I have the most perfect conviction that your presence here, before the departure of the
ministers, would afford great satisfaction to the best disposed
and best informed men in that part of the country with which
I am best acquainted; and I believe, to the great mass of good
men all over the United States.

To this Adams replied:

You urge me to join you and the other public officers at
Trenton before our ministers depart for France, and this from
considerations which relate more immediately to myself as
well as others of a public nature. For myself, I have neither
hopes nor fears. But if I could see any public necessity or
utility in my presence at Trenton, I would undertake the journey, however inconvenient to myself or my family. I would
not, indeed, hesitate, if it were only to give any reasonable
satisfaction to the "best disposed and best informed men."
. . . If any considerable difference should unexpectedly arise
between the heads of department, I will come at all events.
Otherwise, I see no necessity for taking a step that will give
more *éclat* to the business than I think it deserves.

When Stoddert reiterated his plea to his chief, with emphasis on
the possible political consequences of his absence, Adams retorted

that he would come by mid-October, but that the upcoming election was not a consideration.

I HAVE ONLY ONE FAVOR to beg, and that is that a certain election may be wholly laid out of this question and all others. I know the people of America so well, and the light in which I stand in their eyes, that no alternative will ever be left to me but to be a President of three votes or no President at all, and the difference, in my estimation, is not worth three farthings.

When Adams arrived in Trenton he listened to a long harangue from Hamilton to the effect that the envoys should not be sent because the Bourbons were about to be restored to the French throne. He then went over the details of the instructions to the envoys with his cabinet and sent a peremptory note to Pickering:

I REQUEST YOU to order fair copies of the instructions, as corrected last evening, to be prepared and delivered to Judge Ellsworth and Governor Davie, with another for Mr. Murray, without loss of time, and to write a letter to those gentlemen, as envoys extraordinary to the French Republic, expressing, with the affectionate respects of the President, his desire that they would take thier passage for France on board the frigate the *United States,* Captain Barry, now lying at Rhode Island, by the 1st of November, or sooner, if consistent with their conveniences. . . . As their visit to France is at one of the most critical, important, and interesting moments that ever have occurred, it cannot fail to be highly entertaining and instructive to them, and useful to their country, whether it terminates in peace and reconciliation or not. The President sincerely prays God to have them in His holy keeping.

Six weeks later he delivered an annual address to the Sixth Congress in a speech which had none of the belligerency of previous messages. He told the legislators that:

. . . when indications were made, on the part of the French Republic, of a disposition to accommodate the existing differences between the two countries, I felt it to be my duty to prepare for meeting their advances by a nomination of ministers upon certain conditions, which the honor of our country dictated. . . . They have full power to conclude a treaty, subject to the constitutional advice and consent of the Senate.

He reviewed the activities of boards of American and British commissioners negotiating claims covered by the Jay treaty and concluded:

WITH SUCH DISPOSITIONS on both sides, I cannot entertain a doubt that all difficulties will soon be removed, and that the two boards will then proceed, and bring the business committed to them, respectively, to a satisfactory conclusion.

He still felt that:

. . . a steady perseverance in a system of national defense, commensurate with our resources and the situation of our country, is an obvious dictate of wisdom." [But, he added:] Although the period is not arrived when the measures adopted to secure our country against foreign attacks can be renounced, yet it is alike necessary for the honor of the government and the satisfaction of the community that an exact economy should be maintained. I invite you, gentlemen, to investigate the different branches of the public expenditure. The examination will lead to beneficial retrenchments.

In short, the war fever was over; the country could get back to "business as usual."

A few days later the President again addressed the Senate on a sad occasion, the death of George Washington.

THE LIFE OF our Washington cannot suffer by comparison with those of other countries who have been most celebrated and exalted by fame. The attributes and decorations of royalty could have only served to eclipse the majesty of those virtues which made him, from being a modest citizen, a more resplendent luminary. . . . Malice could never blast his honor, and envy made him a singular exception to her universal rule. For himself, he had lived enough to life and to glory. For his fellow citizens, if their prayers could have been answered, he would have been immortal. For me, his departure is at a most unfortunate moment. Trusting, however, in the wise and righteous dominion of Providence over the passions of men, and the results of their counsels and actions, as well as over their lives, nothing remains for me but humble resignation.

His example is now complete, and it will teach wisdom and virtue to magistrates, citizens, and men, not only in the present age, but in future generations, as long as our history shall be read.

As the election year dawned the political situation was paradoxical. Adams' action with regard to France was universally popular with the people; but the removal of the French bugaboo deprived his party of a campaign issue—the Federalists could no longer thunder that the Francophile Republicans were endangering the country. The indignity of the XYZ Affair was forgotten, but the taxes which the Federalists had imposed to support the army and the navy were not, and they were very unpopular. Further, trials of editors under the Sedition Act continued, and the Republican claim that they were aimed at a restriction of the freedom of the press rather than the protection of national security now carried conviction.

Adams seemed to have changed sides politically. The Federalist leaders were confused and irate. Wrote Treasury Secretary Wolcott:

THE PRESIDENT'S MIND is in a state which renders it difficult to determine what prudence and duty require from those about him. He considers Col. Pickering, Mr. McHenry, and myself as his enemies; his resentments against General Hamilton are excessive; he declares his belief of the existence of a British faction in the United States.

Adams did not leave the Hamiltonians in his cabinet long in doubt about his new state of mind. In the midst of a conversation with McHenry on a routine matter he suddenly lost his temper, accused the War Secretary of being a tool of Hamilton's and roared, "No head of department shall be permitted to oppose me." When McHenry tried to deny that he was controlled by the New Yorker, Adams retorted, "I know it, sir, to be so. . . . You are subservient to him. It was you who biased General Washington's mind . . . and induced him to place Hamilton on the list of major generals before Generals Knox and Pinckney." In mounting wrath the President called Hamilton "an intriguant, the greatest intriguant in the world—a man devoid of every moral principle—a bastard and as much a foreigner as Gallatin." His rage spread to include Wolcott and Pickering. "How could such men," he demanded, "dictate to me on such matters, or dare to recommend a suspension of the mission to France." When he could get a word in, McHenry offered to resign. Adams accepted.

While Adams' manner of firing McHenry was most irregular and undignified, the act itself was long overdue on the basis of both disloyalty and incompetency. Washington, who had appointed the Secretary of War, summed up his capabilities by writing to Hamilton:

YOUR OPINION respecting the unfitness of a certain gentleman for the office he holds accords with mine; and it is to be regretted, surely, at this time, that these opinions are so well founded. I early discovered, after he entered upon the duties of his office, that his talents were unequal to great exertions or deep resources. In truth they were not expected; for the fact is, it was a Hobson's choice.

Adams' dismissal of Pickering was more polite but no less peremptory. Without warning the Secretary of State received a letter saying:

As I PERCEIVE a necessity of introducing a change in the administration of the office of State, I think it proper to make this communication of it to the present Secretary of State, that he might have an opportunity of resigning, if he chooses. I should wish the day on which his resignation is to take place to be named by himself. I wish for an answer to this letter on or before Monday morning.

Pickering refused to resign, saying, "I had indeed, contemplated a continuance in office until the 4th of March next; when, if Mr. Jefferson were elected President (an event which, in your conversation with me last week, you considered as certain) I expected to go out, of course." He added that in the meantime he hoped to save enough money to "enable me to subsist my family a few months longer, and perhaps aid me in transporting them into the woods, where I had land, though all wild and unproductive." He concluded, ". . . after deliberately reflecting on the overture you have been pleased to make to me, I do not feel it to be my duty to resign." To this Adams brusquely replied, "Divers causes and considerations, essential to the administration of the government, in my judgment, requiring a change in the Department of State, you are hereby discharged from any further service as Secretary of State."

The dismissal of the secretaries was the last straw in the confusion of the Federalists. The Hamilton faction took a strong stand against Adams. Wolcott wrote:

HOWEVER DANGEROUS the election of Mr. Jefferson may prove

to the community I do not perceive that any portion of the mischief would be avoided by the election of Mr. Adams. We know the temper of his mind to be revolutionary, violent and vindictive. . . . His passions and selfishness would continually gain strength; his pride and interest would concur in rendering his administration favorable to the views of democrats and Jacobins . . . the example of a selfish attention to personal and family interests would spread like a leprosy in our political system.

The moderates felt that the New Englander had too much popular strength to be discarded. George Cabot did not "see how it will be practicable to discard Mr. Adams as a candidate at this period without confounding us in this quarter, and consequently exposing the whole party to a defeat."

Adams was convinced that if the election was lost the Federalists themselves would be to blame for their opposition to his French policy. He wrote:

THESE FEDERALISTS may yet have their fill at fighting. They may see our envoys without peace; and if they do, what has been lost? Certainly nothing, unless it be the influence of some of the Federalists by their own imprudent and disorganizing opposition and clamor. Much time has been gained. If the election of a Federal President is lost by it, they who performed the exploit will be the greatest losers. They must take the consequences. They will attempt to throw the blame of it upon me, but they will not succeed. They have recorded their own intemperance and indiscretion in characters too legible and too public. For myself, age, infirmities, family misfortunes have conspired with the unreasonable conduct of Jacobins and insolent Federalists, to make me too indifferent to whatever can happen.

Then, in August 1800, Hamilton's rage at Adams overcame his

political judgment and he lashed out personally at the President. He first wrote Adams demanding to know whether he had spoken

. . . on different occasions of the existence of a *British faction* in this country . . . and that you have sometimes named me as one of this description of persons. . . . I must, sir, take it for granted, that you cannot have made such assertions or insinuations without being willing to avow them, and to assign the reasons to a party who may conceive himself injured by them.

When he received no reply Hamilton wrote, in late September, a lengthy circular letter titled, *The Public Conduct and Character of John Adams, Esq., President of the United States.* This was supposed to be privately circulated among Federalist leaders, but it quickly found its way into a gleeful Republican press. Wrote Hamilton:

NOT DENYING to Mr. Adams' patriotism and integrity, and even talents of a certain kind, I should be deficient in candor were I to conceal the conviction that he does not possess the talents adapted to the administration of government, and that there are great and intrinsic defects in his character, which unfit him for the office of Chief Magistrate.

Further, said the New Yorker, Adams' great vanity and personal jealousy made it impossible for him to decide issues on their merits. He has, said Hamilton, "an imagination sublimated and eccentric, propitious neither to the regular display of sound judgment nor to steady perseverance in a systematic plan of conduct." Hamilton also referred to the "ungovernable temper of Mr. Adams. It is a fact that he is often liable to paroxysms of anger which deprive him of self-command, and produce very outrageous behavior to those who approach him."

The letter traced Adams' career from the days of the Revolution, when, according to Hamilton, he advocated a "blind and infatuated policy" of short enlistments, directly contrary to the urgent recommendations of General Washington." He had ignored Congress' instructions on the British peace treaty, had shown his lack of understanding of the French by interpreting the reference to himself as the *"Washington de negociation"* as a compliment instead of the sarcasm which it really was, had demanded an equal vote with Washington in the first election, and much more. During his own administration he had not consulted his ministers, had humiliated the country by sending ministers to France, and, particularly, he had opposed Hamilton as second in command of the army and unjustly fired two of his stooges.

Adams made no retort to Hamilton's slander until after the election, and then his comment was surprisingly mild. To a correspondent who sent him a copy of the letter he wrote:

THIS LAST PAMPHLET I regret more on account of its author than on my own, because I am confident it will do him more harm than me. I am not his enemy, and never was. I have not adored him, like his idolators, and have had great cause to disapprove of some of his politics. He has talents, if he would correct himself, which might be useful. There is more burnish, however, on the outside, than sterling in the substance. . . . I dread neither his menaces of pamphlets nor the execution of them. It would take a large volume to answer him completely. I have not the time, and, if I had, I would not employ it in such a work while I am in public office. The public indignation he has excited is punishment enough.

During the election campaign there were the usual incidental scurrilous charges, some of them amusing. One rumor had it that Adams planned to marry one of his sons to a daughter of George III and thus reunite the two countries under an Adams dynasty. In another story Adams was supposed to have sent General Pinckney to England in a frigate to procure four pretty girls as mistresses, two for each of them. Adams replied to this with a rare flash of humor by charging Pinckney with cheating him because he never got his two.

Late in October 1800, Adams returned to the new Federal Capital on the Potomac. From the "President's House, Washington City" he wrote to Abigail begging her to join him because:

IT IS FIT and proper that you and I should retire together, and not one before the other. Before I end my letter, I pray heaven to bestow the best of blessings on this house, and on all that hereafter inhabit it. May none but honest and wise men ever rule under this roof! I shall not attempt a description of it. You will form the best idea of it from inspection.

When she arrived Abby wrote her impression of Washington, D.C., and the White House to Nabby.

WOODS ARE ALL you see, from Baltimore until you reach *the city,* which is only so in name. Here and there is a small cot, without a glass window, interspersed amongst the forests, through which you travel miles without seeing any human being. In the city there are buildings enough, if they were compact and finished, to accommodate Congress and those attached to it; but as they are, and scattered as they are, I see no great comfort for them. The river, which runs up to Alexandria, is in full view of my window, and I see the vessels as they pass and repass. The house is upon a grand and superb scale, requiring about thirty servants to attend and keep the apartments in proper order and perform the ordinary business of the house and stables. . . . To assist us in this great castle, and render less attendance necessary, bells are wholly wanting, not one single one being hung through the whole house, and promises are all you can obtain. . . . But no comparisons—if they will put me up some bells, and let me have wood enough to keep fires, I design to be pleased. I could content myself almost anywhere three months; but, surrounded with forests, can you believe that wood is not to be had, because people cannot be found to cut and cart it! . . .

You must keep all this to yourself, and, when asked how I like it, say that I write you the situation is beautiful, which is true. The house is made habitable, but there is not a single apartment finished. . . . We have not the least fence, yard, or other convenience, without, and the great unfinished audience-room I make a drying-room of, to hang up the clothes in. The principal stairs are not up, and will not be this winter. . . . If the twelve years in which this place has been considered as the future seat of government had been improved as they would have been if in New England, very many of the present inconveniences would have been removed.

Two weeks before the electoral votes were counted, Adams addressed his last annual message to Congress. He did not seek to summarize his administration or justify it. He started by asking Divine blessing on the new city:

IT WOULD BE UNBECOMING the representatives of this nation to assemble, for the first time, in this solemn temple, without looking up to the Supreme Ruler of the universe, and imploring His blessing.

May this territory be the residence of virtue and happiness! In this city may that piety and virtue, that wisdom and magnanimity, that constancy and self-government, which adorned the great character whose name it bears, be forever held in veneration! Here, and throughout our country, may simple manners, pure morals, and true religion, flourish forever!

He advised the Congress that "The envoys extraordinary and ministers plenipotentiary from the United States to France were received by the first Consul [Napoleon] with the respect due to their character; and three persons, with equal powers, were appointed to treat with them." He told them that "the officers and soldiers of the temporary army have been discharged," but recommended the maintainance of "a navy adapted to defensive war. . . . The present navy of the United States, called suddenly into existence by a great national exigency, has raised us in our own esteem; and by the protection afforded to our commerce has effected to the extent of our expectations the objects for which it was created."

It is somewhat strange that Adams, who was usually so avid for acclaim and quick to demand credit for his accomplishments, did not better defend his administration, for, on the whole, it was a successful one. History is still reluctant to criticize the great Washington, but, in fact, the critical problem with which Adams successfully coped was inherited from his predecessor. The Neutrality Proclamation, the Jay Treaty, and the peremptory recall of Monroe were all acts of Washington's which brought America to the brink of war with France. Adams "kept us out of war"—a war which, at that time, might well have brought internal disunion. During a critical period in the emergence of the young nation he trod a middle path between Jeffersonian and Hamiltonian extremists, either of whom might have brought disaster. He left a united country, a solvent treasury, and a Navy that would soon earn for the United States world respect.

Considering the dissolution of the Federalist party, the result of the election was surprisingly close. Jefferson and Aaron Burr tied with seventy-three votes; a tie which was finally resolved in Jefferson's favor by the House of Representatives. Adams received sixty-five and Pinckney sixty-four. Adams' defeat was largely caused by the magnificent political engineering of Burr, plus liberal campaign funds, which threw New York's twelve electoral votes into the Republican column for the first time. Outside of New York, Adams ran stronger in 1800 than he did in 1796. The defeated President resented Burr's success more than that of Jefferson and wrote of the political newcomer:

SEVENTY-THREE for Mr. Jefferson and seventy-three for Mr. Burr. May the peace and welfare of the country be promoted by this result! But I see not the way yet. In the case of Mr. Jefferson, there is nothing wonderful; but Mr. Burr's good fortune surpasses all ordinary rules, and exceeds that of Bonaparte. All the old patriots, all the splendid talents, the long experience, both of Federalists and anti-Federalists, must be subjected to the humiliation of seeing this dexterous gentleman rise, like a balloon, filled with inflammable air, over their heads. And this is not the worst. What a discouragement to all virtuous exertion, and what an encouragement to party intrigue, and corruption! What course is it we steer, and to what harbor are we bound?

In a letter to Benjamin Stoddert, John attributed his defeat to the delinquencies of the Federalist party, of which he said:

NO PARTY that ever existed knew itself so little, or so vainly overrated its own influence and popularity, as ours. None ever understood so ill the causes of its own power, or so wantonly destroyed them. If we had been blessed with common sense we should not have been overthrown by Philip Freneau, Duane, Callender, Cooper, and Lyon [Republican writers] or their great patron and protector [Jefferson]. A group of foreign liars, encouraged by a few ambitious native gentlemen, have discomfited the education, the talents, the virtues, and the property of the country. The reason is, we have no Americans in America. The Federalists have been no more Americans than the antis.

Of the election Abigail wrote to her son Thomas:

THE CONSEQUENCE TO US, personally, is that we retire from public life. For myself and family, I have few regrets. At my age, and with my bodily infirmities, I shall be happier at Quincy. Neither my habits, nor my education or inclinations have led me to an expensive style of living, so that on that score I have little to mourn over. If I did not rise with dignity, I can at least fall down with ease, which is the more difficult task. I wish your father's circumstances were not so limited and circumscribed, as they must be, because he cannot indulge himself in those improvements upon his farm which his inclination leads him to, and which would serve to amuse him, and contribute to his health. I feel not any resentment against those who are coming into power, and only wish the future administration of the government may be as productive of the peace, happiness, and prosperity of the nation as the two former ones have been. I leave to time the unfolding of a drama. I leave to posterity to reflect upon the times past; and I leave them characters to contemplate. . . .

What must be the thoughts and the reflections of those who, calling themselves Federalists, have placed their country in a situation full of dangers and perils; who have wantonly thrown away the blessings Heaven seemed to have in reserve for them? The defection of New York has been the source. That defection was produced by the intrigues of two men. One of them [Hamilton] sowed the seeds of discontent and division amongst the Federalists, and the other [Burr] seized the lucky moment of mounting into power upon the shoulders of Jefferson. The triumph of the Jacobins is immoderate, and the Federalists deserve it. It is an old and a just proverb, "Never halloo until you are out of the woods." So completely have they gulled one another by their southern promises, which have no more faith, when made to Northern men, than lover's vows.

John had some misgivings about his future. He could not go back to the bar, he said, because "I have forgotten all my law and lost my organs of speech and besides that I have given my books away." And he would find it difficult to

. . . exchange a routine of domestic life, without much exercise, for a life of long journeys and distant voyages, in one or other of which I have been monthly or at least yearly engaged for two and forty years. When such long-continued and violent exercise, such frequent agitations of the body, are succeeded by stillness, it may shake an old frame. Rapid motion ought not to be succeeded by sudden rest. But, at any rate, I have not many years before me, and those few are not very enchanting in prospect.

He had another grief to bear during his last months in Washington.

THE AFFLICTION in my family from the melancholy death of a once-beloved son has been very great, and has required the consolation of religion, as well as philosophy, to enable us to support it. The prospects of that unfortunate youth were very pleasing and promising, but have been cut off, and a wife and two very young children are left with their grandparents to bewail a fate which neither could avert, and to which all ought in patience to submit.

He was referring to the death, in his early thirties, of his son Charles, a debt-ridden drunkard.

It was some satisfaction to the outgoing President to send to the Senate, in January 1802, a proposed "convention" between the United States and France which meant an end to the undeclared war which had lasted through most of his administration. But even in this his victory was limited. Final negotiations on the definitive treaty could not be completed before his term ended and he advised the Senate: "I shall take no further measures relative to this business, and leave the convention with all the documents in the office of State, that my successor may proceed with them according to his wisdom." He had partly to share the credit with Jefferson, but he believed that this was the memorable act of his career. Fifteen years later he would write: "I desire no other inscription over my gravestone than: 'Here lies John Adams, who took upon himself the responsibility of the peace with France in the year 1800.' "

Two of Adams' last acts in office would plague his successor for years. When Chief Justice Ellsworth of the Supreme Court resigned he replaced him with John Marshall, well knowing that Marshall was an implacable foe of Jefferson's. Also, the lame-duck Federalist Congress had passed a bill reforming the national judiciary and creating twenty-three new federal judgeships. Adams spent his last days sending to the Senate the names of stanch Federalists to fill these posts and sat until nine o'clock on his last night in the White House signing their commissions. Of this Jefferson later said: ". . . that one act of Mr. Adams' life, and one only, ever gave me a moment's personal displeasure. I did consider his last appointments to office as personally unkind. . . . It seems but common justice to leave a successor free to act by instruments of his own choice."

Before the city was awake on the morning of March 4 the retiring President called for his coach and left the capital for Quincy, without waiting to turn the reins over to his successor or to participate in his inauguration. For this seeming rudeness he has always been criticized, although there is no assurance that he was invited to the ceremony—which had not yet become traditionalized —and the sensitive Adams would not have pushed himself forward without an invitation.

CHAPTER VIII

THE OLD MAN

❦

I LIVE . . . with my family in a rural, solitary place of retirement, after an uninterrupted toil of six-and-twenty years in the service of the public. Like you, also, "I preserve the love, the doctrines, and the independence of true liberty." It is a lamentable truth that mankind has always been ill treated by government, and a most unfortunate circumstance, which renders the evil totally desperate, is that they are never so ill used as when they take the government into their own hands. . . .

Your country by adoption has grown and prospered since you saw it. You would scarcely know it if you should make it a visit. It would be a great pleasure to the farmer of Stonyfield to take you by the hand in his little *chaumière*.

So wrote Adams, a month after his retirement, in reply to a rare correspondent, the Marquis de La Fayette. To a closer friend, Christopher Gadsen, he confided:

THE ONLY CONSOLATION I shall want will be that of employment. Ennui, when it rains on a man in large drops, is worse than one of our north-east storms; but the labors of agriculture and amusement of letters will shelter me. My greatest grief is that I cannot return to the bar. There I should forget in a moment that I was ever a member of Congress, a foreign minister, or President of the United States. But I cannot speak. . . . I am approaching sixty-five, and what are ten or eleven years after that age? I shall arrive soon after you [in the hereafter], and it is my sincere, devout wish that we may be better acquainted and never separated in our new country.

To Mr. Jefferson's administration I wish prosperity and felicity; but the commencement of it is too strongly infected with the spirit of party to give much encouragement to men who are merely national.

John gave the impression that he had returned to Quincy to await an early grave, but, in the next breath, expressed an opinion on politics. This he would continue to do, in great volume, for twenty-six years. Early in his retirement he was rather reticent and brooded about his rejection by the people whom he had served so long and so faithfully and those whom he considered false friends who had deserted or opposed him. He was proud that he was still honored by addresses from every city and town in Massachusetts and content to be the first citizen of Quincy. He revived his bruised spirit with manual work on his farm.

It was a few years before he started to write again in his old style, tempered somewhat by age. And then his pen poured forth a stream of comment on politics, morals, philosophy, history, religion, and much more to several correspondents, among them Benjamin Rush, friend and physician, Benjamin Waterhouse, physician and scientist, Thomas McKean, William Tudor, David Sewall, fellow farmer F. A. Van der Kemp, and, at long last, Thomas Jefferson. In 1804 he started the autobiography which he never finished. He wrote a series of articles reviewing his administration for the Boston *Patriot*. When South Carolinian John Taylor wrote a book which criticized *Defense,* Adams defended his old treatise with thirty-two letters to Taylor; and when Mercy Otis

Warren wrote a *History of the Revolution* which said that his revolutionary principles had become corrupted in England, he retorted, "Corruption is a charge that I cannot and will not bear—I challenge the whole human race, and angels and devils too, to produce an instance of it from my cradle to this hour!" He then continued to blast her with a series of letters in which he corrected all of what he considered the mistakes in her volume.

The Van der Kemp correspondence was casual, intermittent, sometimes amusing, and widely ranging. A typical early letter answered the Dutchman's query on natural science:

BUFFON, I presume, from all I have heard or read of him, believed in nothing but matter, which he thought was eternal and self-existent. The universe had been from eternity as it is now, with all its good and evil, intelligence and accident, beauty and deformity, harmony and dissonance, order and confusion, virtue and vice, wisdom and folly, equity and inequity, truth and lies; that planets and suns, systems and systems of systems, are born and die, like animals and vegetables, and that this process will go on to all eternity. . . . All this, I think, is neither more nor less than the creed of Epicurus set to music by Lucretius.

"The movements of nature" mean the movements of matter; but can matter move itself? "The renovating power of matter," what does this mean? Can matter, if annihilated, recreate itself? Matter, if at rest, can it set itself in motion? A German ambassador once told me, he could not bear St. Paul, he was so severe against fornication. On the same principle these philosophers cannot bear a God, because he is just.

You could not apply more unfortunately than to me for any knowledge of natural history. A little law, a little ethics, and a little history constitute all the circle of my knowledge, and I am too old to acquire anything new. . . .

In the wisdom, power, and goodness of our Maker is all the security we have against roasting in volcanoes and writhing with the tortures of gout, stone, colic, and cancers . . . to all eternity.

And in another letter to Van der Kemp he skipped blithely from current international relations to the importance of Hebraic religious culture in this manner:

WE MAY BE REDUCED to hard necessities. The two most powerful, active and enterprising nations that ever existed are now contending with us. The two nations to whom mankind are under more obligation for the progress of science and civilization than to any others, except the Hebrews. . . . I excepted the Hebrews for, in spite of Bolingbroke and Voltaire, I will insist that the Hebrews have done more to civilize men than any other nation. If I were an atheist, and believed in blind eternal fate, I should still believe that fate had ordained the Jews to be the most essential instrument for civilizing nations. If I were an atheist of the other sect, who believe or pretend to believe that all is ordered by chance, I should believe that chance had ordered the Jews to preserve and propagate to all mankind the doctrine of a supreme, intelligent, wise, almighty Sovereign of the universe, which I believe to be the great essential principle of all morality, and consequently of all civilization. I cannot say that I love the Jews very much neither, nor the French, nor the English, nor the Romans, nor the Greeks. We must love all nations as well as we can, but it is very hard to love most of them.

Evidences of his age creep into his letters.

HAPPY ARE YOU in your various learning, and the enjoyment of your books; I can read little, on account of my eyes. My wife and children and grandchildren are very good to read to me, but they cannot always read when I want, nor always such books as I should choose.

But this reminds him of Abigail's literary ability and he adds:

IT IS REMARKABLE that you never heard the literary character of my consort. There have been few ladies in the world of a more correct or elegant taste. A collection of her letters, for the forty-five years that we have been married, would be worth ten times more than Madame de Sévengné's, though not so perfectly measured in syllables and letters, and would, or at least ought to, put to the blush Lady Mary Wortley Montagu and all her admirers. So much you will say, for conjugal complaisance. So much, I say, for simple justice to her merit.

The first correspondent to bring the old man out of his political shell was a remote cousin, William Cunningham, who tried to induce Adams to make specific accusations against Jefferson. At first, the best that he got from Adams was the comment: "I wish him no ill. I envy him not. I shudder at the calamities which I fear his conduct is preparing for his country; from a mean thirst of popularity, an inordinate ambition, and a want of sincerity." The democracy which Jefferson stood for he would willingly condemn. Democracy, said Adams:

. . . is a young rake who thinks himself handsome and well made, and who has little faith in virtue—When the people once admit his courtship, and permit him the least familiarity, they soon find themselves in the condition of the poor girl who told her own story in this affecting style.

> *Le Lendemain il osa davantage:*
> *Il me promit Le Foi de marriage.*
> *Le Lendemain . . . il fut entreprenant.*
> *Le Lendemain il me fit un enfant.*

The next day he grew a little bolder—but promised me marriage. The next day—he began to be enterprising; But the next day—O Sir! the next day he got me with child. Democracy is Lovelace, and the people are Clarissa. The artful villain will pursue the innocent lovely girl to her ruin and her death.

In a later letter, Adams expressed his opinion of some of the measures of Jefferson's administration. Cunningham had reported to him some Federalist claim that he supported the administration, to which he replied:

THE FEDERALISTS, I think, might suffer my old lamp to go out, without administering their nauseous oil merely to excite a momentary flash before it expires.

Do you think the Federalists believe themselves when they say that I am on the side of the executive, through the whole of his administration? Do they believe that I approve of the repeal of the judiciary law, which I recommended to Congress? Which I believe to be one of the best of laws? . . . Do they believe that I approve of the neglect and mismanagement of the navy? The omission to build more ships? The neglect to fortify our most important cities and exposed places? Do they believe that I approve of the repeal of the taxes, which would have enabled us not only to make the necessary preparations against the formidable dangers that surrounded us, but gradually to diminish the national debt? Do they believe that I approve of the *removals* of so many of the *best men,* or the appointments of so many of *the worst?* Do they believe that I approve of twenty other things, too many to be enumerated? Oh no! They believe no such things. But they are conscious they have injured me and mine, and are only forging false and awkward excuses for it.

From this he proceeded to blast at his old nemesis, political parties, in their probable effect on the election of 1808.

THE FEDERALISTS, by their intolerance, have gone far toward

justifying, or at least excusing, Jefferson for his; and for the future it seems to be established as a principle that our government is forever to be not a national, but a party government. How long such a maxim can be maintained consistently with any civil government at all, time will determine. While it lasts, all we can hope is that in the game at leap frog, once in eight or twelve years, the party of the OUTS will leap over the head and shoulders of the INS: for, I own to you, I have so little confidence in the wisdom, prudence or virtue of either party, that I should be nearly as willing that one should be absolute and unchecked as the other.

In various letters to Cunningham, Adams castigated Republicans and Federalists alike who had opposed him in years past. Typical was his contemptous description of Pickering:

HE IS, for anything I know, a good son, husband, father, grandfather, brother, uncle, and cousin; but he is a man in a mask, sometimes of silk, sometimes of iron, and sometimes of brass. And he changes them very suddenly and with some dexterity.

After writing hundreds—or thousands—of pages justifying every act of his public career and condemning all who opposed him, Adams naïvely told Cunningham: "As against all the vile slanders which have been published, I have never said or written a word in my own vindication, I am not about to begin." Then he disclosed what he claimed as the objective of the end of life in a description of his proposed tomb.

IF MY ACTIONS have not been sufficient to support my fame, let it perish. No higher ambition remains with me than to build a tomb upon the summit of the hill before my door, covered with a six-foot cube of Quincy granite, with an inscription like this,

Siste Viator!
With much delight these pleasing hills you view.
Where Adams from an envious world withdrew,
Where sick of glory, faction, power and pride,
Sure judge how empty all, who all had tried,
Beneath his shades the weary chief repos'd,
And life's great scene in quiet virtue clos'd.

As Jefferson's administration ended, Adams referred to the decline of his precious navy under his successor's policy of building useless little gunboats instead of tall frigates.

WE MAY RAISE the embargo, repeal the nonintercourse, authorize our merchants to arm their vessels, give them special letters of marque to defend themselves against all unlawful aggressors, and take and burn or destroy all vessels, or make prize of them as enemies that shall attack them. In the meantime apply all our resources to build frigates, some in every principal seaport. These frigates ought not to be assembled in any one port to become an object of a hostile expedition to destroy them. They should be separated and scattered as much as possible from New Orleans to Passamquoddy. I never was fond of the plan of building line of battleships. Our policy is not to fight squadrons at sea, but to have fast-sailing frigates to scour the seas and make impression on the enemy's commerce; and in this way we can do great things.

This, written in 1808, was a fine forcast of what the few frigates would do four years later.

In 1809 Skelton Jones sent him twenty queries to elicit information to be used in a biographical article, the answers to some of which are interesting. In reply to a question as to the "part you acted during the time in which you were in public station." Adams succinctly replied:

AN INFLEXIBLE COURSE of studies and labors to promote, preserve, and secure that independence of my country, which I so early saw to be inevitable, against all parties, factions, and nations that have shown themselves unfriendly to it.

To the next question, "When and why did you retire?" The answer was:

THE 4TH OF MARCH, 1801. The causes of my retirement are to be found in the writings of Freneau, Markoe, Ned Church, Andrew Brown, Paine, Callender, Hamilton, Cobbet, and John Ward Fenno and many others. . . . Without a complete collection of all these libels, no faithful history of the last twenty years can ever be written, nor any adequate account given of the causes of my retirement from public life.

Five other answers read:

MY LIFE for the last eight years has been spent in the bosom of my family, surrounded by my children and grandchildren; on my farm, in my garden and library. But in all this there is nothing interesting to the public.

Five feet, seven or nine inches, I really know not which.

I have one head, four limbs, and five senses, like any other man, and nothing peculiar in any of them.

I have been married forty-four years. . . .

My temper in general has been tranquil, except when any instance of extraordinary madness, deceit, hypocrisy, ingratitude, treachery, or perfidy has suddenly struck me. Then I have always been irascible enough, and in three or four instances, very extraordinary ones, too much so. The storm, however, never lasted for half an hour, and anger never rested in the bosom.

For an example of erudite name-dropping there is probably none better than an excerpt from a letter to John Taylor, who had criticized Adams' theory of a natural aristocracy as expressed in *Defense*. In support of his theory, Adams quoted some thirty examples and authorities in two paragraphs:

WOULD ANY MAN SAY, would Helvètius say, that all men are born equal in strength? Was Hercules no stronger than his neighbors? How many nations, for how many ages, have been governed by his strength and by the reputation and renown of it by his posterity? If you have lately read Hume, Robertson, or the Scottish chiefs, let me ask you if Sir William Wallace was no more than equal in strength to the average of Scotchmen, and whether Wallace could have done what he did without that extraordinary strength? Will Helvètius or Rousseau say that all men and women are born equal in beauty? Will any philosopher say that beauty has no influence in human society? If he does, let him read the histories of Eve, Judith, Helen, the fair Gabrielle, Diana of Poitiers, Pompadour, du Barry, Susanna, Abigail, Lady Hamilton, Mrs. Clark, and a million others. Are not despots, monarchs, aristocrats, and democrats equally liable to be seduced by beauty to confer favors and influence suffrages?

Socrates calls beauty a short-lived tyranny; Plato, the privilege of nature; Theophrastus, a mute eloquence; Diogenes, the best letter of recommendation; Carneades, a queen without soldiers; Theocritus, a serpent covered with flowers; Bion, a good that does not belong to the possessor, because it is impossible to give ourselves beauty or to preserve it. Madame du Barry expressed the philosophy of Carneades in more laconic language when she said, "La véritable royauté, c'est la beauté"—the genuine royalty is beauty. And she might have said with equal truth that it is genuine aristocracy, for it has as much influence in one form of government as in any other and produces aristocracy in the deepest democracy that ever was known or imagined, as infallibly as in any other form of government. What shall we say to all these philosophers, male and female? Is not beauty a privilege granted by nature, according to Plato and to truth, often more influential in society, and even upon laws and government, than stars, garters, crosses, eagles, golden fleeces, or any hereditary titles or other distinctions? The grave elders were not proof against the charms of Susanna. The Grecian sages wondered not at the Trojan war when they saw Helen. Holofernes' guards, when they saw Judith, said, "One such woman let go would deceive the whole earth."

His most constant correspondent was kindly Benjamin Rush, friend of all men. When Rush queried him about a recently published life of Thomas Paine, all Adams' rancor against that writer returned, and from this he slipped into an opinion on Christianity.

I HAVE NOT SEEN, but am impatient to see, Mr. Cheetham's life of Mr. Paine. His political writings, I am singular enough to believe, have done more harm than his irreligious ones. He understood neither government nor religion. From a malignant heart he wrote virulent declamations, which the enthusiastic fury of the times intimidated all men, even Mr. Burke, from answering as he ought. His deism, as it appears to me, has promoted rather than retarded the cause of revolution in America, and indeed in Europe. His Billingsgate, stolen from Blount's Oracles of Reason, from Bolingbroke, Voltaire, Berenger, etc., will never discredit Christianity, which will hold its ground in some degree as long as human nature shall have anything moral or intellectual left in it. The Christian religion, as I understand it, is the brightness of the glory and the express portrait of the character of the eternal, self-existent, independent, benevolent, all powerful and all merciful Creator, Preserver, and Father of the universe; the first good, first perfect, and first fair. It will last as long as the world. Neither savage nor civilized man, without a revelation, could ever have discovered or invented it. Ask me not, then, whether I

am a Catholic or Protestant, Calvinist or Arminian. As far as
they are Christians, I wish to be a fellow disciple with them all.

In 1809 Rush sought to induce Adams to write his autobigra-
phy, to which John replied, "I have made several attempts, but
it is so dull an employment that I cannot endure it. I look so
much like a small boy in my own eyes, that, with all my vanity,
I cannot endure the sight of the picture." However, he continued,
"I am determined to vindicate myself in some points while I
live." There followed nine points which he presented in a manner
typical of much of his later writing. Everything which he had
ever done was, in his mind, right; nobody appreciated this and
he was consequently condemned and reviled; he had suffered this
with heroic stoicism, conscious of the virtue of his acts. His points
were:

1. When I went home to my family in May 1770, from the
town meeting in Boston, which was the first I had ever attended, and where I had been chosen in my absence, without
any solicitation, one of their representatives, I said to my wife,
"I have accepted a seat in the House of Representatives, and
thereby have consented to my own ruin, to your ruin, and the
ruin of our children. I give you this warning, that you may
prepare your mind for your fate." She burst into tears, but
instantly cried out in a transport of magnanimity, "Well, I am
willing in this cause to run all risks with you, and be ruined
with you, if you are ruined." These were times, my friend, in
Boston, which tried women's souls as well as men's.
2. I saw the awful prospect before me and my country in
all its horrors, and, notwithstanding all my vanity, was conscious of a thousand defects in my own character as well as
health, which made me despair of going through and weather-
ing the storms in which I must be tossed.
3. In the same year, 1770, my sense of equity and humanity
impelled me, against a torrent of unpopularity and the inclina-

tion of all my friends, to engage in defense of Captain Preston and the soldiers. My successful exertions in that cause, though the result was perfectly conformable to law and justice, brought upon me a load of indignation and unpopularity, which I knew would never be forgotten, nor entirely forgiven. . . .

4. You can testify for me that in 1774 my conduct in Congress drew upon me the jealousy and aversion, not only of the Tories in Congress, who were neither few nor feeble, but of the whole body of Quakers and proprietary gentlemen in Pennsylvania. I have seen and felt the consequences of these prejudices to this day.

5. I call you to witness that I was the first member of Congress who ventured to come out in public, as I did in January 1776, in my "Thoughts on Government" . . . in favor of a government, in three branches, with an independent judiciary. This pamphlet, you know, was very unpopular. . . . Franklin leaned against it. . . . Paine's wrath was excited because my plan of government was essentially different from the silly projects that he had published in his "Common Sense." By this means I became suspected and unpopular with the leading demagogues and the whole constitutional party in Pennsylvania.

6. Upon my return from France in 1779, I found myself elected by my native town of Braintree a member of the Convention for forming a Constitution for the state of Massachusetts. . . . Here I found such a chaos of absurd sentiments concerning government, that I was obliged daily . . . to propose plans and advocate doctrines, which were extremely unpopular with the greatest number. . . . They made me, however, draw up the Constitution, and it was finally adopted, with some amendments very much for the worse. The bold, decided, and determined part I took in this assembly in favor of a good government, acquired me the reputation of a man of high principles and strong notions in government, scarcely compatible with republicanism. A foundation was here laid of

much jealousy and unpopularity among the democratical people in this state.

7. In Holland, I had driven the English party and the stockholder's party before me, like clouds before the wind, and had brought that power to unite cordially with America, France, and Spain against England. If I had not before alienated the whole English nation from me, this would have been enough to produce an eternal jealousy of me. . . .

8. In all my negotiations in France and Holland in 1778, 1779, 1780, 1781, 1782, 1783, and 1784, I had so uniformly resisted all the arts and intrigues of the Count de Vergennes and M. de Sartine and all their satellites, and that with such perfect success, that I well knew, although they treated me with great external respect, yet in their hearts they had conceived an incredible jealousy and aversion to me. I well knew, therefore, that French influence in America would do all in its power to trip me up.

9. Dr. Franklin's behavior had been so excessively complaisant to the French ministry . . . that I had been frequently obliged to differ from him, and sometimes to withstand him to his face; so that I knew he had conceived an irreconcilable hatred of me, and that he had propagated and would continue to propagate prejudices, if nothing worse, against me in America from one end of it to the other.

This feeling that he was the instrument of Providence for his country's salvation is again expressed in the conclusion of the summary of his administration which he wrote for the Boston *Patriot*.

I HAVE NOW finished all I had to say on the negotiations and peace with France in 1800.

In the meantime, when I look back on the opposition and embarrassments I had to overcome, from the faction of British subjects, from that large body of Americans who revere the

English and abhor the French, from some of the heads of department, from so many gentlemen in the Senate, and so many more in the House of Representatives, and from the insidious and dark intrigues as well as open remonstrances of Mr. Hamilton, I am astonished at the event.

Rush next urged him to write a political testament for posterity, "in which shall be inculcated all those great national, social, domestic, and religious virtues, which alone can make a people free, great, and happy." Adams said he would do so if "I could have any rational assurance of doing any real good to my fellow citizens." But, he added, "there are difficulties and embarrassments in the way, which to me, at present, appear insuperable." He went on to point out that nobody would believe that his motives were pure, even after he was dead.

IF THEY SHOULD NOT suspect me of sinning in the grave, they will charge me with selfishness and hypocrisy before my death, in preparing an address to move the passions of the people, and excite them to promote my children, and perhaps to make my son a king. Washington and Franklin could never do anything but what was imputed to pure, disinterested patriotism; I never could do anything but what was ascribed to sinister motives.

In such a document he might say that:

. . . religion and virtue are the only foundations . . . of social felicity under all governments and in all the combinations of human society. But if I should inculcate this doctrine in my will, I should be charged with hypocrisy and a desire to conciliate the good will of the clergy. [Or:] If I should inculcate "fidelity to the marriage bed," it would be said that it proceeded from resentment to General Hamilton, and a malicious desire to hold up to posterity his libertinism. Others would say

that it is only a vainglorious ostentation of my own conti-
nence. . . .

If I should recommend the sanctification of the sabbath . . .
I should be charged with vain ostentation again, and a selfish
desire to revive the remembrance of my own punctuality in
this respect. . . .

Fifty-three years ago I was fired with a zeal, amounting to
enthusiasm, against ardent spirits, the multiplication of taverns, retailers, and dram-shops, and tippling houses. . . . I only
acquired the reputation of a hypocrite and an ambitious dema-
gogue by it. . . .

If I should then in my will, my dying legacy, my post-
humous exhortation, call it what you will, recommend heavy,
prohibitory taxes upon spirituous liquors, which I believe to
be the only remedy against their deleterious qualities in society, every one of your brother Republicans and nine tenths
of the Federalists would say that I was a canting Puritan, a
profound hypocrite, setting up standards of morality, frugality,
economy, temperance, simplicity, and sobriety, that I knew the
age was incapable of.

And if he should write such a thing, people would think that
many of his ideas were ridiculous.

MY OPINION is that a circulating medium of gold and silver
only ought to be introduced and established; that a national
bank of deposit only, with a branch in each state, should be
allowed; that every bank in the Union ought to be annihilated,
and every bank of discount prohibited to all eternity. Not one
farthing of profit should ever be allowed on any money deposited in the bank. [No, he said:] I am not qualified to write
such an address. . . . If I could persuade my friend Rush, or
my friend Jay, my friend Trumbull, or my friend Humphreys,
or perhaps my friend Jefferson to write such a thing for me, I
know not why I might not transcribe it, as Washington did so

often. Borrowed eloquence, if it contains as good stuff, is as good as own eloquence.

For twelve years after Adams left the White House, he and Jefferson were completely estranged. In 1804 Abigail had written the Virginian to offer condolences on the death of his daughter Maria, whom she had known and loved as a child in London. It was in answer to this letter that Jefferson mentioned that the only act of Adams' which ever hurt him was the appointment of the judges. This led to three long letters from Abby in which she castigated Jefferson for what she considered two unforgivable instances of personal enmity. He had pardoned the "venomous" Callender, jailed under the Sedition Act and one of John's bitterest critics, and he had removed John Quincy from a political job in Boston. She ended her last letter by writing:

I WILL NOT any further intrude upon your time; but close this correspondence by my wishes that you may be directed to that path which may terminate in the prosperity and happiness of the people over whom you are placed, by administering the government with justice and impartiality.

On the bottom of a copy of this letter was a note in John's hand: "The whole of this correspondence was begun and conducted without my knowledge or suspicion. Last evening and this morning at the desire of Mrs. Adams, I read the whole. I have no remarks to make upon it, at this time and in this place."

In 1809 the basis for a reconciliation was laid when Jefferson's disciple and successor, James Madison, appointed John Quincy as the first minister to Russia. Then, during 1811, Benjamin Rush quietly started to press both old men to resume their ancient friendship. His efforts were brought to fruition when Madison's secretary, after visiting Adams, told Jefferson that he had said, "I always loved Jefferson and still love him." This caused Jefferson to write to Rush:

THIS IS ENOUGH for me. I only needed this knowledge to revive toward him all the affections of the most cordial moment of our lives. . . . I knew him to be always an honest man, often a great one, but sometimes incorrect and precipitate in his judgments.

I wish therefore, but for an opposite occasion to express to Mr. Adams my unchanged affections for him. There is an awkwardness which hangs over the resuming a correspondence so long discontinued, unless something could arise which should call for a letter.

Adams was almost, but not quite as coy as Jefferson. Rush wrote him of Jefferson's letter and added: ". . . fellow laborers in erecting the great fabric of American independence . . . embrace—embrace each other." To which John replied:

I PERCEIVE PLAINLY enough, Rush, that you have been teasing Jefferson to write to me, as you did me some time ago to write to him. You gravely advise me "to receive the olive branch," as if there had been war; but there has never been any hostility on my part, nor that I know, on his. When there has been no war, there can be no room for negotiations of peace. Mr. Jefferson speaks of my political opinions; but I know of no difference between him and myself relative to the Constitution, or to forms of government in general.

After stating that there were "no differences" he then proceeded to enumerate some of them: the repeal of the judiciary law, the neglect of the navy, Jefferson's disapproval of the undeclared war with France, "which I believed . . . to be a holy war. . . . He disapproved of taxes, and perhaps the whole scheme of my administration. . . . We differed in opinion about the French Revolution." Adams then concluded, in a jocular vein:

IN POINT OF REPUBLICANISM, all the difference I ever knew

or could discover between you and me, or between Jefferson and me, consisted:

1. In the difference between speeches and messages. I was a monarchist because I thought a speech more manly, more respectful to Congress and the nation. Jefferson and Rush preferred messages.

2. I held levees once a week, that all my time might not be wasted by idle visits. Jefferson's whole eight years was a levee.

3. I dined a large company once or twice a week. Jefferson dined a dozen every day.

4. Jefferson and Rush were for liberty and straight hair. I thought curled hair was as Republican as straight. . . .

But why do you make so much ado about nothing? Of what use can it be for Jefferson and me to exchange letters? I have nothing to say to him but to wish him an easy journey to heaven, when he goes, which I wish may be delayed as long as life shall be agreeable to him. And he can have nothing to say to me but to bid me make haste and be ready. Time and chance, however, or possibly design, may produce ere long a letter between us.

The above was written on Christmas Day, 1811, and seemed to politely slam the door on a reconciliation. But on New Year's Day, John picked up his pen and started one of the most memorable correspondences in American history with a little note that started:

As you are a friend to American manufacturers under proper restrictions, especially manufacturers of a domestic kind, I take the liberty of sending you by the post a packet containing two pieces of homespun lately produced in this quarter by one who was honored in his youth with some of your attention and much of your kindness.

Jefferson could not know that the two pieces of homespun

were two volumes of John Quincy's *Lecture on Rhetoric and Oratory.* He started his reply, before he had received the books, with a serious comparison of New England and Virginia weaving. Then he continued:

A LETTER FROM YOU calls up recollections very dear to my mind. It carries me back to the times when, beset with difficulties and dangers, we were fellow laborers in the same cause, struggling for what is most valuable to man, his right of self-government. Laboring always at the same oar . . . we knew not how we rode through the storm with heart and hand and made a happy port. Still we did not expect to be without rubs and difficulties; and we have had them. . . . In your day, French depredations; in mine, English. . . . And so we have gone on, and so we shall go on, puzzled and prospering beyond example in the history of men.

After saying that he was now more interested in "Tacitus and Thucydides, . . . Newton and Euclid," than in politics, he concluded:

NO CIRCUMSTANCES have lessened the interest I feel in these particulars respecting yourself; none have suspended for one moment my sincere esteem for you, and I now salute you with unchanged affection and respect.

For fourteen years the old friends would continue to correspond, with Adams writing about three letters to Jefferson's one. There was hardly a conceivable topic on which they did not exchange ideas; they wrote about books and philosophers, people they had known, events they had shared, Western learning, history, religion, man, society, eternal truths. Adams was more prone than Jefferson to discuss politics, particularly political differences. Jefferson refused to rise to his baits; all this was long behind them. As one of many instances of this, Jefferson had referred to the alien laws, in a letter to Dr. Priestley, as "that libel on legislation." Adams could not let that pass, particularly since, during the War of 1812, the Republican administration had imposed strict regulations on English aliens. Adams wrote:

As YOUR NAME is subscribed to that law, as Vice-President, and mine as President, I know not why you are not as responsible for it as I am. Neither of us was concerned in the formation of it. We were then at war with France. French spies then swarmed in our cities and our country; some of them were intolerably impudent, turbulent, and seditious. To check these was the design of this law. Was there ever a government which had not authority to defend itself against spies in its own bosom—spies of an enemy at war? This law was never executed by me in any instance.

But what is the conduct of our government now? Aliens are ordered to report their names and obtain certificates once a month; and an industrious Scotchman, at this moment industriously laboring in my garden, is obliged to walk once a month to Boston, eight miles at least, to renew his certificate from the marshal. And a fat organist is ordered into the country, etc. All this is right. Every government has, by the law of nations a right to make prisoners of war of every subject of an enemy. But a war with England differs not from a war with France. The law of nations is the same in both.

On most things that were fundamentally important they agreed. In religion, for instance, by two different routes, they had both arrived at an approximation of present-day Unitarianism. In one letter Adams wrote:

THE HUMAN UNDERSTANDING is a revelation from its Maker, which can never be disputed or doubted. There can be no scepticism, Pyrrhonism, or incredulity or infidelity here. No prophecies, no miracles are necessary to prove this celestial communication. This revelation has made it certain that two and one make three, and that one is not three nor can three be one. We can never be so certain of any prophecy, or the fulfillment of any prophecy, or of any miracle, or the design of any miracle, as we are from the revelation of nature, that is, nature's God, that two and two are equal to four. Miracles or prophecies might frighten us out of our wits, might scare us to death, might induce us to lie, to say that we believe that two and two make five, but we should not believe it; we should know the contrary.

Had you and I been forty days with Moses on Mount Sinai, and admitted to behold the divine Shechinah, and there told that one was three and three one, we might not have had courage to deny it, but we could not have believed it. The thunders and lightnings and earthquakes, and the transcendent splendors and glories, might have overwhelmed us with terror and amazement, but we could not have believed the doctrine. We should be more likely to say in our hearts—whatever we might say with our lips—This is chance. There is no God, no truth. This is all delusion, fiction, and a lie, or it is all chance. But what is chance? It is motion; it is action; it is event; it is phenomenon without cause. Chance is no cause at all; it is nothing, and nothing has produced all this pomp and splendor, and nothing may produce our eternal damnation in the flames of hell-fire and brimstone, for what we know, as well as this tremendous exhibition of terror and falsehoods.

God has infinite wisdom, goodness, and power; he created the universe; his duration is eternal, *a parte ante* and *a parte post*. His presence is as extensive as space. What is space? An infinite spherical *vacuum*. He created this speck of dirt and the human species for his glory, and with the deliberate design of making nine tenths of our species miserable forever for His glory. This is the doctrine of Christian theologians, in general, ten to one. Now, my friend, can prophecies or miracles convince you or me that infinite benevolence, wisdom, and power created—and preserves for a time—innumerable millions [solely] to make them miserable forever for His own glory? Wretch! What is His glory? Is He ambitious? Does He want promotion? Is He vain, tickled with adulation, exulting and triumphing in His power and the sweetness of His vengeance? Pardon me, my Maker, for these awful questions. My answer to them is always ready. I believe no such things. My adoration of the Author of the Universe is too profound and too sincere. The love of God and his creation—delight, joy, triumph, exultation in my own existence—though but an atom, a *molécule organique* in the universe—are my religion.

Howl, snarl, bite, ye Calvinistic, ye Athanasian divines, if you will; ye will say I am no Christian; I say ye are no Christians, and there the account is balanced. Yet I believe all the honest men among you are Christians, in my sense of the word.

On some things they never saw eye to eye: political parties, for instance. On this the more tolerant Jefferson wrote:

MEN HAVE DIFFERED in opinion, and been divided into parties by these opinions, from the first origin of societies, and in all governments where they have been permitted freely to think and to speak. The same political parties which now agitate the U. S. have existed thro' all time. Whether the power of the people, or that of the [aristocrats] should prevail, were questions which kept the states of Greece and Rome in eternal convulsions; as they now schismatize every people whose minds and mouths are not shut up by the gag of a despot. And in fact the terms of Whig and Tory belong to natural, as well as to civil history. They denote the temper and constitution of mind of different individuals.

To which Adams replied:

THE REAL TERRORS of both parties have always been, and now

are, the fear that they shall lose the elections and consequently the loaves and fishes; and that their antagonists will obtain them. Both parties have excited artificial terrors and if I were summoned as a witness to say upon oath which party had excited, Machiavellialy, the most terror, and which had really felt the most, I could not give a more sincere answer than, in the vulgar style, "Put them in a bag and shake them, and then see which comes out first."

Adams virtually wore Jefferson down with his defense of his theory of aristocracy. Jefferson started by saying:

I AGREE WITH YOU that there is a natural aristocracy among men. The grounds of this are virtue and talents. Formerly bodily powers gave place among the aristoi. But since the invention of gunpowder has armed the weak as well as the strong with missile death, bodily strength, like beauty, good humor, politeness, and other accomplishments, has become but an auxiliary ground of distinction. There is also an artificial aristocracy founded on wealth and birth; without either virtue or talents; for with these it would belong to the first class. . . . The artificial aristocracy is a michievous ingredient in government, and provision should be made to prevent its ascendency.

Adams, the better lawyer of the two, rode roughly over this by replying:

WE ARE NOW explicitly agreed in one important point, viz., that "there is a natural aristocracy among men; the grounds of which are virtue and talents." . . . But tho' we have agreed in one point, in words, it is not yet certain that we are perfectly agreed in sense. Fashion has introduced an indeterminate use of the word "talents." Education, wealth, strength, beauty, stature, birth, marriage, graceful attitudes and motions, gait, air, complexion, physiognomy, are talents, as well as genius and science and learning. Any one of these talents that in fact commands or influences two votes in society, gives to the man who possesses it the character of an aristocrat in my sense of the word.

Pick up the first 100 men you meet, and make a republic. Every man will have an equal vote. But when deliberations and discussions are opened it will be found that 25, by their talents, virtues being equal, will be able to carry 50 votes. Every one of these 25 is an aristocrat, in my sense of the word, whether he obtains his one vote in addition to his own by his birth, fortune, figure, eloquence, science, learning, craft, cunning, or even his character for good fellowship and a bon vivant.

I will select a single example, for female aristocrats are nearly as formidable as males. A daughter of a greengrocer walks the streets of London daily with a basket of cabbage sprouts, dandelions, and spinach, on her head. She is observed by the painters to have a beautiful face, an elegant figure, a graceful step, and a debonair. They hire her to sit. She complies, and is painted by forty artists in a circle around her. The scientific Dr. William Hamilton outbids the painters, sends her to school for a genteel education, and marries her. This lady not only causes the triumphs of the Nile, Copenhagen, and Trafalgar, but separated Naples from France, and finally banishes the king and queen from Sicily. Such is the aristocracy of the natural talent of beauty.

Although his eyesight and speech were impaired and he shook with palsy, Adams was by no means an invalid as he approached his eighties in the early teen years of the nineteenth century. He still had some interests besides his books, his correspondence, and his farm. He made frequent trips to Boston as President of the American Academy of Arts and Sciences, the Massachusetts Society for promoting Agriculture, and a member of the Board of Visitors for Harvard.

Even though President James Madison was a Republican brought up under Jefferson's wing, Adams approved of him, and followed the War of 1812 with keen interest. He was not discouraged by the ineptness of the American campaigns on land. "We do not make more mistakes now than we did in 1774, 5,6,7,8,9,80, 81,82,83," he wrote Rush. "It was patched and piebald policy then, as it is now, ever was, and ever will me, world without end." The few successes of the American frigates delighted him, but they would have been much greater, he wrote Rush, if the Congresses of the Jefferson administrations, "who, by mud-docking my navy have disarmed themselves at sea." He was irate at the Essex Junto of New England Federalists who refused to support the war effort and talked of secession. And he was proud and pleased when John Quincy was named as a peace commissioner to negotiate the Treaty of Ghent.

John's feelings on the war and the conduct of his native state are reflected in a letter from Abigail to Mercy Warren. Incidentally, the fact that Abby and Mercy were still on friendly terms is an indication of how the Adamses mellowed somewhat in old age. Mrs. Warren had already written her *History of the Revolution* in which she criticized John; in former years this would have put her on the Adamses' black list. Now Abby wrote, of the War of 1812:

WE HAVE OUR FIRESIDES, our comfortable habitations, our cities, our churches and our country to defend, our rights, privileges and independence to preserve. And for these are we not justly contending? Thus it appears to me; yet I hear from our pulpits and read from our presses that it is an unjust, a wicked, a ruinous and unnecessary war. If I give an opinion with respect to the conduct of our native state, I cannot do it with approbation. She has had much to complain of as it respected a refusal of naval protection, yet that cannot justify her in paralyzing the arm of government when raised for her defense and that of the nation. A house divided against itself—and upon that foundation do our enemies build their hopes of subduing us. May it prove a sandy one to them.

The year 1812 was a "good" year for the Adams. A long, otherwise inconsequential, letter from Abigail to Nabby's daughter Caroline gives an inkling of contented, hard-working domesticity:

YOUR NEAT, pretty letter, looking small but containing much, reached me this day. I have a good mind to give you the journal of the day.

Six o'clock. Rose, and, in imitation of his Britannic Majesty, kindled my own fire. Went to the stairs, as usual, to summon George and Charles. Returned to my chamber, dressed myself. No one stirred. Called a second time, with voice a little raised.

Seven o'clock. Blockheads not out of bed. Girls in motion. Mean, when I hire another man-servant, that he shall come for *one call.*

Eight o'clock. Fires made, breakfast prepared . . . Mrs. A—— at the tea board. Forgot the sausages. Susan's recollection brought them upon the table.

Enter ANN. "Ma'am, the man is come with coals."

"Go, call George to assist him." *Exit* ANN.

Enter CHARLES. "Mr. B—— is come with cheese, turnips, etc. Where are they to be put?" "I will attend to him myself." *Exit* CHARLES.

Just seated at the table again.

Enter GEORGE with, "Ma'am, here is a man with a drove of pigs." A consultation is held upon this important subject, the result of which is the purchase of two spotted swine.

Nine o'clock. *Enter* NATHANIEL, from upper house, with a message for sundries, and black Thomas's daughter for sundries. Attended to all these concerns. A little out of sorts that I could not finish my breakfast. Note: never to be incommoded with trifles.

Enter GEORGE ADAMS, from the post office—a large packet from Russia, and from the valley also. Avaunt, all cares —I put all aside—and thus I find good news from a far country—children, grandchildren, all well. . . . For this blessing give I thanks.

At twelve o'clock, by a previous engagement, I was to call at Mrs. G——'s for Cousin B. Smith to accompany me to the bridge at Quincy-port, being the first day of passing it. The day was pleasant, the scenery delightful. Passed both bridges, and entered Hingham. Returned before three o'clock. Dined, and;

At five, went to Mr. T.G——'s, with your grandfather; the third visit he has made with us in the week; and let me whisper to you he played at whist with Mr. J.G——, who was as ready and accurate as though he had both eyes to see with. Returned.

At nine, sat down and wrote a letter.

At eleven, retired to bed.

The "Adams mansion" at Quincy was bulging at the seams with daughters-in-law, grandchildren, and great-grandchildren. John wrote to Van der Kemp:

YOU ASK, "What! have you more grandchildren about you?" Yes, I have four pretty little creatures, who, though they disarrange my writing-table, give me much of my enjoyment. Why, you seem to know nothing about me. I have grandchildren and great-grandchildren, multiplying like the seed of Abraham. You have no idea of the prolific quality of the New England Adamses. Why, we have contributed more to the population of North America, and cut down more trees, than any other race; and I hope will furnish hereafter, if they should be wanted, more soldiers and sailors for the defense of their country.

The news of Napoleon's return from Moscow, and the speech which he made in Paris, reminded Adams to reread *Discourses on Davila,* and he found to his delight that the Emperor's speech was an endorsement of *Discourses*—although it is most unlikely that Napoleon ever heard of the work. In any event, Adams wrote on the flyleaf of his copy:

THE CONTENTS of the foregoing volume are summarily comprehended in a few sentences in the following comment by Napoleon, Emperor of France:

"It is to ideology, to that obscure metaphysics, which, searching with subtlety after first causes, wishes to found upon them the legislation of nations, instead of adapting the laws to the knowledge of the human heart and to the lessons of history, that we are to attribute all the calamities that our beloved France has experienced. Those errors necessarily produced the government of the men of blood. Indeed who proclaimed the principle of insurrection as a duty? Who flattered the people by proclaiming for them a sovereignty which they were incapable of exercising? Who destroyed the sanctity and the respect to the laws, by making them to depend not upon the sacred principles of justice, upon the nature of things and upon civil justice, but only upon the will of an assembly composed of men strangers to the knowledge of the civil, criminal, administrative, political, and military laws? When we are called to regenerate a state, we must act upon opposite principles. History paints the human heart. It is in history that we are to seek for the advantages and disadvantages of different systems of laws."

It was characteristic of Adams to reply to Napoleon and he wrote a "comment on the comment" below the quotation from the Emperor: "Napoleon! . . . This book is a prophecy of your empire before your name was heard." After rereading the book he wrote, at the end:

THIS DULL, heavy volume still excites the wonder of its author, first that he could find amidst the constant scenes of business and dissipation in which he was enveloped time to write it. Secondly that he had the courage to oppose and publish his own opinions to the universal opinion of all America, and indeed of almost all mankind. Not one man in America then believed him. He knew not one then, and has not heard of one since, who then believed him.

Death started to strike around John Adams in 1813 when old friend Benjamin Rush passed on. Then, in the middle of a learned dissertation to Jefferson, John dropped his pen. When he resumed the next day he wrote:

I CAN PROCEED no farther with this letter as I intended. Your friend, my only daughter, expired yesterday morning in the arms of her husband, her son, her daughter, her father and mother, her husband's two sisters, and two of her nieces, in the 49th year of her age, 46 of which she was the healthiest and firmest of us all; since which, she has been a monument to suffering and patience.

He was referring to the demise of Nabby, who had returned to Quincy to die after an operation for cancer. Nabby's married life had not been a happy one. William Smith had been a promising young man when he was Adams' secretary in London, but performance never equaled the promise. He was prone to follow nebulous, get-rich-quick schemes, and after service as a colonel—an appointment which his father-in-law secured from a somewhat reluctant Hamilton—he had eked out a bare subsistence of a farm in western New York.

Greater grief occurred in 1818, when Abigail died after being immobilized by a stroke. John wrote to John Quincy: ". . . the grim spoiler so terrible to human nature has no sting left for me." In his letter of condolence Jefferson said:

IT IS OF SOME COMFORT to us both that the term is not very distant at which we are to deposit in the same cerement our sorrows and suffering bodies, and to ascend in essence to an ecstatic meeting with the friends we have loved and lost, and whom we shall still love and never lose again.

To which Adams replied:

I BELIEVE IN GOD and in his wisdom and benevolence; and I cannot conceive that such a being could make such a species as the human merely to live and die on this earth. If I did not believe in a future state I should believe in no God. This universe, this all . . . would appear with all its swelling pomp a boyish firework. And if there be a future state why should the Almighty dissolve forever all the tender ties which unite us so delightfully in this world and forbid us to see each other in the next?

In later letters Jefferson expressed himself as being not quite so sure of an afterlife as his first letter intimated, and Adams defended this belief vigorously, ending with a characteristic admonition: "Vain man! Mind your own business! Do no wrong! Do all the good you can! Eat your canvasback ducks! drink your Burgundy! Sleep your siesta, when necessary, and TRUST IN GOD."

In 1820 John, aged eighty-five, performed his last public service. The Constitution which he had written for Massachusetts had served the state well for forty years, but now a convention was called to revise it, on which Adams was asked to serve; an appointment of which he wrote:

AS A MEMBER to the convention I can be but the shadow of a man. An election, however, to this situation, at my great age and feeble condition of body and mind, I esteem the purest honor of my life, and shall endeavor to do as much of my duty as my strength will permit. I presume it will not be made a question now, as it was forty years ago, whether we should have a governor, or a senate, or judges during good behavior. What questions will be moved, I cannot say; but I hope that no essential flaw will be found or made in the good old forty-two pounder, though it should be tried over again after forty years' usage, by a double charge of powder and ball.

To the son of old friend Benjamin Rush he wrote:

IN THE COURSE of forty years I have been called twice to assist in the formation of a constitution for this state. This kind of architecture, I find, is an art or mystery very difficult to learn, and still harder to practice. The attention of mankind at large seems now to be drawn to this interesting subject. It gives me more solicitude than, at my age, it ought to do; for nothing remains for me but submission and resignation. Nevertheless, I cannot wholly divest myself of anxiety for my children, my country, and my species. The probability is that the fabrication of constitutions will be the occupation or the sport, the tragedy, comedy, or farce, for the entertainment of the world for a century to come. There is little appearance of the prevalence of correct notions of the indispensable machinery of a free government. . . .

But hazardous as it may be, I will venture one remark upon our national and state institutions. The legislative and executive authorities are too much blended together. While the Senate of the United States have a negative on all appointments to office, we can never have a national President. In spite of his own judgment, he must be the President, not to say the tool, of a party. . . .

Strait is the gate and narrow is the way that leads to liberty, and few nations, if any, have found it.

Barely able to enunciate, Adams spoke but once at the convention. The question had to do with universal suffrage versus a property qualification for voting. Still defending his aristocracy, the octogenarian poured forth some of the old fire in describing the horrors of the French revolution when the propertyless *sans-culottes* had a voice. He accepted defeat with better grace than of yore, mildly remarking that if universal suffrage would work anywhere, the United States offered the best grounds.

What might me called Adams' last public appearance took place in 1821. The Cadets of the Military Academy had come to Boston for some occasion and they took a day to march to Quincy and pay their respects to the old man. He stood on his porch while they performed military evolutions and fired guns. Then he laboriously delivered a brief address on glory. He asked:

As your profession is at least as solemn and sacred as any in human life, it behooves you seriously to consider, *what is glory?*

There is no real glory in this world or any other but such as arises from wisdom and benevolence. There can be no solid glory among men but that which springs from equity and humanity; from the constant observance of prudence, temperance, justice, and fortitude. Battles, victories, and conquests, abstracted from their only justifiable object and end, which is justice and peace, are the glory of fraud, violence, and usurpation. What was the glory of Alexander and Caesar? "The glimmering" which those "livid flames" in Milton "cast, pale and dreadful," or "the sudden blaze," which "far round illumin'd Hell."

Different—far different is the glory of Washington and his faithful colleagues! Excited by no ambition of conquest or avaricious desire of wealth; irritated by no jealousy, envy, malice, or revenge; prompted only by the love of their country, by the purest patriotism and philanthropy, they persevered, with invincible constancy, in defense of their country, her fundamental laws, her natural, essential and inalienable rights and liberties, against the lawless and ruthless violence of tyranny and usurpation. The biography of these immortal captains, and the history of their great actions, you will read and ruminate night and day. You need not investigate antiquity, or travel into foreign countries, to find models of excellence in military commanders, without a stain of ambition or avarice, tyranny, cruelty, or oppression toward friends or enemies.

Even in his final years Adams was not free from the political mud-slinging which had so infuriated him during his active life. In 1824 John Quincy, who had served as James Monroe's Secretary of State, was an obvious candidate for the presidency. A competitor was Andrew Jackson, hero of New Orleans. William Cunningham, who had elicited letters from Adams almost twenty-five years before in which he criticized Jefferson, had promised not to publish them. But Cunningham had recently committed suicide. His son, an ardent Jacksonian, published the letters. Adams feared that his renewed friendship with Jefferson might again be disturbed, but the Virginian mildly noted: "It would be strange indeed, if, at our years, we were to go an age back to hunt up imaginary or forgotten facts to disturb the repose of affections so sweetening to the evening of our lives." This, said Adams, was "the best letter that was ever written."

When John Quincy was elected there was a touching and almost formal exchange of notes between father and son. A letter from Rufus King advised John Quincy of his election and he sent this to his father with a covering note: "My Dear and Honored Father, The inclosed note from Mr. King will inform you of the event of this day, upon which I can only offer *you* my congratulations, and ask your blessings and prayers. Your affectionate and dutiful son, John Quincy Adams." To which the old man replied:

MY DEAR SON,

I have received your letter of the 9th. Never did I feel so much solemnity as upon this occasion. The multitude of my thoughts, and the intensity of my feelings are too much for a mind like mine, in its ninetieth year. May the blessing of God Almighty continue to protect you to the end of your life, as it has heretofore protected you in so remarkable a manner from your cradle! I offer the same prayer for your lady and your family, and am your affectionate father.

John Adams.

And to Thomas Jefferson he wrote:

THE PRESIDENTIAL ELECTION has given me less anxiety than I myself could have imagined. The next administration will be a troublesome one, to whomsoever it falls, and our John has been too much worn to contend much longer with conflicting factions. I call him our John, because, when you were at the cul de sac at Paris, he appeared to me to be almost as much your boy as mine. I have often speculated upon the consequences that would have ensued from my taking your advice, to send him to William and Mary College in Virginia for an education.

As the year 1826 dawned, Adams was virtually immobilized, unable to even walk in his garden. There is no record that he suffered from any particular fatal disease. Palsy had long plagued him, and to this was now added sciatica and rheumatism. He breathed with difficulty, but his mind was clear. He sat surrounded by cushions in an armchair while somebody read to him. His preference was for the classics, ancient history, or profound philosophical speculation. But, if needs must, he willingly listened to the contemporary fiction of Walter Scott, the sea stories of Cooper, or the vigorous poetry of Byron. In one of the last letters which he wrote—or, rather dictated—to Jefferson he said:

I HAD RATHER go forward and meet whatever is to come—I have met in this life with great trials—I have had a father and lost him—I have had a mother and lost her—I have had a wife and lost her—I have had children and lost them—I have had honorable and worthy friends and lost them—and instead of suffering these griefs again, I had rather go forward and meet my destiny.

As July 4, 1826, approached there were great plans to celebrate the fiftieth anniversary of the signing of the Declaration of Independence. Many had an idea for the supreme celebration: a meeting of Jefferson and Adams. The thought of these two great drafters of the document, shaking hands after more than twenty-five years of separation, was a sublime contemplation. But neither Adams at ninety nor Jefferson at eighty-four could travel. Boston invited Adams to attend its celebration, as did New York. In refusing the latter he wrote:

NOT THE UNITED STATES ALONE, but a mighty continent, the last discovered, but the largest quarter of the globe, is destined to date the period of its birth and emancipation from the 4th of July 1776. Visions of future bliss in prospect, for the better condition of the human race, resulting from this unparalleled event, might be indulged, but sufficient unto the day be the glory thereof.

The principal speaker for the Quincy celebration, Reverend Henry Ware, visited him and noted in his diary:

SPENT A FEW MINUTES with him in conversation, and took from him a toast to be presented on the Fourth of July as coming from him. I should have liked a longer one; but as it is, this will be acceptable. "I will give you," said he, "Independence Forever!"

He was asked if he would not add anything to it, and he replied, "not a word."

On the morning of July 4 it was evident that death was near.

Shortly before noon he whispered his last words: "Thomas Jefferson survives." At the time he said them they were true. An hour later they were not. Jefferson died at 12:50 P.M. Adams outlived his old friend by about five hours and quietly passed away at about six o'clock.

John was laid away, without much fanfare, beside Abigail. Later the bodies were removed to the new, marble First Church and the sepulcher was marked with a lengthy epitaph written by John Quincy.

LIBERTATEM, AMICITIAM, FIDEM, RETINEBIS

D. O. M.

Beneath these walls

Are deposited the mortal remains of

JOHN ADAMS.

Son of John and Susanna (Boylston) Adams

Second President of the United States;

Born $\frac{19}{30}$ October, 1735

On the Fourth of July, 1776,

He pledged his Life, Fortune, and sacred Honor

To the INDEPENDENCE OF HIS COUNTRY

On the third of September, 1783,

He affixed his seal to the definitive treaty with Great Britain

Which acknowledged that independence,

And consummated the redemption of his pledge.

On the Fourth of July, 1826,

He was summoned

To the Independence of Immortality,

And to the JUDGMENT OF HIS GOD.

This House will bear witness to his piety;

This Town, his birthplace, to his munificence;

History to his patriotism;

Posterity to the depth and compass of his mind.

INDEX

 જી